Praise for *Sodomy Gods*

I have known David Lauterstein and his husband Frederick Kearney for many years now, and everyone knows about their brand Nasty Pig, cuz it's a queer household name! Reading *Sodomy Gods* gave me so much insight into what inspired David to set out on his journey in the first place. It's a powerful story that exposes the hardships we faced in the nineties, and how he transformed that trauma into triumph. Sexy, authentic and real as hell, it's a must read for 2024.

Billy Porter
Grammy, Emmy, and 2X Tony Award Winner
Author of *Unprotected: A Memoir*

David has always been a storyteller...a visionary, and Fred knew how to bring it all to life. They changed homosexuality, how we dressed, and that is such a major thing in faggotry. Younger generations can be cute, but they need to recognize the shoulders they stand on, allowing them to be so free. We didn't have that, because our people died, but they can learn what it took to get here.

Kevin Aviance
Legendary drag queen, musician, and nightlife personality

For nearly two decades, I've known Nasty Pig's David Lauterstein and Fred Kearney as business leaders and larger-than-life characters in the community of kinky queers. David's raw and often hilarious memoir is a uniquely American account of how commerce can be used in service of style, transgression, activism, love, community, and gay sex. It's a must-read for aspiring businesspigs everywhere.

Josh Barro
National journalist, commentator, and podcast host

As a Gay man who came out in the late 70s, survived the AIDS epidemic, then found the love of my life, I knew I would identify with David and Fred's story. I've always been a big fan of them as a couple. I've admired their leadership within the community and have long been a regular patron of their groundbreaking company, Nasty Pig. I was not, however, prepared for how moved I would feel reading the book itself.

David Lauterstein's *Sodomy Gods* is a rich, emotional ride from start to finish. It's a gorgeous love story, giving the reader a bird's eye view of the good, the bad, and the ugly that goes into forging a future together, not just for years, but for decades. *Sodomy Gods* is also a tale of love for oneself and community, and the courage to step outside the comfort zone in the name of personal and professional authenticity. David's voice in the book is every bit as poetic, vivacious, audacious, and real as the man himself.

Having lived through a generation that lost its elders, the fact that David "passes the torch" to younger generations with this story resonates with me deeply. I encourage everyone, young and old, out-and-proud, or an ally in the making, to buckle up and enjoy this journey. It's a tale for the ages that will stay with you.

Brad Carpenter
Emmy-nominated producer

I have known David Lauterstein for some time as a friend and kindred soul, and now readers of *Sodomy Gods* will too. He is a warm light of a person, a man who earned his stripes in the darkest days of the AIDS crisis, and is now here to teach the children. More relatable and vulnerable than you might expect, the fully revealed Lauterstein writes about nothing more or less than the "poetry of the universe," in his words — that gay magic that happens in threesomes and after-hours clubs, the mystery stuff that queer people live, die, and dance for. It's fun to experience, through his eyes, clubbing at Sound Factory and the Roxy, and this book — ostensibly a memoir, sex diary, and brand story all at once — is also a time capsule of lost New York. It is, almost incidentally, a useful guide for any creative person wondering how a successful project happens, how little exchanges between friends and lovers (in bed, in a club) and a lot of grunt work (shopping, stitching) come together to make something that hits. Nasty Pig was a passion project between two men forced to navigate love and fear in a rapidly changing world. Their passion ignites every page.

Alexander Cheves

Bestselling author, *My Love Is a Beast: Confessions*

Sodomy Gods

Sodomy Gods David Lauterstein

ed.

UNBOUND EDITION PRESS

Atlanta

FIRST EDITION

Printed in the United States of America

LIBRARY OF CONGRESS RECORD

Name: Lauterstein, David, 1969 — author.
Title: Sodomy Gods / David Lauterstein.
Edition: First edition.
Published: Atlanta : Unbound Edition Press, 2024.

LCCN: 2024937418
LCCN Permalink: https://lccn.loc.gov/2024937418
ISBN: 979-8-9892333-8-0 (fine softcover)

Designed by Eleanor Safe and Joseph Floresca
Printed by Bookmobile, Minneapolis, MN
Distributed by Itasca Books

23456789

Unbound Edition Press
1270 Caroline Street, Suite D120
Box 448
Atlanta, GA 30307

for Frederick

Contents

Sodomy Gods

Sodomy Gods is a memoir.

Everything shared within these pages is true.
The specific details are recounted through the lens
of personal memory by the author.

Some names have been changed for privacy,
and some events have been compressed
or combined for brevity.

Prologue

My staff and I showed up for a private tour of the White House, courtesy of Dr. Demetre Daskalakis, President Biden's pick to coordinate the federal government's response to the Mpox viral outbreak. I had gone from being a 90s New York City club kid to the founder and CEO of Nasty Pig, a globally recognized, if often controversial, queer clothing brand. Along that journey, between Upper East Side penthouse fundraisers to downtown loft apartment after-hours kikis, I had found myself welcomed to an incredible mix of eclectic house parties. *But the White House?* I didn't think people like me, who spent decades being fearlessly sex-positive in the public eye, could make it past the door of this particular house. Yet there I was, on my way in.

After going through multiple security checks, Dr. Demetre came down the stairs through the brisk January air and we embraced one another: two queer men with three virulent plagues beneath our belts, wearing Nasty Pig jockstraps beneath our pants. We had fought hard against those plagues, but thankfully we didn't have to do any fighting that evening. The worst was behind us for now, and Dr. Demetre was leading me and my team from Nasty Pig on a presidential victory lap.

"Thank you so much, David. You're amazing," Dr. Demetre said to me as we held each other close.

"No, you're the one who's amazing, Doctor," I replied.

"No, you are, David."

"No, you are, Doctor."

We both laughed as we both cried. Calling each other amazing was how we ritualistically ended our conversations during those awful times. We were joking, but not fully. We held tremendous respect for each other, and we were united in transforming the traumas of our past to shape the trajectory of our queer community's future. From HIV to COVID to MPox, we shared a lived experience that taught us when it comes to public health, it's best to meet people where they are.

With my input, Dr. Demetre added common-sense solutions to government messaging that addressed clinical problems arising from the latest virus attacking our community. I'd share the official information with my customer base through my "Letter from the CEO" emails. Thanks to my 30 years of informal leadership within our community, I'm blessed that they would often listen. I never set out to be a part of the White House communications apparatus, but I wasn't mad at it either. We had come a long way from those dark days when the White House didn't communicate with us at all. Standing there in my Nasty Pig jock, I hoped Ronald and Nancy Reagan were rolling over in their graves.

Demetre led us through the hallways and into rooms where our country's history was often shaped. Everything felt weighted with the past, from the carved wood walls to the tiled floors to the Colonial desks with their upholstered chairs and gilded sofas. As visually impressive as it was, my awareness of my country's complicated history made it difficult to feel truly moved.

That all changed, however, when we got to the room dedicated to Dr. Martin Luther King, Jr. Standing on the ground on which he stood, sitting in a chair upon which he sat — *that* moved my soul. Dr. King is one of my heroes, as is Dr. Demetre, who instructed us all to sit down at a long wooden conference table. Another man — another queer man — entered the room, and introduced himself as Harold Phillips, Director of the Office of National AIDS Policy. He requested that I stand up and join him and Dr. Demetre at the head of the table.

"David, this is long overdue," Dr. Demetre began. "We at the White House would like to honor you for your 30 years of leadership and tireless commitment to sex positivity and public health advocacy for our queer community."

I proceeded to break down and cry. Being recognized for my work was never something that I needed, and up until that moment, it was never something I was afforded. To be formally recognized *at all* was something I had learned not to expect. It comes with being ahead of one's time, and for me, that was just fine. To be honored for being a sex-positive queer man, by two sex-positive queer men, in front of my sex-positive queer staff, *at the fucking White House,* was all too overwhelming. The poetry of the moment had me weeping. I guess my time — or rather, *our* time — had finally come.

Times were so different at the start of my life's journey. When I grew up there was almost no representation of queer people in film or on TV. Occasionally, a gay or lesbian character was written into a plotline, but they were usually tragic at best and villainous at worst. Men like Freddie Mercury, Boy George, and George Michael — men who were clearly queer — never talked about it, nor was that questioned. No one even spoke of being gay, because being gay was just about the worst thing anyone could be. Any progress and visibility that was made after Stonewall had practically been erased by AIDS. Being gay meant being sick, both physically and morally. The closet held most of our community incarcerated behind its doors. The closet held me prisoner as well, until I came out in 1992 — the start of my queer journey.

Times were different at the start of my queer journey, as well. Queer people were not equals in society. We couldn't donate blood. We couldn't serve openly in the military, and we were dishonorably discharged if our truth was revealed. We weren't legally permitted to get married. We couldn't legally adopt children. In many states we could be arrested for having sex under discriminatory sodomy laws used almost exclusively to humiliate, punish, and even jail queer people.

Our sex could also be deadly. AIDS, the plague that ran rampant in our community because of who it inflicted, decimated our ranks and killed off generations of our queer ancestors. It was ever-present in our psyches and we had adopted the stigmas that were unfairly placed upon us. Our own leadership encouraged us to blend in and be "normal," in the hope that society would forget about who we were and tolerate us for who we pretended to be.

That was our reality when I first came out. I wanted to pretend I wasn't different, but thankfully the powers that be had other plans for me. They shook me out of the closet of internalized homophobia. They woke me up to my queer identity and showed me my lineage. They put me on my authentic path, instilled in me my purpose, and inspired me to manifest it through Nasty Pig, my own great American Wet Dream.

There are many misconceptions about Nasty Pig. Some people think we make porn. Some people think we're an underwear brand. Some people think we're tired and cheap, while others think we're overpriced sheep. Some think we're all about kink. Some think we're a sham, or a scam, or a flash in the pan, glorifying dick as a means to get rich quick. I've heard it all, trust me.

But if you want to know the honest truth . . .

One

Nasty Pig is a love story.

It all began in New York City on May 6, 1993 at The Break, one of the many bars and clubs in Chelsea, the consummate gay ghetto of the 90s. I was there that Thursday night to meet a guy named Steve for a date and to have a few of The Break's infamous dollar margaritas. I was 23, just out of the closet, and ready to find a boyfriend and fall in love. I imagined my future man to be an upwardly mobile Wall Street guy with a six-figure salary, his own place in Manhattan, and a worked-out body. Someone acceptable to my straight friends and family. I just wanted to hang out with him in our underwear while we cuddled up on the couch in our high-rise apartment watching *Friends*. I'd talk to him about hip-hop while he talked to me about this new Internet thing that people were starting to invest in. I had it all figured out.

Except for this: *You can't figure out love. She just shows the fuck up and your job is to be ready for her.*

Although The Break wasn't particularly large, the lure of margarita madness packed the place with local hotties every Thursday night. Making your way through the wall-to-wall crowd took quite a bit of effort. I knew Steve liked to hang out toward the back so I did my best to maneuver my way in as I set off to find him. I detoured to the bar to get myself a cocktail. The sheer number of people trying to get drinks at once made waiting for service something to be expected. Since coming out, however, I had become aware of this powerful set of secret weapons my dad had gifted me at conception that often got me what I wanted: my crazy pale eyes. I managed to carve out about 10 inches of space at the bar, and just as my favorite bartender looked in my direction, I took off my baseball cap and flashed him the greenish-gray windows to my soul. He went to the cash register to make change for another customer, and on his way back he put a drink down in front of me, on the house. I tipped him a five and left him a business card with my beeper number on it.

I grabbed my drink, and just as I was about to go find Steve, I noticed a guy across the bar staring in my direction. Guess my weapons were causing some collateral damage that night, because we locked eyes and he smiled at me. I smiled back and he giggled like a schoolgirl. There was something about his reaction that caught my attention. This guy felt different than all the other stand-offish guys hanging out and posing there. He felt warm.

I did my best to find Steve, but he wasn't in his usual spot, and after about 20 minutes I figured I was being stood up. I decided to cut my losses early, leave the bar alone, and chalk the experience up to another failed attempt at meeting Mr. Right. On my way out, I bumped into the warm, giggling man, who introduced himself as Fred, a recent transplant from New Jersey. He had just moved to Chelsea a week ago.

He wasn't exactly my type. He was on the lean side, not the jock I pictured myself with. And his style was way more Wyckoff than Wall Street. After a few minutes of small talk, I told him it was time for me to head out. He mentioned that he lived a block away and was ready to leave too, so I figured I'd walk him to his apartment. By the time we got there, I decided I might as well end the night with a bit of fun. I asked him if I could come up to use his bathroom before I headed home. So original of me, I know. His pouty lips parted with a "yes," and I followed him into his building.

He opened the door to his apartment and the first thing I noticed were the walls. They were beautiful. I had never seen anything like them. The colors were all shades of what felt like fall leaves, and they blended to create an effect that was warm and dimensional. I mentioned to him how much I liked them and told him he was fortunate to have moved into a place that came with so much character. "Oh, I painted them myself," he said, "but I'm not happy with how they came out. I'll repaint them when I get a chance."

The walls may have been the first thing to grab my attention, but as I looked around I noticed that pretty much everything in his place was incredibly beautiful and detailed. I asked more questions, all of which got the same response.

"Yeah, I took that photo but when I developed it the blacks didn't come out rich enough and I need to do it again once I set up my darkroom."

"I covered that couch and added the trim, but I don't think it works so I'm going to get more fabric and make it better."

"I found those cabinets at a garage sale and sanded them down and refinished them then added new drawer pulls. I don't know if I like the final color that much, though."

He had made everything in his place and was satisfied with none of it.

I checked my beeper for the time and realized it was getting late, so I stopped asking questions and decided to leave him satisfied with something. We made out. I went down on him. He blew his load on my face. The end.

Or so I thought.

* * *

As I was getting dressed to leave, the small talk turned to the quintessential New Yorker question: "So what do you do?"

He proceeded to tell me he was a pattern maker at a clothing manufacturer in Brooklyn, an okay job he'd had for eight years because he really liked the "world of *fayashun.*"

Maybe it was his lowbrow pronunciation of such a highbrow statement, but suddenly I became hyper aware of his New Jersey accent, which perfectly matched his high-waisted New Jersey jeans, and his very New Jersey choice of New Balance sneakers. At 32 years old, he was just moving into Manhattan for the first time in his life, and he was doing so in a converted one bedroom with a roommate who arrived there as I was putting on my shoes. This loud, flamboyant character stormed in wearing micro-denim Daisy Duke shorts and a tank top that was two sizes too small. I looked at Fred, who now embodied the opposite of that Wall Street white-collar jock dream man I had in mind, and I said goodbye and ran out of that New Jersey nightmare as quickly as my fly-ass Jordans could carry me.

That night I got home and wrote the following in my journal about the man I had met:

> *i talked to fred. back to his place. meaningless sex. fears about aids. the whole nine. during the walk of shame i questioned a lot of shit about my life. i think i need to experience some real emotion attached to sex. that hasn't happened yet and it won't happen with fred. that's not to say that I didn't have a good time. and he was hung like a motherfucker. that's a bonus.*

Like I said . . . love just shows up when she's ready. I didn't know it yet, but there she was.

Two

Sometime in the fall of 1979, I would make an unforgivable mistake that would define the rest of my adolescent life. While walking down the hallway of my elementary school, I held my notebook up against my chest as opposed to loosely at my side. I didn't know that was the "girls' way" of carrying books. From that day forward, I was permanently branded as gay.

Prior to that moment, I was a creative little kid with a strong sense of identity who fearlessly did his own thing. In second grade, we were given an assignment to make fantasy dioramas, and mine was filled with miniature girl dolls on a tropical vacation. The following year, my Boy Scout troop leader had us decorate pumpkins for Halloween using Magic Markers and construction paper, but given my passion for origami, I took a stand against taking a pair of scissors to mutilate my favorite medium, and instead, I folded my way to success. I knew I was different, but being different made me happy.

Once I became known as gay, it put an end to me publicly making anything at all, because art was what gay boys did instead of playing sports. My entire life became focused around not giving the bullies any ammunition because being permanently marked as their target was truly terrifying. All I wanted to do was silently blend into invisibility, hoping that I wouldn't be killed before I made it to junior high.

I stopped going outside to play with the other kids and found myself spending most of my time alone in my room, reading about dinosaurs and butterflies and outer space. My favorite book of all time was a masterpiece called *Some of Us Walk, Some Fly, Some Swim,* which revealed the wonders of the animal kingdom through vibrant illustrations and explanatory rhymes. One afternoon, while listening to the shrieks and laughter of the other kids playing in the street, I found myself wishing I could be one of the birds in that book and just take to the sky, looking down at my torturers while they all screamed with jealousy that I could fly. That would make them like me. I grabbed my crayons and a piece of paper to draw what I imagined, but in a moment of sudden inspiration, rather than illustrate my feelings, I wrote them down in a poem.

In that instant, I was able to talk about what I was going through without revealing my horrible truth. I began writing poems to express my sadness, my dreams, and my fears. I put my thoughts and feelings into these cryptic little puzzles that safely gave a voice to my anxiety. I found my very own magic language and with it came a newfound creative happiness. Then, one day, my secret was revealed when my fifth-grade teacher unexpectedly called upon me to stand in front of my classmates and recite what she thought was a note I was scribbling – to the menacing delight of my bullies.

After reading those 16 rhyming lines, my effort to blend into invisibility was officially over. Just as I was finally feeling like I no longer had a handwritten "Kick Me, I'm Gay!" note taped to my back, it was replaced by a neon target with the most intimidating and humiliating insult possible in the lexicon of bullying. From that day forward, I was permanently branded a *faggot*.

But something else happened that year that would change my world and the rest of culture along with it: The Sugar Hill Gang released "Rapper's Delight," considered to be the first rap song commercially pressed. Critics wrote the song off as a novelty and declared that it would join the ranks of the other one-hit wonders that collectively defined pop music's ongoing joke. But I was lucky enough to live in New York City, and a couple of radio stations began giving airtime to this new form of music. I couldn't get enough of the driving break beats that grounded the sound. It was like my favorite parts of my dad's disco and soul records looped over and over again. The next year I went on to junior high and I noticed the Black kids who went to my new school embracing it just like I did. They blasted it from their boom boxes and recited the words to each other, while wearing their Fila track suits and permanent-crease, cranberry Lee Jeans. Even though the white kids made fun of rap music, I knew it was incredibly cool. That made something else incredibly cool along with it: Poetry.

Three

The only full-time job I ever had before starting Nasty Pig was a two-year stint at a company called Sonic Assembly, a music merchandising firm that had the innovative idea of producing clothing lines for bands and singers. You might be asking yourself what's so innovative about that, being that every major artist today has a portfolio of branded cosmetics, alcohol, restaurants, and marijuana, not to mention a fashion line. It makes perfect sense. Musicians have always been tastemakers, and capitalizing on that status in multiple markets morphs them from cultural icons into financial moguls. Jay-Z and Taylor Swift are billionaires — and if Cardi B put out toilet paper, the public would line up to wipe their WAPs in her name.

Things, however, were very different in 1992. The idea of musicians selling *anything* other than music still carried an air of "selling out," unless the star was Madonna or Michael Jackson. This, compounded by the fact that the early-90s were dominated by grunge rock with its decidedly anti-commercial aesthetic, made Sonic Assembly a challenging concept at the time. They still managed to ink deals with the companies that owned the rights to produce merchandise for bands like Nirvana and Alice In Chains, but that didn't mean their fans would take to buying pricey sleeveless flannels and polo shirts emblazoned with their names. The bands themselves weren't thrilled with the idea either. Almost everyone was content to offer tour tees and ill-fitting baseball caps at concerts and call it a profitable day. The appetite for Pearl Jam jeans didn't exist.

There was a sector of the music industry that the CEO at Sonic Assembly felt was on the cusp of exploding musically and had the breakthrough potential to make his idea work. His name was Paul, a recent transplant from Norway, which limited his knowledge of American music. His vision for how to capitalize on it, however, was spot on. After applying and being rejected for a job at Sonic Assembly as a graphic artist (because I had zero qualifications), I got a call from Paul to come back to discuss a different position. He told me he was looking for someone to act as an assistant to the A&R rep he had on staff.

In the music industry, A&R — which stands for Artists and Repertoire — is the division of a record label that is responsible for scouting talent and the artistic and commercial development of the artists who were signed. It also acts as a liaison between the artist and the record label. A&R rep was the coolest job you could possibly have in the industry other than actually being the recording artist. While Sonic Assembly was in the business of making clothing, not music, they needed to find and court the right artists just the same.

During my interview, he told me that he was interested in branching out into hip-hop, but there was no one on his team who had any idea what the culture was about. He knew of my interest in hip-hop from my first (failed) interview, so we talked about it. I told him that in terms of culture, hip-hop was about where grunge was right before Nirvana blew the entire scene into the mainstream — and that I loved it. Impressed with my answer, he asked me what I thought about "this new song Naughty By Nature" that was released a couple of days prior. I promptly informed him that the song was called "O.P.P.," and the band was Naughty By Nature. I predicted it would blow up as a crossover hit, especially with Queen Latifah's Flavor Unit label behind it. I confidently smiled at him, and he nodded and smiled back. We both knew I nailed it.

Three weeks later, "O.P.P." was climbing the *Billboard Hot 100* and I got a call from Sonic Assembly offering me the job of Assistant A&R Rep. Of all the offers my bachelor's degree in poetry got me, this was the coolest — as well as the only one. I took it and never looked back.

Not too bad for a poet.

Four

Working at Sonic Assembly was exciting, to say the least. I went from a directionless college grad with a poetry degree to being the protégé of the CEO at a company on the forefront of music and fashion, two things I loved as much as writing. I found myself doing everything from smoking blunts with Cypress Hill, to flying around the country installing shop-in-shops in chain stores like Musicland and Sam Goody's, to being in meetings as deals were closed with executives at the major record labels. I even had the honor of being present as Suge Knight unexpectedly showed up at our offices to "renegotiate" the terms of our deal with Death Row Records artists Dr. Dre and Snoop Dogg. The negotiations went as follows: He showed up strapped with his terrifying crew. He told us what we would accept. We agreed, they left, and we exhaled. It was pretty scary, but being intimidated by Suge Knight felt really fucking official.

While music merchandising was Sonic Assembly's bread and butter, my gut was telling me that there was another space in the market that was complementary and even cooler: Streetwear. Sure, people would want to wear a Beastie Boys shirt, but damn that Phillies Blunt shirt AdRock wore on MTV was the shit! It was the brainchild of three graffiti artists who formed a company called GFS. Along with brands like Triple Five Soul, Pervert, Fuct, PNB Nation, Carhartt, and Stüssy, they were setting the style for the hip-hop scene. The artists themselves were starting to get in on the game, with the Beastie Boys "XLarge" line selling side-by-side with these red-hot brands. Cypress Hill was fine with us making their merchandise, but they really wanted us to help with their signature "Weedwear" line.

I convinced the CEO that we should be exploring the possibility of partnering with these companies, and he gave me the green light to set up some meetings. At the top of my list was GFS because the Phillies Blunt tee was the coolest shirt of 1992, and they had the business chops to negotiate a licensing deal with JR Cigars, which owned the trademark. I reached out to them, set up an introductory meeting, and three days later took a train to Mott Street to check out their offices. But here's the thing: I didn't end up at an office. I knocked on their industrial bolted metal door and found myself welcomed into a vision for my future.

* * *

New York City in 1992 was still very gritty. Space was cheap. You didn't need much more than creativity and drive to set up shop and make shit happen. And at GFS, shit *was happening.* One room was filled with boxes of freshly screen-printed tees and newly embroidered baseball caps and woolies, ready to be sold and shipped to stores. The walls of the other room were covered in graffiti and cans of Krylon spray paint were strewn on just about every flat surface that wasn't housing the latest Mac desktop. Reggeaton was booming through the sound system and the smell of blazing weed saturated the air. These guys were more than a company and less than a company at the same time. They were three artists generating culture and making money as a byproduct of doing what they loved — all for a scene in which they were immersed.

The thrill of closing deals at Sonic Assembly was nothing compared to the excitement I felt being in that room. I spent the next year knee-deep in New York's vibrant, underground hip-hop scene, soaking up the physical explosive ambition of the music I had loved since junior high.

That was my last year in the closet. I didn't know it at the time, but I was being primed to spend the rest of my life creating what would become Nasty Pig.

Five

A couple of days after I fled Fred's apartment, he called me and asked if I wanted to go out to dinner. I wasn't quite sure about Fred, but I had never been on a second date before — and I was definitely sure about giving his dick a second chance.

About that second date thing: I met Fred five months after I kissed my first boy — more of a man, actually. His name was Thor. He was big, blond, and when I brought him back to my place and asked him to take my virginity, he was kind enough to explain to me that the hair conditioner I grabbed from my shower wouldn't work as lube. A lifetime of denying my desires had me ready to obliterate my cherry the first chance I got. I may have lived in the closet, but while I was in there I sure did entertain myself from a very early age, figuring out all sorts of things I could do to my body. By the time I met Thor I was more than ready for someone else to do those things *to me*.

Fred came to my apartment on 34th and Park, and when I opened the door, he greeted me with a dozen white roses. It was the first time anyone had ever brought me flowers, and it moved me to feeling quite sure about going on my very first second date *with him* — and not just his impressively huge cock. I don't remember much about that dinner other than Fred knocking his glass over and spilling water across the table into my lap. He got so frazzled, desperately using his napkin to mitigate the damage while nervously apologizing for his blunder. I found it adorable. I couldn't believe someone was so concerned with making a good impression on me. It felt special. I also remember the poetry of the universe coming into my head, telling me to pay attention because this guy was going to get me very wet, very often.

The poetry of the universe is the only thing that's real in this world to me. It's this massive amount of unknown stuff that somehow governs what we do. Some people refer to it as God. Others call it quantum physics. Maybe it's dark matter. I don't know. But to me it's simply magic. The stuff we see and do as we go about our day-to-day lives is basically bullshit. It's our mind's attempt to process something we don't have the capacity to truly understand. But if you open yourself up, pay attention, and let your natural energy guide you, you get tuned into her frequency. She brings you along with her, and every now and again, sometimes in small whispers and sometimes in grand performances, she reveals herself as truth.

This is the poetry of the universe. It's magic. It's love. I spend my life present for it every single day.

After dinner, Fred came back with me to my studio and before I could open the door he grabbed me and kissed me with the softest lips and the strongest intent. I could feel how much he wanted me. He was tender and aggressive at once, and that combo floored me. I fumbled with my keys to get us inside and we stripped down to our underwear. He led me to the couch, laid me down, got on top of me, and made out with me for what felt like forever.

There was something so innocent about it, the two of us in our white Calvin Klein briefs rubbing up against each other. I could feel his amazing dick pressed up against mine. Finally, we lost the undies. He flipped my legs over my shoulders and ate my ass until I came. I then got down on my knees and blew his monster until Fred sensed he was about to cum and lifted my head up. I finished him off with a hand job, and he blew his load all over my face. I grabbed my shirt and wiped the cum off me as he got dressed. I walked him to the door and before he left, he said, "I guess spilling things on you is kind of my thing so far." It was funny, so I laughed as I shut the door behind him.

But it wasn't funny at all. It was terrifying. What if he started to shoot his load an instant before I took him out of my mouth? What if some of his cum had gotten into my eye? I didn't know anything about Fred's HIV status, and his fluids might have entered my body. I ran to the bathroom and washed my eyes out with soap and gargled with hydrogen peroxide. I gargled with vodka, which I then proceeded to drink. I fell to the floor of my tiny galley kitchen and cried my eyes out.

I had spent 22 years of my life terrified of admitting to myself and to the world that I was gay. It took every ounce of courage I had to finally accept myself and be free from living in fear of my desires. Yet here I was, more scared than ever. The intimacy that I had denied myself was finally mine to have and the thrill of giving in to it came with the terror of dying from it. It was bad enough that the world generally hated gay people. Whatever nascent acceptance we forged in the 70s had been wiped out by the plague of AIDS. AIDS defined gay people, and suddenly I realized it would define me as well, whether I had it or not.

I went into work the next day and ducked right into my office and closed the door behind me to avoid any contact with my coworkers. You know that annoying morning person who has more energy at 7 a.m. than the motherfucking sun? That's me. So normally I'd make my rounds and say hello to everyone and crack a joke and think I was amazing. They all probably hated my toxic positivity as they downed their coffee, trying to gather up the strength to simply turn on their computers. But not this day. I didn't have the strength to face my fears, let alone my fellow employees.

It wasn't long before there was a knock at my door; I assumed it was my boss, Paul. We had a meeting at noon with Great Entertainment Merchandising to discuss rolling out a line for Madonna after the success we had with her iconic crown jacket from the Blond Ambition Tour. I was his go-to guy to make sure he knew what we were talking about. Paul was very smart about a lot of things when it came to business, but he didn't know shit about music.

I opened the door and fortunately it was Carl, the boyfriend of my best friend from high school who had connected me to Sonic Assembly. My eyes began to water as soon as I saw him, and sensing my dispair he cheerfully said, "Let's grab a coffee!" Everyone knew Carl was gay. So was Paul, for that matter. But some of the employees didn't appreciate us queers being around. I was perfectly okay to be pretty public about such discriminatory views, so Carl got me out of there so we could talk openly.

We got in the elevator, took it down to the lobby, left the building, and walked all the way to a bodega on 55th and 9th before I felt safe enough to even whisper about what had happened with Fred. Through my gasping and choking I gave him all the details, and once I was done, he pulled me in close and held me. This was something, I later realized, he had probably done before for other baby gays like me, and something I would one day find myself doing for other newcomers. We pass queer knowledge and comfort from one heart to the next, because no one teaches you about this stuff as you grow up. Once I calmed down enough that a normal rhythm to my breathing returned, Carl gently held my shoulders, and looked into my eyes:

"David. Girl. First things first. It sounds like Fred didn't cum in your mouth, right?"

"No, he didn't."

"So, let's take that off the table. Even if he did, there is still a very small chance that you could get HIV that way, but he didn't, so you won't. As for wiping his cum off your face and into your eye, well you'd know if that happened. Trust me, I've gotten sprayed in the face a few times and you know when you're seeing white. And the odds of getting HIV that way are practically zero. So relax. Go get tested and you'll see that you're still negative. Besides, Fred didn't try to cum in your mouth, right?"

"Right"

"Well then that's great. It's a sign that he's not a fucking asshole. And he's the one with the gigantic dick, right?"

"Yes"

"So he's not an asshole, and he's hung. As far as gay guys go, it sounds like you scored so pull yourself together girl!" We both laughed. "Have you talked to him about his status yet?"

"No. I just assumed he is negative. He's not sick or anything."

"David, anyone can have HIV and be perfectly fine until it develops into AIDS. You'd be surprised how quickly it happens sometimes. I'm talking months, sometimes even weeks." I couldn't believe what I was hearing. I knew about AIDS from seeing it on the news in the 80s. I saw what *those* people looked like. They looked like lepers. They looked like death. To hear that someone could get that sick that fast was news to me.

"So, what do I do, Carl? Do I ask when he last got tested?"

"Honestly there are no easy answers here. But you have to look out for yourself. You have to know what you are dealing with so that you make good choices. Everyone I know practices safe sex, and if you don't let guys cum in your ass while wearing a condom, you're likely fine. But it's not just about protecting your health. You need to protect your heart. I've lost a lot of friends. Everyone I know has. That level of grief, it's just . . . it takes a toll. Nowadays when I meet positive guys, I'm friendly enough. I certainly won't have sex with them, but I'm also at a point where I won't even invest too much energy into getting to know them. I've been to enough burials and I'm done. I know it sounds cold, but it's where I'm at. It's kind of where we're all at."

I stood in that bodega realizing that my fear of dying from sex was only half the hell neatly packaged with coming out of the closet. Now I had to be afraid of love and affection too. Loss loomed large everywhere for us.

Carl put his arm around me again and said, "Alright, let's get back to work. And cheer the fuck up. You're going to meet Madonna today! Between that and Fred's dick, you've basically won the gay lottery, and you've only been playing it for five months."

As we got into the elevator to head back to our office I turned to Carl and said, "It's gonna be weird the first time I meet someone positive."

"Honey, you already have," he replied. "Don't tell anyone I told you this, but Paul's friend Josh who we were hanging out with last Friday . . . He's positive."

Josh became the first gay man I met who was both victimized by and convicted for a crime he didn't commit. There was no appealing his verdict. He was sentenced to die with zero chance for parole.

Josh was my first. He wouldn't be my last.

Six

For our third date, Fred suggested we go rollerblading together. He didn't need to ask me if I had a pair of roller blades because absolutely everyone did. They were a very convenient way to get around the city, and they reminded me of going roller skating as a kid, another activity that I cut from my repertoire of faggot behavior.

To be clear, roller skating itself wasn't inherently faggoty. All types of kids on Staten Island went to Skate Odyssey on the weekends and went around in circles listening to disco and Top 40. But it was my fateful decision one Saturday to attend wearing one of my mother's favorite shirts, an oversized blue tee with a giant roller skate screen printed onto the front. I tied it off in a knot on the side at the waist and debuted my choreographed rendition of "Keep On Loving You" by REO Speedwagon. Under the disco ball and the flashing lights I felt myself merge with the moment, gracefully maneuvering between the other kids as I hit my spins and my jumps, glory coursing through my veins as I mouthed the crescendo to the final chorus. *And I meant every word I said, when I said that I loved you, I meant that I loved you forever. And I'm gonna keep on lov . . .* But my debut performance became my swan song as some teenage guido intentionally clocked me in the stomach as he passed me going the other way.

I put on my blades and skated from my place in Murray Hill down to Fred's place in Chelsea. While I lived on my own in an upscale, double-doorman, pre-war building on the corner of Park Avenue and 34th Street, I only did so thanks to my aunt and uncle, who owned the place and allowed me to live there for a ridiculously low $750 a month. I felt like a baller: 23 years old and being greeted by four separate doormen as "Mr. Lauterstein" every time I came and left. But Murray Hill wasn't exactly the epicenter of New York City's gay scene. That was Chelsea, and Fred was located right in the thick of it.

Fred's doorman buzzed me in and when I got off the elevator on his floor, I quickly bladed down the hallway to his apartment. There was something in me that was anxious to get to his door. I guess I was excited to see this guy who I had all but written off just a couple of weeks ago. It was a new feeling. Something joyous. It reminded me of the skipping I eliminated from my behaviors back in fifth grade. I guess it was okay to feel this way again, because based upon how much I enjoyed penises, I was indeed the faggot that all those former bullies thought me to be — and happily so for the first time. I did a jump spin pulled straight from my REO Speedwagon routine and hit my mark right outside of Fred's front door. I felt *super* gay at that moment, and I was not one bit mad about it.

Fred opened the door and gave me one of his incredible kisses before he let me in. This was my second time at his place, my first time sober, and it was even better than I remembered. Everything in there felt like *something*. My college friends had furnished their apartments with reclining chairs upholstered in beige fake leather, torn Phish posters standing in as art, and half-smoked water bongs that hadn't been cleaned since our freshman year. But Fred's place surrounded me with intention. His intention. It was like he saw everything around him and made sure it had a reason to be there.

"I love your apartment, Fred. It's so put together. This couch is so cool."

"I don't like it. I'm going to cover it with black velvet fabric that I saw in the garment center and add some gold trim and make it look like a couch from the Roxy." The Roxy was a mega-club located on 18th and 10th. I had been there a couple of times over the past year with my best friend from high school, prior to coming out. When he would take me there and introduce me to his gay friends, they would all lean in to kiss me and I would say, "Sorry, I don't do kisses."

But that was then. I sure as hell did kisses now, and I was particularly fond of doing them with Fred. I knew the couches he was talking about, too. They were kind of over-the-top and grand but I could see exactly how that vibe would work with the rest of his furniture. Not that his surroundings were over the top — well, except for his roommate Eddie, who was thankfully nowhere to be seen. Or heard, for that matter.

Fred put his blades on and asked me where I wanted to go. He suggested Central Park or maybe down through the Village to the West Side Piers. "Why don't we go look at that fabric?" I suggested. I can't really explain the smile that appeared on his face. I could tell that he was so happy that I took an interest in what he was doing, but at the same time there was something restrained in his expression. It caught me off guard because Fred seemed so genuine, but his smile made it seem as if he had something to hide. I didn't think much about it after that. It's not like we had been on more than a couple of dates and the idea of red flags wasn't even something that had entered my thought process.

We made our way up 7th Avenue to 37th Street and I found myself in a part of town I hadn't really explored before: The Garment District. Even though it was Saturday, the streets were wildly chaotic, with people pushing large canvas bins on wheels loaded with fabric and what Fred referred to as "cut goods".

He went on to explain what cut goods were as part of a meticulous crash course he delivered to me on how clothing was manufactured. He detailed each step of the process: from the sketching of designs, to the drafting, correcting, and grading of patterns, to the knitting and spreading of fabric for bulk production, to the different machines used for sewing and hardware application. He spoke at length, to say the least, and after a good 20 minutes of uninterrupted education, he apologized for boring me.

But I wasn't bored, I was *fascinated*. I had always loved clothing and used it to express myself since my early teens. I used to sketch out designs when I wasn't writing poetry. But beyond knowing that people used sewing machines, I never really thought about how clothing was actually made. I suddenly realized that my co-worker Vince, who was Sonic Assembly's manager of production, oversaw all of this kind of work. I literally worked at a company that made clothing and I had no idea how any of it happened.

But Fred knew. I was getting the feeling that Fred knew how to make just about anything. Well maybe not lawnmowers or nuclear reactors, but he might as well have. I had never encountered anyone like him. He was nothing like the Wall Street man I had fantasized about, making so much money that he could walk into any art gallery and drop six figures on a painting just for bragging rights while diversifying his portfolio. Fred wasn't the consumer — he was the *creator*.

Fred took me in and out of all the fabric stores in the garment center until we found the exact material he envisioned for his couch. We bought a roll of it, along with all the trims and some batting to firm up the cushions, and for the next few days I was at his side as he taught me how to recover a couch. It came out amazing, but much like everything else in the apartment, he wasn't happy with it once it was done.

Fortunately, there was one thing he seemed to be happy with in his apartment, and that was me. Unlike everything else he had refinished, Fred and I were just getting started.

Seven

While waiting in LaGuardia Airport for my flight to San Francisco, the first stop on a West Coast business trip that would take me from Fresno to San Diego, I found myself picking up a few magazines to occupy my brain while in the air. I mostly read *The Source, Paper, Vibe,* and *High Times,* along with local NYC gay rags *HX* and *Next.* The mix of music, fashion, drugs, and sex they provided seemed to cover all my bases. But when I got to the bookstore in Terminal B, right there in the front on full display, was a book titled *Queer in America* by the journalist and gay activist Michelangelo Signorile. I had known of the author from his controversial policy of "outing" people in the public eye who were openly homophobic while being secretly gay. Most of the gay people I had met felt that this was a dangerous invasion of privacy. They defended their position by asking whether or not any of us would want the most personal and pivotal moment of our lives to be taken away by another. I thought outing was a declaration of war against our own kind who were knowingly oppressing us for their own advancement, and it spoke to me with its militancy. I learned more about the true history of racism from "militant" hip-hop artists like Public Enemy than I did from the public school system. Feeling militant about my own culture was nothing short of empowering.

Reading *Queer in America* was life-changing. Up until that moment, I had seen the closet as a space where I had been hiding for the first two decades of my life. It was a self-centered place that I fought to escape from so that I could have the same things that my straight friends had: love, acceptance, and sex without shame. I had no idea that the closet was actually a societal prison largely guarded and policed by members of my own community. The depth of hypocrisy coming from within our own ranks made the hatred of those who didn't really know us seem practically acceptable. From New York to Los Angeles to Washington DC, queer people in media, entertainment, and politics were largely responsible for reinforcing the stereotypes and stigmas used against us. They leveraged their platforms to deflect attention from themselves by putting a spotlight on us, on me, and I was fucking pissed off at the status quo of traitors within our ranks.

My days of wanting to blend in for the sake of not being noticed were over. I wanted to be noticed. I wanted to be seen. I wanted to be heard. In that moment, I realized that there were millions of gay people living in their own closets, their own private hellscapes, and I was not going to be part of their problem. I wanted to be part of our solution. I had no idea how, but I was going to help set us free.

Halfway through my trip, I finished *Queer in America* and picked up a copy of *And the Band Played On* by Randy Shilts, and my experience as a gay man exploded. I learned that AIDS wasn't a gay disease; it was a disease that was allowed to happen to gay people, often by gay people. This plague dominated so much of how gay people, including myself, saw one another, and it was all part of the closet, designed to stigmatize us back into silence. The phrase "Silence = Death," born out of the work of six courageous activists in New York, suddenly held even more meaning than solely referring to the tragic deaths of those who were my literal queer ancestors. Silence would lead to the cultural death for our community. I was done being silenced, with being silent. I wanted to be *loud*. My life depended on it. I wanted everyone in the world to know that I was gay, and that being gay had nothing to do with living in Chelsea or idolizing Madonna or covering couches in velvet and tassles. Being gay meant I loved dick — a lot — and I was going to wear my status as a faggot on my sleeve. I was going to do whatever I could to move beyond fitting in to be accepted. I didn't need to fit in. I needed my community to live and be celebrated for exactly who we are. No more hiding. No more closets. No more silence. And, I hoped, one day, for no more death.

I got home from my trip to the West Coast and decided I was going to start a one-man activist group called the Metropolitan Faggot Authority, or the M.F.A. for short. I bought a box of crayons and began scribbling out ideas for posters and artwork, combining the influences of Jean Michel Basquiat, Public Enemy, and GFS with the history of AIDS, my heroes like Michelangelo Signorile, and the language of house music. I admit that the artwork was shitty, but it was the best I could do to channel my anger into some sort of mission. The world had picked a fight with me, and things were about to get nasty.

I didn't realize it at the time, but Nasty Pig was being born.

Eight

The bar where I first met Fred was a variation on the places I had frequented in the five months since I came out of the closet. They were gathering spots where guys came to stand around, drink, and focus their attention on screens showing cable news, or sports, or gay porn. I found the experience to be disappointing to say the least. I don't know what I was expecting, but it was something more than what I got. I was never really someone who was so into bars in the first place. While I had made my way into the bar scene at college, I had been going to clubs since I was 15, sneaking into spots like The Palladium and The Tunnel and The Limelight. I even managed, as a junior in high school, to experience The Saint when I went to see Dead or Alive perform "You Spin Me Round" for a riled-up crowd of gay men of legal age. "Look at all these faggots," I said to my fellow Staten Islander crew who had snuck in with me. I didn't realize until much later that I had gotten the chance to experience one of the most legendary gay clubs in New York City just months before it closed.

Going out dancing was in my blood, and this practice continued into college when I dove a bit deeper into Manhattan's thriving underground scene. During the summer and on winter breaks, while my fraternity brothers went to Florida to be disgusting to women and drink until they puked, I was pressed up in Mars, Red Zone, and Love Machine for the house music, and Powerhouse at Building for the hip-hop. I would show up to Michael Alig's outlaw parties on subway cars and at unsuspecting McDonald's restaurants. While all these spots had very different vibes, the common thread for me was that they all were so authentic, and despite being closeted, or perhaps because of it, I gravitated to everything that was honest and real.

Fred shared my appreciation for going out dancing, and from the earliest days of our budding relationship we would spend pretty much every Saturday night at the Roxy, Chelsea's legendary gay nightclub on 10th Avenue and 18th Street. The Roxy felt like a spectacle, packed with all sorts of colorful characters who gave the space a carnival-like atmosphere. Lina and Candis, Bunny and RuPaul, Lahoma and Perfidia, along with countless other nightlife fixtures would parade around the space and bring some much-needed atmosphere to the overall vibe. The Roxy was definitely an upgrade from the gay bars that I had found myself in prior to meeting Fred, but despite it being the go-to spot for all of gay New York on a Saturday night, and undeniably fun, I still had hoped for something *more*.

"I want to show you Sound Factory," Fred practically screamed into my ear over the music blaring through the Roxy sound system. It was extremely tough to converse on the dancefloor, and I had made it clear to Fred on a few occasions that his predilection for chatting with me while I was throwing down was a no-no. When I was dancing I was not to be disturbed, so his decision to violate my headspace meant what he had to say was important. I had heard about Sound Factory, an after-hours club located someplace within walking distance of the Roxy. Fred and his friends, who were becoming my friends, had talked about it, and on a few occasions, they had departed for Factory as Roxy wound down around 4 a.m. I was never interested in going. I wanted to get home with Fred as quickly as possible. Given the choice between continuing the night with more dancing (something I had been doing for the past seven or eight years) or trying to take Fred's dick and lose my virginity (something I had been doing for the past seven or eight weeks) more dancing always took a back seat.

But that night, something else I had been doing for the past seven or eight weeks, ketamine, had me in a spin, and the thought of checking out Factory seemed appealing. Additionally, any time Fred prefaced something with "I want to show you . . . " I paid attention. Fred had shown me how to cover a couch, refinish a cabinet, cook chili con carne, and make my own candles. Each time I learned something cool, and each time it made me appreciate him more, so I knew I was going to experience something of value. We found our friends, stumbled out of Roxy, and headed north to what would one day become my favorite block in Manhattan, West 27th between 10th and 11th.

Factory felt different before we even got through the door. Unlike almost every other club I had been to, there was a line to get in, and we willingly got in it. I was used to getting into clubs by being picked out of a crowd by a doorman, a chaotic scene where you vied for the attention of one person who held the power to make or break your night, hoping they would let you in. I was accustomed to this rite of passage, and I had mastered it. Waiting in line to get into clubs was something that I associated with, well, places that would let anyone in — and those weren't places I wanted to be. Strike one for Sound Factory.

Strike two came when Fred's roommate Eddie shushed me for speaking above a whisper, like everyone around us. I knew I was loud, but to have Eddie of all people try to quiet me down felt downright hypocritical. Eddie was loud even when he was quiet, and just as I began to serve him a full-throated take-down, Fred grabbed me and said, "David, please keep it down." I didn't like being told what to do and quietly waiting in line as we slowly made our way toward the entrance had me *definitely* wishing I was back at Fred's apartment getting loud with his dick.

"Fred, why isn't anyone allowed to talk out here?"

"I have no idea. It's just the way things happen at Factory so please be quiet so we don't have any problems getting in."

As we got closer to the entrance, I could hear a large man, who looked more like head of security than doorkeeper, tell a group of girls ahead of us that they weren't going to be admitted because it was a gay club. The girls insisted that they were let in just last week, to which he replied, "That was last week. This is a gay club. You're not getting in." I was so confused because from what I heard Sound Factory wasn't exactly a gay club at all, and the same DJ spun there every Saturday night. In a whisper I asked Fred what was going on?

"I have no idea. It's just the way things happen at Factory."

Whatever was going on at this place, I suddenly wanted to get in, and badly so. Something about it set off my authenticity radar. I also became concerned because within our crew of boys we had two of our girls with us, and if they didn't get in Fred wouldn't leave them to walk home alone on their own. Fred was the perfect gentleman. But as we approached, the rope lifted and we all got in without issue.

The silence we left behind outside gave way to the thump of the bass that reverberated through the walls of a dark hallway. We paid the $20 entrance fee and walked down another hallway until we emerged into a large well-lit room where people were sitting on bleacher style seats and hanging out. That place was a fucking scene. The crowd was mixed in every possible way. Boys, girls, and everything in between. Black and white and brown and even green thanks to one jacked-up girl standing on a table with a painted body and hair dyed to match, looking like the daughter of The Jolly Green Giant and She-Hulk. Everyone was serving some sort of look and I was suddenly grateful that I even got in. I thought to myself that I was going to get totally dressed up to come again the following week, and laughed to myself

that I was already becoming a "factory rat," a term I had heard to describe the people who came religiously every weekend. They came to be seen, or to be the scene, or *something*. I couldn't quite yet tell. But unlike the Roxy, where the drag queens brought the drama, the drama was everywhere I looked at Factory.

The walls of the lounge were covered in giant 10-foot-tall canvases, each one exploding with mixed-up imagery from pop culture, the animal kingdom, nightlife, and history. I could immediately tell that they were all done by the same artist, and the "Keck" signature in the corner of each painting confirmed my instinct. The style was so distinct. It carried the signatures of graffiti but nothing about it was derivative. It felt authentically queer. Whatever I had clumsily tried to capture with my Metropolitan Faggot Authority crayon drawings, this artist had nailed it at a scale that was larger-than-life. It fit perfectly with the energy of the looks that the patrons were serving up. In that one room I felt more connected with the gay energy that was being stirred up in my soul than in all the clubs and bars I had been to over the past eight years combined. This was something truly beyond. It felt unreal and like home. I was immersed in a magic that was nothing less than palpable.

Ultimately though, like every other club I went to, I was there for the music and to dance. I had heard a lot about the resident DJ, Junior Vasquez, and as a dedicated househead, I was excited to hear what all the fuss was about. I got turned on to house music in the summer of '88 by my friend Emily. She lent me a mixtape of a set by Frankie Knuckles and it blew my mind. Not since I began listening to hip-hop did a style of music connect with me so deeply. It held elements of the disco and funk records my dad would play, but the beats and the loops kept it deeper. It had more of a drive. I loved it and I was hooked. The summer of '89 was when I really connected with the house scene in New York City, and the very first house record I bought was a song I heard at Mars called "Tears," which turned out to be produced by Frankie Knuckles himself. I guess some people would call that a coincidence. For me, it was poetry, and I doubled down on house from that moment on.

Fred took my hand and led me through the crowded dancefloor. It was a good thing he was in charge because I was completely overwhelmed by the sounds I was hearing. The beats were aggressive, and they came at me in attack mode. I felt the rhythm pulsating through the air around me. It was present and it was progressing, and it was alive. It was heaving. Fred found us a spot and I dropped a pill and for the next two hours I dissolved into the sonic energy that was surging through my body. I became part of it. I was moving and I was being moved and it was all so frenetic and intense. The drums were unlimited and complex, and the entire place would build and release and build and release, a volcanic series of flows and eruptions. The beats densified and piled in on themselves as the music climbed higher and higher, forming a sonic tidal wave that swept through the room, from the rafters to the floor, until it all became so immense that it finally exploded, crashing in upon us, disintegrating into a downpour as the sounds of a rainfall doused our ears from the speakers, stacked 20 feet tall. The lights went out. There was total darkness. All I could hear was rain.

Then, suddenly a spotlight shot through the club, landing upon and illuminating this towering, imperial Black queen, unironically bald, with a perfectly painted face and oversized hoop earrings, wrapped in a skintight red dress that revealed a set of gorgeous, muscular legs, descending downward into the strictest pair of matching red stilettos I had ever seen. She held her pose with ferocity, a seriousness in her gaze, arms extended outward, each finger angled with its own specific intention. With the skill of a ringmaster, without saying a word, she captivated every single one of us. Then precisely as a chorus of electronic voices came through the speakers, her face transformed, eyes opening with such expression and drama that it felt as if she was lifting the curtain on her own performance. Her mouth blossomed open into the most welcoming of smiles as she lip-synched to the track:

IT'S GONNA BE. A LOVELY DAY. FOR YOU AND ME.
JUST WAIT AND SEE

IT'S GONNA BE. A LOVELY DAY. FOR YOU AND ME.
JUST WAIT AND SEE

IT'S GONNA BE. A LOVELY DAY. FOR YOU AND ME.
JUST WAIT AND SEE

IT'S GONNA BE. A LOVELY DAY. FOR YOU AND ME.
JUST WAIT AND SEE

One after another, doors opened above the dancefloor and sunlight came beaming into the room. It was as if the skies had risen and drenched us in the warmth of nature. Everyone's hands lifted into the air and people were applauding and screaming with joy: *WORK JUNIOR! WORK KEVIN!*

WORK!! The music resumed, deeper and organic — and one after another, I heard the voices of women singing about struggles and pain and joy and God. The Factory transformed itself from something secular into something spiritual. It became a temple. People were there to vanquish the pain of bigotry and the devastation of AIDS. They gathered to connect to something glorious and profound. Something that was *theirs*, something that was *ours*.

I wasn't just connecting, though. I was reconnecting. Reconnecting to something that was always there, though unseen. In that moment I understood that queer people had been doing this exact same thing for thousands and thousands of years. I was convinced I had ancestors in Africa and Asia and South America who danced around the flickering lights of a fire while people pounded on drums, just as I did that night and that day. They danced and altered their states until the sun came up and they bathed in the warmth of the magic of the universe.

At that moment I felt that I was no longer doing something new. I was doing something old. I was doing something sacred, something special. It was purposeful, it was powerful, and above all else, it was entirely, beautifully queer.

Nine

"I want to show you The Pines," Fred said as we woke up on a Saturday morning. The sun was warm on our bodies as it came through the windows and fed the palm trees and ivy that filled his bedroom. It amazed me that even on 23rd Street and 7th Avenue his room emanated this natural, organic presence that felt dreamlike. The sponged terra cotta-colored walls and the green leaves and the black and cream mud cloth patterned blanket that we slept beneath made his 10-foot by 12-foot space seem otherworldly. Lying quietly within that jungle-like aesthetic was another thing I had never pictured when I imagined myself with a man, because I didn't know that men like Fred even existed.

He got out of bed, tall and lean with skin golden brown from the summer sun, and put on a pair of white Calvin Klein briefs that framed his beautiful ass and pushed his morning wood to the left. It was long enough to practically reach his hip and thick enough that the elastic of his underwear stood away from his waist. While Fred's upper body was on the thin side, he had incredible legs (three of them to be exact) and I loved to watch him simply walk around the apartment in his tighty-whities, brushing his teeth and tidying up, going about his life next to me as I went about mine.

Fred exited the bedroom and went into the bathroom. I heard him lift the toilet seat and unleash his piss, and my morning wood began to throb. I followed him and stood in the doorway and watched him holding his giant dick until he was done, then shaking it up and down before he tucked it back into his underwear. He flushed and turned to me with that smile, the one that never seemed to fully express the emotions in his eyes, and he giggled and said, "What?" I got on my knees and pulled his briefs down and proceeded to blow him until he came on my chest. I could fit maybe half his dick in my mouth, and I always hoped I was satisfying him. I couldn't deep throat the way I had seen guys in porn suck dick, but I was still new to all of this, and with each passing day I was getting the feeling that I would be hanging out with Fred for a lot longer than I wrote in my journal the night we met, so there would be lots of time to practice.

I stood up and he kissed me. "Go back to bed, Angel. Let me thank you with some breakfast," he whispered in my ear as he held me close. He had started calling me Angel a couple of weeks prior, and I began signing my little notes to him that way, adding a halo with horns around the A and little pointed tail to the l, an appropriate nod to my constant state of horniness. Whatever shame I had about gay sex during the first two decades of my life had quickly been shed. What Fred and I were doing felt natural to me; it was perfectly normal. I went from being afraid that any of my straight friends would think I was gay, to proudly talking about my commitment to mastering fellatio, like an Angel getting his wings.

I went back into the bedroom, got under the blanket, and stared up at the black velvet canopy that Fred had sewn and mounted above our heads. It was grand and dramatic, made of the same fabric we used to cover the couch. He had trimmed the edges with a gold tassel fringe, framing the space above our headboard, making our bed feel almost regal. I loved everything about it, but I was puzzled by the three inches of fringe that hung down, unattached, with a needle and thread dangling from it like a spider descending on a strand of silk. He had put the canopy up weeks ago but left it in this oddly unfinished state. It made no sense, adding to a small but growing list of what seemed like evidence pointing to something about Fred that wasn't quite right — or at least that wasn't quite right with me. As we got to know each other, I learned that Fred had been working at his job as a patternmaker for years without ever getting a raise or a promotion, and without any reservations about that situation either. He was in a large amount of debt by which he was unfazed, and that was the opposite of how I was raised to view money. It quietly bothered me that it didn't bother him. When he had gotten sick toward the end of June, he didn't go to see a doctor. I wondered if he couldn't afford health insurance. Or maybe he didn't have a doctor. Or he didn't care. He just slept for four days straight until he woke up and felt better. That needle and thread hung above my head like a thought bubble filled with question marks.

The bedroom door opened and in walked Fred with breakfast for both of us on a large wooden tray. It smelled amazing, somewhat sweet, oddly familiar, and I quickly forgot about any misgivings I had about this man who was becoming part of my heart. "So, the omelet has this cheese in it that I bought for you from the farmers market in Union Square. You mentioned that you liked it in your appetizer the last time we ate at Intermezzo."

"What smells kind of sweet?" I asked him.

"That's chicken apple sausage. When we went out to breakfast last weekend you asked the same question when our waitress passed by and brought food to another table. So, when you got up to go to the bathroom, I asked her what it was so I could make it for you. Try it." It was delicious. So was the omelet. So were the biscuits he made, and so was Fred. The level of attention he paid to making me happy, to making me feel special, remembering these little details about what I liked and putting them into my breakfast in bed, made my eyes tear up as I ate beside him. He was so sweet. I had found a good man, so rather than speculate about my assumptions I decided to ask him his truth. I pointed upward and asked, "Fred, why haven't you finished sewing up the tassel? I don't get it. It's like ninety-nine-point-nine percent of the way there so why not just finish it?"

"Because then it would be done and I wouldn't be able to work on it anymore." His answer was so simple, so pure, the answer of a true artist. I removed this from my list of concerns. I decided to stop being concerned at all. I had found a good man, and I was going to learn to trust him.

"Let's shower and get dressed," he said. "I want to show you The Pines." He lifted the tray off us, brought it into the kitchen and put the dishes in the dishwasher. I got out of bed, went into the bathroom, and turned on the faucet, careful to adjust the knobs to the temperature I knew that he liked. I got under the water, and he got in right after me, washing my back then turning me around to shampoo my hair. I stood there sudsy and smiling. He shut off the water, grabbed a towel, wrapped it around me and dried me off. There was something paternal about it, and it felt incredibly right. We went into the bedroom and got dressed: tank tops and cut off shorts with scrunchy E.G. Smith socks and Tims. It was the gay clone look of 1993, and I loved that the Tims I wore to hip-hop clubs did double-duty for my emerging faggot identity.

Fred packed a bag with sunblock, towels, some snacks and blue Gatorades, and we headed out of the apartment. I grabbed his hand and held it as we walked together. The weather was NYC August at its best: 85 degrees and sunny, with no humidity. We passed by a street vendor selling sunglasses and I grabbed a pair of Louis Vuitton knockoffs. They were ostentatious as fuck and added a bit more hip-hop flare to my Chelsea boy style.

We got to 8th Avenue and headed north toward Penn Station, but right around 25th Street Fred let go of my hand. We walked a few more feet, Fred continuing to talk to me like nothing had changed. When I realized he didn't let go of me to get something out of his pocket, I stopped dead in my tracks and asked him angrily, "Why did you just do that?"

"David, we're not in Chelsea anymore and I don't want anyone to see us ho . . ." but by that point I was seeing red and I cut him off.

Raising my voice I said, "*Fuck that!* I don't give a fuck what anyone thinks. I've lived my whole life in the closet and I'm not going back so this isn't going to cut it with me. If you want to be with me then you need to be *proud* of us and not give a shit about what other people think!" I was irate. All the rage that had been building inside me came spewing out at Fred. I quickly started walking away from him, that paternal feeling I bathed in earlier now gone, furious at his rejection. He stood there calling out to me, but at some point he realized I wasn't stopping, so he ran after me and grabbed my arm and turned me around.

"If you want to be with me David then don't walk away from me and don't fucking cut me off. You're acting like a child and I'm not having it." I guess he was the one feeling paternal now. "We're above 23rd Street and I know you want to be in everyone's face but that's you, not me. I've been out for a long time, and I've experienced a lot of hatred and violence and I'm not interested in attracting it because I don't want anything to happen to you." He started crying. "I don't want anyone to hurt you, especially because of me. You're my Angel and I can't lose you." He was sobbing uncontrollably, and I went to pull him in close, but he shouted, "No! Don't!" I wasn't sure if he didn't want to hug me because of my behavior or because of where we were, but I held back and put my hand on his shoulder instead. He shook it off. Whatever rage I was feeling, Fred's felt twice as big and ten times as deep.

"Fred, honey, I'm sorry. Please stop crying." I reached into his bag and pulled out a Gatorade. "Drink this. Calm down." He took a few sips and started to breathe easier, and we resumed our walk to Penn Station, but he stayed mostly quiet for the rest of the train trip that followed. I kept trying to talk to him, to better understand what he was feeling, but he wasn't open to it. As someone who values language and communication as tools for resolution, his silence confused me. It also pissed me off. Why the fuck were we sitting there not speaking, trapped on a train to Long Island, when we could just talk things out and move on?

We pulled up to Sayville, where Fred indicated that it was time for us to get off. As we exited the train, I noticed that just about everyone else getting off looked pretty damn gay, too. We boarded a white van, and Fred put his hand on my knee as we sat. Progress. We drove through this quaint small town until we reached a ferry terminal and got on board a boat named the Island Princess. As soon as it pulled away from the dock, Fred's energy completely changed. He seemed to light up. It was as if nothing had happened. He began talking about The Pines and its sister community, Cherry Grove, and all the experiences he had enjoyed there over the years. As we pulled into the harbor, he pointed out the different establishments: the Pines Pantry and the Blue Whale and the Pavilion. But all I could see were hot men walking around in the tiniest of speedos.

We got off the ferry, made our way into town, got some ice cream, and in a race against its melting, ate it as quickly as possible. We walked through the harbor and headed toward the beach. He grabbed my hand and talked to me about the different houses lining the shore. "Calvin Klein lives there. That one used to be owned by Tommy Tune. This one coming up has a pool with a glass wall and you can see people swimming inside it." We left the beach and headed to the boardwalks, looking at the houses and the deer. The entire time we were holding hands. He felt safe here, and I don't think I had ever seen Fred so happy.

As we passed the co-ops, Fred turned to me and said, "This place just feels like home to me."

It felt like home to me too, because it was.

Ten

Today, we get to play outside all day by ourselves as much as we want because Mommy said we could and we're in charge. At home someone has to watch us when we play and when we walk to school Mrs. Matae goes with us because we're too little to go by ourselves. But here it's just me and Alisha and Karen and we get to be the ones in charge. Alisha just turned eight in June so she's the oldest and Karen is six and we include her because she's my sister. But I love Alisha the most because she's my favorite cousin and when we play Charlie's Angels she's Jill and I'm Kelly and we make Karen be Sabrina. Karen always wants to be Jill or Kelly but we don't let her even though Mommy told me to in order to be fair. I told Mommy that we would but we don't because Karen cries at first but then she stops and we have fun and me and Alisha are really the ones in charge anyway.

We're staying with Aunt Nina and Uncle Robert in their apartment but for some reason they don't call it an apartment like the one they live in on 96th Street. They call it a co-op and I don't understand the difference except that this apartment is at Fire Island so maybe that's what apartments at the beach are called. The co-op has tall glass windows and a bedroom upstairs that doesn't have a wall and it's so cool cuz you can see downstairs when we play up there! That's where Charlie gives us our assignments and today we need to go build a castle on the beach and then capture horseshoe crabs at the other side where the water comes right up to the grass. We take the ladder down to the living room and run out the door to the deck then down a staircase that goes round and round until we are on the boardwalk and the air smells so good.

We head to the beach and we hide behind the gates with our finger guns drawn in case anyone tries to stop us. We get to Ocean Walk and we head into the sand dunes which are way taller than all the adults and not just Aunt Nina because she's a little person. They're even taller than the snow mountains that the trucks make in front of our home on Staten Island when the plows come through in winter and those mountains go halfway up the lamp posts! The grass is almost as tall as me and we get down on our hands and knees and make our way through the sand dunes that go on and on and this way none of the bad guys spot us cuz we don't want to get shot. Charlie gave us our assignment and we need to win.

The sand dunes get shorter and we stand up and run onto the beach and past the towels where the men are laying out and some of them are always naked. "We see a tushy! We see a tushy!" we scream and laugh and I love to look at their armpits cuz they are hairy and so are their legs and their things are much bigger than mine. So are their balls and they look like the ones on the dog that lives next door to us at home. The men here hold hands and kiss each other and their things get bigger and so does mine when I see them but those are my private parts and I don't talk to Mommy and Daddy about it. I once asked Mommy why the only girls I ever see are Aunt Nina and Alisha and Karen and she said the women were home making food and that made sense. Aunt Nina always made hot dogs for us when we got hungry.

Me and Alisha put ourselves in charge of making drip castles and we run back and forth to the edge of the ocean and scoop up wet sand and let it pour out from our hands to build the towers. We tell Karen to go find clam shells and she comes back with them and then we tell her to go find scallop shells and she gets them too. We press them into the towers like walls and we make patterns and we use one big shell to dig a moat. Karen starts to cry because she wants to be Jill but Alisha is Jill so we tell her to go find a starfish for the top of the castle and that Charlie said it was a special assignment that only Sabrina was pretty enough to do. Me and Alisha know that starfish are a lot harder to find than shells so Karen will be gone for a while and we can play together without her cuz everyone knows Jill and Kelly are the pretty ones.

Two naked men walk up to our castle and Alisha says, "Hi Jim and Michael! This is my cousin David."

"Hi Alisha. We actually met David last summer. It's nice to see you again David. I'm Jim and this is Michael." They both shake my hand and they have hair on their knuckles. "That's a beautiful castle you're building," Michael says.

"It's not done yet," I tell them. "We sent Karen to find a starfish to put on top and then we can tell Charlie that the first part of the assignment is done and then we have to go get the horseshoe crabs next."

"That sounds like a lot of fun!" Jim says. "Alisha, is Charlie one of your parents' friends out here?"

"No, it's Charlie from Charlie's Angels and we're the angels and I'm Jill cuz we both have blond hair," Alisha says.

"And I'm Kelly because I have dark hair and my sister Karen is Sabrina because Jill and Kelly are the pretty ones and we're in charge." Alisha and I stand back-to-back and stick our arms out with our handguns pointed just like when the show starts and the explosions go off and the two naked men start laughing and it makes me smile.

Michael asks me, "David, do you like being Kelly?" and I tell him that she is my favorite even though everyone in the world has a poster of Jill in their rooms. "Kelly has the best hair, and she gets to wear red jumpsuits just like the one Mommy has only we're on assignment at the beach today so we are in our bikinis."

Alisha and I pick up clam shells and hold them up to our chests and shake our hips back and forth as we walk around the castle like grown up girls. The two men are laughing so hard now and Jim says to me "David, I have a feeling when you grow up you're going to be Kelly in real life."

"That's silly because it's on TV and that's not even real!" I tell him and now me and Alisha are laughing hard too.

"Well Angels, good luck with the rest of your assignment and watch out for the bad guys," says Jim. Michael says back "They should be ok. There aren't any bad guys out here in The Pines." And then Jim says back "I beg to differ, girl." They both start laughing even harder and I guess they get to be girls too when they play. They turn around and start walking away and me and Alisha shout out "We see your tushies. We see your tushies."

Alisha tells me, "Those are Mommy and Daddy's friends and they have us over for dinner sometimes. They live with Carl and Jake and Mark and the other Jake at the next house down over there." I can barely see it because it's so far away and the dunes are all around it and the grass comes up even higher there. On Staten Island there are houses everywhere and they are all right next to each other but here there aren't a lot of houses and there are no cars and no real bad guys like the boys at school who want to beat me up. That's why we can be in charge of ourselves with no one watching us.

"And down that way is where Stephen and Mark live with Charles and Randy. And next to them are Adam and Eddie and Doug and Kelly only Kelly is a boy. Not like you Kelly!" Alisha tells me as she laughs.

"I feel like everyone here is a boy except you and Aunt Nina right?" I ask Alisha.

"Well not everybody," she tells me, "but mostly everybody. Most of Mommy and Daddy's friends in Manhattan are boys too. They come over

all the time to look at the pictures and the statues and sometimes they buy them. We have these parties and everyone comes over and we turn on the disco ball in the dining room and put out a lot of snacks and I get to serve everyone. We get dressed up and so does everyone else and we play all the Donna Summer songs." My Daddy doesn't let me listen to Donna Summer cuz he says it's for grown-ups but sometimes when he's not home I put on the record and play it in the headphones and dance all by myself.

Their apartment on 96th Street is like a hundred times bigger than the co-op and there's this really long room they call the gallery with pictures on the walls of naked people and sculptures of private parts. One painting has a bunch of naked people on a horse and there's a huge statue of a man's thingy that's as tall as Mommy! I hug it when the adults aren't around, and we all laugh because we're not supposed to touch it but it feels cold and smooth against my face. And me and Alisha and Karen always get to jump on the big waterbed that's right in the middle of the gallery. It's so fun! Alisha told me that no one sleeps on it which is weird but maybe that's why we get to play on it in the first place. Uncle Robert makes some of the paintings himself, the ones of Marylin Monroe and Barbara Streisand and they look like they're in TV's with knobs sticking out for where you'd change the channel and make the sound louder. Their faces are made of thin little round lines of paint and one time when I was with Uncle Robert in the room where he makes stuff I asked him if I could copy him and use his little tiny brushes. He told me "David you know when you go to the doctor to get a shot? Well, I make those paintings by putting paint in the same needles the doctor uses and squeezing it out onto the canvas, so it's too dangerous for you to do that because needles can hurt. But you can use any of my other brushes" and he got them all out and me and Uncle Robert painted together for hours that day.

Karen comes running back with a starfish and we put it on top of the drip castle and we use our hands to call Charlie and tell him that we are heading to the other water. We climb back through all the dunes and find a boardwalk and run to the other side of the island. The beach side has big waves and lots of people but this side has almost no sand and the water stays flat and there are lots of reeds with big fluffy tails. We pull out all the little seeds and blow them in the air and they float away like dandelions. We make wishes and Alisha wishes for a pony and Karen wishes to be Jill next time and I wish that I could spend every weekend here instead of

playing little league. We go out into the water and look down and I find a horseshoe crab first. I pick it up by its tail and then Alisha finds hers and picks it up and we both sing the notes to the Charlie's Angels theme song at the top of our lungs. But Karen can't find one and she starts to cry, and she is my sister, so I put mine back into the water behind her and she spots it and picks it up. "I found mine too! I found mine too!"

She puts her hand up to her face and calls Charlie and lets him know that we won the assignment. We all sing the song together and run home to the co-op. We climb the stairs and open the door to the living room and there is Uncle Robert and Aunt Nina with a chocolate frosted cake that says "Happy Birthday David" with eight candles on it. Everyone sings happy birthday to me, and I close my eyes and wish for the same thing I did before . . . that I could spend every weekend here instead of playing little league . . . and I blow out my candles all at once.

Eleven

I woke up on my 24th birthday thinking how much had changed for me over the past year. Last August I was closeted, deeply depressed, out of shape, and despite having a large group of friends from college, I felt totally alone. I knew I couldn't live that way anymore, but the thought of coming out carried with it the consequences of possibly losing all my friends and my family.

But so much had changed. I wasn't alone anymore. Every member of my family accepted me as I came out to them, one by one, as did many of my friends. My depression had given way to a level of optimism that some might refer to as toxic, and I had been hitting the gym across the street from my studio five times a week. I even used a trainer to help get me into shape, but admittedly I hired him primarily because he turned me on so much. He wore loose fitting gym shorts without underwear, and the outline of his hefty cock was constantly in my face, quite literally when he spotted me doing bench presses. After our sessions I would run back to my apartment and jerk off furiously.

The biggest change in my life, thankfully, was that I had met the man I needed, and not the one I thought I wanted. Fred brought out the best in me. He had an incredibly strong moral compass, and he was always doing the right thing, even when it meant he would get less. It was so admirable. I loved getting what I wanted, so being around him made me often stop and think when I was about to do something for my personal gain at the expense of my integrity. Rarely did that cause me to change my behavior, but rarely was more than never, and I viewed that as real progress. Fred was also a conduit for my own creativity, as he lived in a constant state of creation and I found that contagious. Being around him inspired me to return to something I hadn't done since college: writing poetry. I didn't think any of it was good, but Fred hated everything he did as well, so I followed my instinct and just let whatever I was feeling at the time come out on the page.

"Good morning, my birthday Angel," Fred whispered in my ear as he wrapped his arm around me and spooned my body with his. Fred was long waisted with shorter legs, and I was short waisted with longer legs, so when he held me from behind, our bodies fit perfectly together like two dovetailed pieces of wood.

He began to kiss my neck and I felt his raging boner pressed up against my ass. He reached around and grabbed mine out of my briefs and started jerking me off. I rolled over and we started kissing furiously. I pulled his briefs down off his body and started sucking his cock, or at least the half of it that I could fit in my mouth. I swung my ass around to his face and sat down on it. Fred was the best kisser, everywhere. He ate my hole and worked me up so hard before he grabbed some lube from his dresser and began to work his fingers in.

I was tight. I knew I was tight. The few guys who had fingered me before I met Fred all told me so. I wanted Fred to fuck me so bad, but getting his dick in my ass was like squeezing ten pounds of meat into a two-ounce shot glass. I had gotten in the habit of trying to open myself up at the gym when I showered at the end of each of my workouts. I would soap up my finger and stick it into my ass. As soon as I felt it clench, I would stop, breathe, relax, and push in further. I did the same thing as I pulled out. I did this religiously, and God it felt good. Eventually I managed to slide not one, not two, but three fingers into and out of my ass without clamping down and practically snapping them off.

Fred lifted me off of him and got me on all fours. I heard him tear the wrapper off a condom and squirt more lube out onto his dick. He pressed the head against my hole, and I felt it give way, but every time he pushed in deeper, I moved away from him on the bed. He chased me around that mattress in circles, until eventually I got on top of him, hoping I could ease my way down toward officially being a bottom. As much as I wanted it mentally, my body just refused to get with the program. I got frustrated. That made things worse. Fred leaned into me and said, "Angel, it's not about the destination. Let's just have fun with the journey." Fred was so wise, but also ... *fuck off! I needed to get nailed.* I pulled off the rubber and sucked the top half of his dick until he came on my face.

Somewhere along the way, I stopped being terrified of having sex. Everything I was doing was widely considered very safe: kissing, sucking with no swallowing, rimming, using rubbers when we tried to fuck. I was comfortable with taking the same risks that all my friends who were negative were taking because they were doing just fine. Being with Fred made it even easier, because more than anything in the world, he was terrified of hurting me or losing me. In the brief time I was in the dating pool before I met Fred, at least two guys had tried to coerce me into swallowing their loads, promising me they were negative. One tried to physically force me, but I pulled my head away in time and his cum landed on his chest. Before he could stop shaking from his orgasm, I told him to get the fuck out of my apartment. I didn't have to worry about any of that with Fred.

"OK, so I know you didn't get exactly what you wanted for your birthday," Fred said to me with a closed-mouth smirk as he stood up and smacked my ass, "but I got you something else that I hope you will like." He reached underneath the bed and pulled out a present, wrapped in beautiful navy and gold paper with a gold ribbon tied around it, finished with a cascading bow that curled and opened like a flower blossom. Attached was a card in a gold envelope with the word "Angel" stylishly penned on its outside in navy ink that matched the paper. Fred's attention to detail was unwavering.

Angel, I know that today is your birthday, but every day I am with you feels like a gift to me. I love watching you grow before my eyes. The past three months have been the best of my life, and I hope I have made them feel the same for you. May you get everything you want today, and every day in the future.
Love, Fred.

It was the first time either of us had used the L-word, and even though it was casually dropped in a signature, Fred never added details without intention. I hugged him tight as my eyes watered up.

I gently untied the ribbon, respecting the work he had put into making the bow himself, but once undone I tore into the wrapping paper like a seven-year-old. I loved opening presents, and I wasn't exactly a delicate person to begin with, so while I'm sure his wrapping job was as immaculate as his bow, it didn't stand a chance against my desire to see what I was getting. I ransacked the paper and inside was a copy of *Thierry Mugler Photographe,* the book I had seen at Fred's friend Louis's apartment. I followed fashion designers throughout college, and I had always loved Mugler for his capacity to present a fantasy world through clothing. His ability to transform the women who wore his designs into futuristic powerful sex Goddesses astounded me, and by the time George Michael released his "Too Funky" video, with every 90s supermodel strutting down the runway in his creations, Mugler had become my favorite. That same year, as the grunge music scene exploded and laid waste to the careers of many pop musicians such as George

Michael, Marc Jacobs picked up the grunge trend for fashion, causing that industry to change direction, too. Mugler's couture fell out of favor with both the industry and the public, replaced by fashion that gave more flannel than fantasy. But I lived for the fantasy, and no one delivered fantasy like Mr. Mugler.

While I may have been a Mugler fan, Fred was a Mugler *fanatic*. As both a patternmaker and someone who was more interested in how things were put together than what they became, Fred saw Mugler as the consummate constructionist. He would buy the collection magazines each season and skip right to Mugler's pieces, studying them, trying to understand how each seam was sewn and in what order the parts were put together. When he would turn the page and come to one of Mugler's pieces made entirely of metal, he would stare in amazement, astounded by both the vision and the execution.

We bonded over our love of Mugler. I loved how he built his own world: designing impeccable haute couture, choosing models no other fashion house would think to cast, then traveling to the planet's most exotic locations to showcase his grand vision. Fred, on the other hand, loved each meticulous detail: every jewel hanging off a gown, every intricate seam, every piece of boning that went into a corset, even the hole in the long fingernail that housed a cigarette. We spent the morning in bed together, astonished by every page, the models, tiny in proportion to their environments, fascinated by the power and the beauty of the work. Looking at his portrait at the end of the book, we both took a moment to bond over how fucking hot he was as well.

"I love it so much Fred. Thank you," I said to him as I put the book aside and kissed his beautiful face. "How about I make us some breakfast?"

"You just wake up and enjoy your birthday. I'll make something light since we're meeting everyone at Benny's for brunch at 2 p.m. Don't want you to fill up before then," he said as he left the room. But three seconds later he popped back in. "Unless you want a big breakfast. It's your birthday, just tell me what you want."

"Something light sounds great, honey," I said to him. He gave me that Fred smile and left for the kitchen. I got myself out of bed and went to the bathroom, turned on the lights, and there I was — so fucking hairy . . . *again*. In the 90s, the prevailing gay aesthetic was very polished, very smooth. From the photos of Bruce Weber all the way to the dancefloor of the Roxy, it seemed that everyone wanted to appear less like men and more like statues of men. I preferred the hairy men who dominated the 70s and the classic pre-condom porn that made up my spank-bank of VHS tapes. But wanting to fit in with my new community, I had adopted the custom of shaving my chest and my back to appear less like me and more like the statue that bore my namesake.

Unable to achieve this feat on my own, I had also adopted the custom of asking Fred to help me shave my body. While I could manage to get rid of all the hair I had on my chest, the hair on my shoulders, sides, and back were very much out of reach. I would stand in the tub and do my front, then Fred would take the clippers and handle the rest. "One day the hair on your torso is going to join the hair on your back and I'll throw them a wedding reception," he told me as he stroked the inch wide strip of bare skin that ran down the sides of my body. From the neck down, that was about the only part of my torso that wasn't covered in fur. I never felt the urge to shave my armpits, my arms, or my legs, and neither did Fred. Hairy arms and legs were a major turn on for me when I'd stare at guys in my high school locker room, so I was glad that Fred left his intact, and I did the same. Shaving me was quite an ordeal, and it needed to be repeated, often, to keep me looking shiny and new. But just like everything else in life, I was much more passionate about the result than the process. I hated having to sit still in the shower as Fred mowed me, watching the hair fall off and accumulate at my feet below, not to mention having to clean it all up once he was finished.

Contemplating a lifetime of this ritual, I walked out of the bathroom, sat down on the couch to eat with Fred, and announced: "I know what else I want to do for my birthday. After breakfast I want to go down to The Village to get electrolysis."

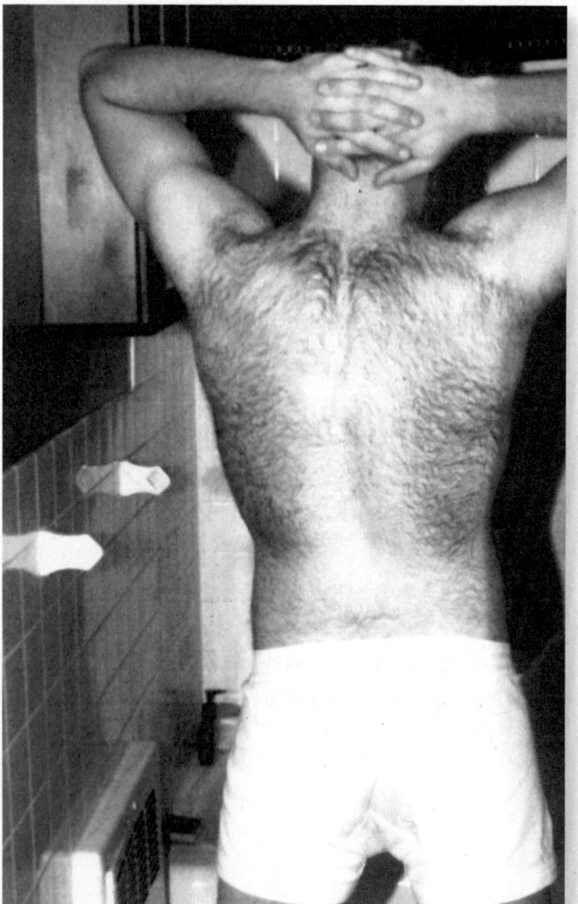

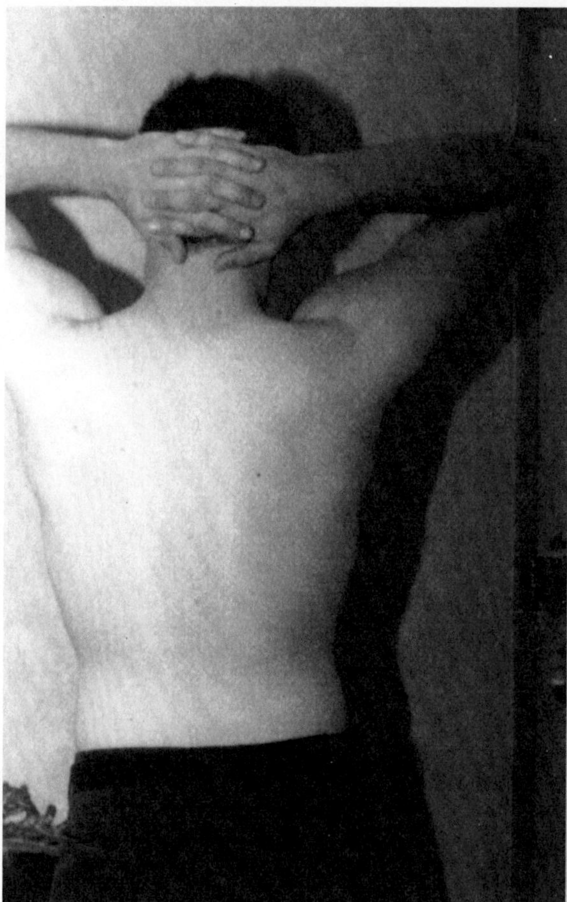

Twelve

As we headed downtown along the West Side Highway, Fred pointed out a few of the crumbling structures that jutted out into the Hudson River. "You know those pictures I took of my ex John that we have hanging in the living room? That's where I shot them back in '81. Guys used to have sex everywhere in those buildings."

The thought of men fucking in public, carefree, no rubbers, buried into my psyche. I imagined them, unbothered by AIDS, pants around the knees, getting off in each other as Manhattan loomed large in the background, going about it's business as those men went about theirs. I imagined it was both extremely hot and incredibly joyous. I also imagined they were all hairy, much like me, but unlike me, they were desired for it. I sometimes thought I was born at the wrong time, that I would have been right at home as a gay man in his 20s in the NYC of the 70s and early-80s. That being said, I would have been dead. 90s New York may have been sanitized of much of its sexual grit, but that meant there was a really good chance I'd survive.

We picked up Louis at the huge loft apartment he shared with Tom in a converted factory building on Horatio Street and the West Side Highway. If Fred's apartment felt like a jungle, Louis's apartment was a fucking rainforest, which was all Tom's doing, according to Fred. There were tapestries hanging on the walls, wooden masks lining the two thick columns that jutted upwards to the high ceilings, and zebra skin rugs under the furniture. Both couches and all the chairs were covered in ornate pillows, and no matter where I would sit, it was always so comfortable. The place was exotic and surreal, characteristics that I noticed as soon as I walked in — and not just after snorting large amounts of ketamine that Tom would procure and sell to us at eight dollars a bottle. Tom was an odd character, one of those gay men who didn't have a job, yet seemed to have everything else, including a prescription authority he had "taken over" from his ex, a veterinarian who had died of AIDS a year prior. While Fred had the strongest moral compass of anyone I had ever met, he didn't seem to mind that there *might* be some strange karma attached to the bumps he gleefully consumed, and neither did I.

"I have to move out of this place," Louis announced as he put on his combat boots. "The only good thing about living here is my unauthorized

access to Tom's hidden stash of powders," I was shocked that anyone would want to leave what was the largest, most well-appointed apartment I had ever seen, especially after Fred told me he was only paying Tom $600 a month to live there. When I asked Louis why he would choose to give up such an amazing set up, he replied, "Girl, the Amazon may be gorgeous, but it loses its appeal when the bitch you share your hut with might be out to shrink your head and steal the beads off your corpse before it's even cold." We all laughed, but Fred laughed the hardest. When Fred and I were together I was always the center of Fred's attention, but when Louis showed up, he stole my spotlight, and I was totally okay with that. I think Louis appreciated that I never felt threatened by their friendship, and he took me under his wing like a gay auntie, side-barring with me whenever we were together, sharing his biting social commentary, and educating me on gay life with a dark sense of humor that rivaled my own.

The three of us headed east until we arrived at an electrolysis place on Bleeker Street that I had seen advertised in *HX*. As we walked in, I was greeted by floor to ceiling images of hairless, chiseled men that I doubt were actual clients, but evoked the results desired by the patrons. Their bodies were so perfect, worked out much harder than mine, and glistening with sweat droplets the size of nail heads at that scale. I wanted to be just like them, just like the guys I would see at the Roxy, and in the Calvin Klein ads, and in the Herb Ritts books Fred had in his living room. That was the ideal, and I wasn't big on settling for less.

"Welcome to Smooth Operator," the woman behind the counter said to us as we made our way to the pricing brochures. "What brings you in here today?"

"My best friend has been dating this gorilla and I'm tired of waiting around every Saturday night for him to be Roxy-ready," Louis said. "I'm not getting any younger and he is definitely getting a lot hairier, so we need to know what it's gonna take to get this problem solved."

She laughed and replied, "Well you're in the right place. Electrolysis is a permanent, effective way to get rid of unwanted hair. Using our state-of-the-art machines, we run a current of electricity through your skin, which breaks down the hair follicles, resulting in the smoothest skin achievable."

"Is it painful?" I inquired.

"We aim to make sure you are as comfortable as possible during the treatments," she replied. That sounded like a *yes* to me.

"Ok, well can you tell me how long it takes and what it costs?" I asked.

"Treatment normally takes 12 to 18 months, but much like the cost, it really depends on the thickness and the amount of hair on the person we are treating." That was the second time she used a variation of the word "treat" and I began to feel less like a potential Adonis and more like a patient that Smooth Operator aimed to heal. That I was looking at a year-and-a-half of visits was the opposite of what my hairy, impatient ass had hoped for in terms of results. "Why don't you step over here behind this curtain and remove your clothes. Let me get a look at you so I can see what we are dealing with and give you a solid estimate."

"I only want my torso done," I told her. She smiled and replied, "Well that's great news in terms of lowering the cost." Upon removing my shirt, her smile faded a bit and the optimistic, exclamation point look to her eyes changed into something resembling more of a mortified question mark.

"Would you mind turning around for me?" Her voice literally wobbled.

I rotated and stood there for what seemed like five minutes as she assessed my back. Finally, without her asking, I turned around on my own to face her. She looked genuinely defeated.

"So, what do you think?" I asked her.

"Ummmm," she paused, "I need to get my manager."

Louis burst out laughing. Lifting his shirt and stroking his chest, he said to me in a strange accent, "Touch this skin honey, touch all of this skin, ok? You can't take it. You're an overgrown orangutan!" Now Fred burst out laughing as well and I didn't quite know what was going on, but I knew they were laughing at me, not with me, so I put my shirt back on and swiftly exited Smooth Operator.

Fred and Louis ran out after me. Fred grabbed my hand and Louis put his arm around me.

"Honey, I don't mind shaving you on the weekends. I love you and I want you to feel good about yourself," Fred said as he kissed my cheek.

"And listen up, orangutan," Louis said in my other ear, "all these men running around with their perfect hairless bodies and you still managed to snag the best man on the planet. You won the gay husband lottery with this one." He pointed at Fred then poked me in the chest. "Play your cards right and I might just let you stick around." He grabbed my face and gave me a big kiss on the lips and hugged me hard, and long, stopping us from walking. "Don't fuck this up," he whispered in my ear, seriously.

I hugged him back and turned around and gave Fred a long kiss on his unbeatable lips. “Ok, now take me to brunch, because after that I'm so ready for a birthday cocktail!” We met the crew at Benny’s, ordered a few rounds of frozen margaritas and maybe had some food. I blacked out, so I can’t say for sure.

Thirteen

I looked at the clock and it was — *fuck!* — 10:54 p.m. "Fred, wake up! We are supposed to meet Louis outside Roxy at midnight!" My head was pounding, and I got out of bed and staggered to the bathroom to down some Tylenol and splash cold water on my face. I wasn't sure how many birthday margaritas I had, but judging by the pain throttling through my brain, it was more than my usual two. Fred joined me in the bathroom and turned on the light, making things that much worse. Not only was I completely hung over, I was still looking like — what had Louis called me? — an overgrown orangutan.

Fred was an introvert so going out in general gave him plenty of anxiety. He also wasn't a "rise and shine" kind of person, so for him, the act of waking up was more like a five-act play than a five minute mission. Being startled out of bed *and* rushed to go out was a recipe for disaster. I could sense that he was in panic mode with only an hour to pull it together, make it out the door, and walk to 18th and 10th. He was doing four things at once, not making progress on any one of them, and I knew that if I didn't put in the work to keep him calm, he would call the whole night off. That was not how I was ending my first birthday as an out gay man.

"Baby," I said to him, "calm down. We have plenty of time. Jump in the shower and don't rush. You already know you're wearing that silver tank top you finished yesterday with your black Calvin Klein Jeans. I'll get the favors together and go get some cash, then I'll take a quick shower once you are done."

"Angel, we still need to shave you. You're definitely ready for another mowing and we didn't have time earlier and I thought you were going to set an alarm and . . . "

"Honey, it's fine. I don't need you to do all that for me so don't stress. I'm going to run to the ATM and I'll shower when I get back." I smiled, put my Tims on and walked out of the apartment, then wiped that smile off my face and replaced it with a pinched, bitchy scowl that matched my displeasure at having to go out dancing with a hairy back. But I only had two options: Fred having a meltdown and calling the night off for both of us or sacrificing my manscaping session so that I could get him out the door and properly turn it up for my birthday. I resigned myself to accepting that if I wanted to be swinging from the rafters at the Roxy, I would need to do so looking like Queen Kong.

We got to the club right on time, and Louis called out to Derek, the doorman, and we walked right in. Louis knew everyone, but not in a social-climber, name-droppy kind of way. He was just such an affable, genuine human being, which was exactly why Fred loved him so dearly. Fred had a lot of friends but didn't let most people truly into his heart the way he did Louis. I used to think Fred was kind of a negative person, often finding fault in others based on the littlest things they said and not giving them the benefit of the doubt. "People tell you who they are very quickly," he told me. "You just need to listen to them."

We made our way past the coat check and to the front bar, which was already packed with boys because Merritt was spinning. Merritt was my favorite DJ of the Saturday night rotation, serving some pretty progressive beats and leaning more on dubs than full vocals. But after experiencing Sound Factory and the futuristic, musical soundscapes Miss Vasquez created with her three turntables, I began referring to Merritt as Junior Mint, much to the delight of all our friends. I may have been a newbie at taking dick, but I had picked up the art of *reading* very quickly.

I learned all about reading after asking Fred what Louis's "overgrown orangutan" comment was all about. Fred sat me down to watch *Paris is Burning*. It turned out "overgrown orangutan" was a phrase used by Venus Xtravaganza to read one of her hairy friends. As Dorian Corey explained, "reading is the real art form of insult." Thanks to my love of language and poetry, I could read like a champ. So, the next time Louis called me an overgrown orangutan, I simply replied, "I used to think the only lines you stole were from Tom's ketamine stash, Miss Venus," and read that bitch right back.

Louis got us a round of Gatorades for free, because of course the bartender knew him. We quickly spotted Lulu, a plus-sized straight girl who always wore a bolero jacket over a bodysuit, a giant circle skirt made of layers of crinoline, and oversized eyelashes. She was easy to pick out of a crowd, which was probably intentional because she was one of the main dealers in the club, and if someone asked you where to get ecstasy, she truly was the only person who fit that description. Her pills were always quality, and Louis asked for three, which he got for free. "I'll take two more," Fred said and gave her forty dollars. He looked at me and smirked. "For later, birthday boy,"

We made our way to the dancefloor and found our crew. They were Fred's crew, but they had become mine too. I still got together with my straight college friends and former frat brothers, but hanging out with them as they drank beer and treated girls poorly was never very appealing to me, especially after I had found the joy of ecstasy, ketamine, and penises.

The pills began to hit, and Tom pulled out his giant vial of ketamine, which he freely passed around to all 12 of us throughout the night. When Fred and I cooked up a bottle of K and put it into a little brown jar, it just about filled it to the top. Tom's vial was as big as a roll of lifesavers, and even with us all doing our best to get twisted, it never seemed to run out. At eight dollars a bottle, I'm sure he wouldn't have cared even if it did.

Merritt was delivering a really great set and we danced and Fred and I kissed. I needed to make my way to the bathroom, so I started to squeeze my way through the dancefloor

As the K started to wear off, I realized that in the sea of glistening homosexuals, my torso had more hair on it than all their bodies combined. And while there were definitely a few guys here and there who rocked some chest hair, I was the only one with a hairy back. Nobody gave me a nod or a wink. There was no hint of cruising. My birthday suit, it seemed, was basically a gorilla costume, and it wasn't Halloween, so no one appreciated my look.

As I made my way through the crowd, I felt someone grab my ass. I turned around and there, holding hands, was by far the sexiest couple of men I had ever seen. Both were shirtless and muscular with hairy chests, their arms covered in tattoos, something I had never seen on anyone who wasn't in an 80s hair metal band. They had on leather chaps, one wearing a pair of jeans beneath his, the other in nothing but a jockstrap. They looked like guys I had seen in some old porn magazines Fred had under his bed. "Those are Leathermen," he told me. "That was a thing in the 70s. Guys used to dress like that, and they'd go to leather bars and sex clubs down in the Meatpacking District, but they're all pretty much shut down now. You know The Spike and The Eagle on the West Side Highway, those are leather bars and they're still open, but no one really goes there anymore. That whole thing kind of got old and died out."

I thought to myself at the time: That "whole thing" didn't die out. It was the men, the beautiful, sexually fearless men, who died out, and they did so long before they got old.

These two men, however, were very much alive — not dated and certainly not dead. They didn't come across as relics or looking like they were wearing Village People costumes. To me, they felt authentically gay, and the way they embraced their sexuality so brazenly stood in stark contrast to the objectified statues that surrounded us, belonging more in a museum to be detachedly admired. These two men were readily available to be touched and desired. I must have been so taken aback by their energy that the one in the chaps and jeans waved his hand in front of my eyes and said to me in a Spanish accent: "That was me who just grabbed your ass, sexy boy." I was stunned. The hottest guy in the club, as far as I was concerned, had just called me sexy, back hair and all. "I'm Julio." He stuck out his hand and I shook it, and he didn't let go, and neither did I. "This is my partner, Marcus,"

"I love your fur," Marcus said to me as he rubbed my torso with both his hands. "I wish I had hair like this." I felt Julio come at me from behind, stroking my back then putting his arms around my chest. "You're such an animal, boy." Pressed in between them, I could smell the leather they were wearing. I smelled their bodies, their sweat. I could almost taste the salt coming off their muscles. My dick was getting hard from the pheromones they were emitting.

"Aren't you going to introduce yourself?" Marcus asked. I suddenly realized I hadn't said a single word to either of them.

"Oh, sorry, I'm David."

"No need to apologize, sexy boy. Just stay here between us and dance." But we weren't really dancing at all. We just rocked back and forth to the music, feeling each other. I felt like I could lift my feet from the ground, and they would just support me between their bodies. I closed my eyes and for a moment wondered if I was floating. Julio whispered in my ear, "So, hairy boy, do you put that ass to use? I love hairy boys like you. Please tell me you're a bottom."

I said yes, then realized I was lying — sort of. "So, honestly, I am a bottom, or I want to be a bottom, but I've only been out of the closet for a few months, and I have a boyfriend and we've been trying, but technically I'm still a virgin. I want it so bad, but he's got a gigantic dick and I can't take it."

"You're still a virgin?" he asked, half laughing. His reaction ended my floating. I came crashing back down to earth and landed somewhere that felt very much out of my league.

"Yeah, it's embarrassing."

But he looked into my eyes and said to me, "Don't be embarrassed, little beast. Thank you for sharing your truth with me. It's actually so fucking hot." He put my hand on his hard cock bulging through his jeans to prove his truth to me. "Can I tell my man too?" I was stunned by his words. He was so gentle with me. So *polite.* The juxtaposition of his hard stance and his soft energy did something to me. At that moment I understood what a girl must feel like when her pussy gets wet. "Of course you can."

"Marcus, this boy is a bottom but he's still a virgin. *Tiene un novio con una verga enorme.* He says he can't take it."

"I wish it was smaller," I said to Marcus, half-jokingly, but mostly not. There had been many nights that I went to bed frustrated, knowing full well that I would have been getting fucked a lot had my boyfriend not been blessed with the biggest dick in Manhattan.

Marcus held my face, looked into my eyes, and said to me, "Ok boy, so two things. Number one, you most definitely can take that dick, or at least your body can. You just have to get your mind to let it happen so your ass can let go. And number two, don't you ever, ever wish that your man had a smaller dick!" He looked at Julio and said, "silly boy," and they both laughed together, but certainly at my expense. It felt like they were laughing *for* me, and I was totally in on the joke.

"Are you a top?" I asked Julio, hoping desperately for an unequivocal yes.

"I am, hairy boy, what gave it away? Me grabbing your ass, or telling you I love using hairy boys? Or was it my armband?" He looked at me so devilishly and I smiled back as if I understood what his armband had to do with being a top. I prided myself on being someone who never went along with something others were saying just to appear smarter than I was. I looked at Julio with a shit-eating grim and playfully replied, "Well grabbing my ass wouldn't do it since even total bottoms want a piece of it. And honestly I have no idea what you mean by your armband." I leaned in, took a deep breath of the leather and his armpit, and looked up at him, flirting with my best set of puppy dog eyes. "I guess I'm just a confused little boy, Papi. *Diga me por favor.*"

"Fuck, boy, you're making me crazy. I'll tell you but you have to grab my cock again." He unzipped his jeans and pulled it out right there on the dancefloor. I'd never seen anyone do that before, but I was all too happy about it, and I stroked his thick uncut dick while everyone around us stared, some in disbelief, others with disdain, but all of them with a whole lot of jealousy as far as I was concerned. "This leather armband — I wear it because it *means* I'm a top." I noticed Marcus was wearing one too, and the thought of both of these men topping me together had me understanding what a girl must feel like when her pussy gets *sopping* wet.

"So you're both tops? Jeez that's so fucking hot!"

"No, no, boy. I'm a top. Marcus is a bottom. I wear mine on my left side. He wears his on his right. Left means top and right means bottom. Same goes for these bandanas in our back pockets."

"It's called flagging," Marcus added. "Makes cruising a lot easier. You tell everyone exactly what you're looking for without saying a word." I wasn't quite sure who "everyone" was, but I wanted to meet these people, and badly so. I was so enthralled by the entire concept of using clothing to communicate sexual preferences that I almost forgot my disappointment in learning both of them weren't tops.

"Here. Take this." Marcus removed his armband and put it on my right bicep. He had to snap it a lot tighter on me because my arms weren't nearly as big as his.

"Trust me," he said as he nodded his head, "you're definitely a bottom, and you're definitely gonna take that huge dick. And one day you'll look back and laugh about wishing it was smaller." He nodded again. "Definitely." Turned out he was right about everything. "Now run back to your man before we keep you all to ourselves." That didn't make it any easier to part ways with them, but Marcus was right.

"Thank you both for being so sweet and so sexy. I do need to find my boyfriend. I'm sure by now he's getting a little upset thinking I'm spending my birthday jerking off at the urinals instead of with him."

"Happy birthday, hairy boy." One at a time, the two hottest guys in the club kissed me with such intensity and passion that it was almost as good as the way Fred kissed. *Almost* my mind echoed back to me because no one could kiss like my man.

I wandered through the packed dancefloor until I found the crew. I leaned in to kiss Fred, but he pulled back and asked me where I was. I could tell he was upset. Fred didn't handle being left alone very well. Sometimes his reactions felt unhinged. He'd take a nap and I'd go out to meet up with one of my friends. When I returned to his apartment he would be furious, hurling accusations at me, none of which were tethered to reality. None of it made any sense, so I wrote it off as one of those things that must come up early in a relationship but then magically disappear. I had no idea how wrong I was about that. *People tell you who they are very quickly. You just need to listen.*

I explained to him what happened, trying not to exude any excitement about meeting Julio and Marcus. I told him that the armband was a spontaneous gift for my birthday, not exactly the truth, but close enough to it to keep Fred from spiraling. His mood had shifted, though, and I knew from experience there was no turning back. He didn't say anything to me for the next hour. He just did his little disassociated clap dance until I gave up trying to make things better. I asked him if we could leave and he said, "It's your birthday and clearly you're going to do whatever you want. So let's go."

We walked back to Fred's place in silence, not holding hands. As my attempts to smooth things over at the club went from trying to show some real empathy to a pathetic display of unnecessary groveling, my mood had shifted as well. By that point I was clearly being punished and my birthday was about to end with the two of us in bed, backs to one another, and no dick for me. I would lay there awake and angry, waiting until he would fall asleep so I could go back into the living room to jerk off to classic porn where no one had to use rubbers. And all I could think about was the fact that if Fred wasn't around, I could have gone home with Julio and Marcus, and ended my night in my birthday suit with them banging my ass until dawn.

But once in bed, unexpectedly, Fred chose to let go of his grudge and hold me instead. He spooned me, pulling me in close and gently. He kissed the back of my hairy neck, made his way around to my cheek, then rolled me over and kissed me with those unmistakable lips. He got on top of me and pressed his cock up against mine, bearing down on me and spreading my legs with his. He pulled his underwear off, then did the same with mine, and put my legs up over my head so he could devour my ass, winding me up like a child's toy and sending me spinning. After feasting on me for a good 20 minutes, he stood up to grab the lube and some condoms. Much to my surprise he went into the pocket of my shorts and returned with the armband as well.

He put it on my right bicep, unrolled a rubber onto his dick, lubed it up, and pressed the head against my hole. He looked into my eyes and said to me, "Angel, I know how bad you want this, and I know you can take it. You know you can take it too, so it's happening tonight. It's gonna happen now. OK?" He posed that "OK" as a question but we both knew it was rhetorical. Beneath him, I looked up, overwhelmed by his compassion, completely seduced by the words that came from his lips, and shaking with anticipation. "OK," I agreed. He gently slid the head in, then then next inch, then the next, until he was completely inside me. He slowly worked it in and out, telling me to relax every time I tensed up, and no matter how long he went without feeling me grip down on him, as soon as I did again, he would stop until I let go. He kept at it until my body finally and fully submitted. He thrust away at me, and I felt his rhythm change as he used my hole to work up a load from his balls. He pounded at me harder, faster, and I held onto him like he was the only thing tethering me to the earth. "I'm gonna cum," he shouted and he pulled out and jerked his dick until he came into the rubber. He fell back down on top of me, breathing heavier than I had ever heard before. I could feel his heart beating into mine. I was no longer a virgin, and I cried with uncontrollable joy in the arms of my man.

He slid off me but didn't let go, rolling me sideways with him and spooning me until my tears quieted and gave way to steadied breathing. Only then did he fall asleep, and with my man's lean body wrapped around mine, I thought back to how I had started that day, reflecting upon just how much had changed for me over the past year of my life. I realized I had one more line item to add to my list of achievements, and I must have fallen asleep with the biggest smile on my face. I ended my birthday as a very happy, very hairy, very hungry bottom boy.

Fourteen

Things at Sonic Assembly were changing, both for me and for the company. I had basically come out to all my coworkers, and unsurprisingly, my manager Mark went from being my buddy to being a jerk, no longer able to confide in me about his disapproval of the sexual orientations of his co-workers. In the past he had made offhanded comments about Carl getting everything he wanted from Paul because he was probably "smoking his pole." I had asked Carl how he dealt with the harassment that Mark displayed toward him at the office, and he told me, "Mark's just bitter because I've got Paul's ear and he will always take my advice over his. He thinks because this company is run by the pink mafia that I made consigliere because I'm gay, but I got to where I am because I've got more business acumen in my pole than he has in his giant doughy body."

The other big change at Sonic Assembly came in the form of a potential buyer for the business.

A huge company called HBN that specialized in selling massive amounts of product through infomercials was interested in acquiring us. Paul was always very open about his intent to sell the company. It had been backed by a small group of Norwegian investors who were in it for the money, and a couple of high-profile musicians who wanted artists to be able to put out top-quality merchandise, and who were also in it for the money. I had gone with Paul and Carl to meet with a few potential buyers in the past. I was the guy who looked cool and could speak to why this would work from a cultural standpoint, while Paul and Carl presented the financials, which I understood as little about as I cared. Numbers bored me, other than the number of zeros I fantasized would accompany my salary once a deal went through.

One after the other, those deals all fell apart, much to everyone's disappointment, except for mine. I loved my job. One day I was on a plane to Los Angeles, the next I was jamming with the team at Tommy Boy or Def Jam Records, and the next I was sent to a hotel suite where Cypress Hill was staying. For that particular meeting, my job was to grease the wheels of capitalism and get them to understand why they should partner with Sonic Assembly and use their name to sell clothing. I went in armed with an M-65 Alpha Industries Field Jacket embroidered with their logo on the back, easily the coolest thing we had ever designed, and a quarter ounce of the best weed money could buy. I rolled a fat blunt, lit it up, and we passed it around and talked about hip-hop as we got totally baked. "You sure know your shit," B-Real said, as he inhaled a massive toke. "For a white boy," I added, finishing what he meant and causing everyone in the room to break out in laughter.

"You alright," Muggs said to me as he passed me the blunt. I took a big hit, exhaled, and with all the confidence in the world replied, "Oh, I'm better than alright." I opened my messenger bag and pulled out the jacket. Practically in unison the three of them said "WHOA!" B-Real grabbed it from me, tried it on, and stood in front of the mirror, nodding his head in approval because that jacket was dope as hell, and everyone there, including me, knew it. They passed it around, along with another blunt that I rolled while they talked about different styles they wanted us to make for them. I left that meeting with their buy-in on the deal and a hand-crafted, metal Cypress Hill roach clip, one of a couple dozen that they made as a very limited-edition promotional item. Shit just didn't get any cooler than that for me. Whether Sonic Assembly got sold or not, I was living my best life.

The next day I strutted into work, feeling like a king at the age of 24. I said hello to Rich, my best friend from college who I had gotten a job at the front desk when he found himself unemployed after graduation. "How did it go last night?" he asked me, eagerly. Rich was raised in the Bronx and began listening to hip-hop around the same time I did. It was one of the things that initially bonded us at college, and we were both huge Cypress Hill fans. I pulled out the roach clip and waved it in his face. "How do you think it went?"

"No fucking way!" He went to snatch it from my hand, and I pulled it back. He managed to grab it anyway. "Maybe you should have played some sports at school and developed your reflexes, homo," he said to me jokingly.

"You want to talk about reflexes? Maybe you should suck my dick and learn to lose one of yours," I snapped back.

"Gross," he said genuinely, as his face pinched up with disgust. I loved him for his reaction. My biggest fear about coming out of the closet was that everything would change with my friends. Moments like this meant we could both truly be ourselves around each other. Rich was totally accepting of my homosexuality, but I knew the thought of fellatio held as much appeal for him as cunnilingus did for me, and any other reaction would have been dishonest. I loved him for keeping it real.

I made my way to my office, and there standing between mine and Paul's was Mark. He gave me a smug, condescending smirk hello, and I returned the insincerity with one of my own. Back when I started at Sonic Assembly I was not only closeted, I was also his assistant, and we got along really well. He took me under his wing, probably because he needed as many straight allies as possible at a company that employed such a large number of gays and lesbians. We would go to strip clubs after work, and he would buy me drinks and cocaine. He even arranged for me to travel with him to New Orleans on a business trip that neither of us really had to go on. Referencing Paul and Carl, he said, "Why should *the girls* have all the fun?" as we racked up a huge dinner bill eating tenderloin and lobster tails, drinking Goldschläger, and doing lines on the bathroom sink, all of which he expensed to the company.

But those days were over now that I was openly gay with my co-workers, and so were my days of being Mark's assistant. I was promoted to the role of Head of A&R, a job I knew he was gunning for, right around the time I came out at work. He openly joked about me getting the position because I "let the boss butt-pirate my ass," but we both knew he wasn't joking. He was being a dick.

The first time he said it to me I thought about reading him. "Mark, honey, the reason I got the job over you isn't because I'm a butt pirate. I got it because *your* ship has sailed." While running his mouth in New Orleans about Paul and Carl, he admitted to me that he felt like music was changing a lot and he didn't understand "hip-hop crap" or half the bands we were signing. "I can't relate to the shit that kids like you are listening to today." In the music business, this was code for, "I'm terrified that at 40 I'm getting too old to effectively do my job." Since then, I found Mark to be rather sad, so I decided to keep my brilliant read regarding his seaworthiness to myself and save him the public humiliation.

I quietly threw him shade instead.

Shade was another concept I learned from Dorian Corey while watching *Paris Is Burning*. "Shade is I don't tell you you're ugly, but I don't have to tell you because you know you're ugly." So why read Mark's pitiful little lie with such a hard truth when I could be a shady bitch instead? The next time Paul called me into his office, I sashayed by Mark's desk, hand on hip, and shot him a look while gleefully announcing, "On my way, Paul!" As I closed the door to Paul's office behind me, I blew Mark a kiss and watched his face get pinched.

* * *

Paul was sitting behind his desk, looking almost as pinched as Mark. I was relieved that I had good news for him. "Cypress Hill are on board, and they're going to put in a good word about us with House of Pain, that Irish hip-hop group I've been telling you about. I think they are going to be big, Paul. Trust me."

"That's nice David. Now, sit down." Paul wasn't one to pat you on the back for your successes when he needed to be upfront with you about your failures. "That company HBN is getting serious about buying us."

"And you need me to meet with them to make you look cool." I blurted out my words with equal amounts of confidence and cockiness, hoping the combination would somehow help me dodge whatever bullet he had coming my way.

"No, David. They don't care about House of Pain or N.W.A. or O.P.P or whatever. They think it's a trend that will come and go, and that's a problem. That's *your* problem, David."

"Well, they're wrong," I hit back.

"It doesn't matter what you think. What matters is what *they* think, and they are questioning the risk of making tons of inventory for a bunch of one-hit-wonders." He paused, then continued, "But they do see the big picture. They get the *vision*. So we need a big idea to bring them back to the table, David. We need something that's going to be *around*," he practically shouted. I could tell by the sternness in his tone that he now had his doubts about the groups I was signing. Or, if he didn't have them before, he sure as hell did after some higher ups at HBN told him to. Their doubts about hip-hop were now his doubts about me, and I suddenly didn't feel like the king who walked into work 15 minutes earlier. I felt like a 24-year-old poetry major who was about to lose the dream job I knew I would never find again.

"I don't know what to tell you Paul. The days of New Kids On The Block are over." New Kids was the band that inspired the idea of Sonic Assembly in the first place, and they made buckets of money selling practically anything with the NKOTB logo on it to teenage girls who worshiped the band with their young hearts and their parent's credit cards. But music had moved on. Grunge was huge, and even I knew selling Nirvana hoodies and Nine Inch Nails windbreakers was the opposite of what that scene was all about. It was destined to fail. Hip-hop was the next thing coming, and I knew it was going to set the style for the entire world. I knew it in my bones, and up until that moment I thought Paul knew it too. But the only thing Paul really knew was money. I realized I was a means to that end, and if I couldn't deliver, I was at the end of my employment with Sonic Assembly.

"Well, you better think of something to tell me. I need this deal to go through. This is *your* job and the Norwegians are tired of losing *their* money." Losing money? We were losing money? My head was spinning as my world turned upside down. How could we be in financial hardship? We had Madonna on the roster, for God's sake.

"What about Madonna?" I asked.

"We already have Madonna! She's part of your generation. I need to know what's coming! Tell me what 11-year-olds want. That's where the money is!" Paul was truly shouting by this point, and I knew he was loud enough for Mark to hear our conversation. I could picture him standing outside the door thinking, "Who's ship has sailed now, butt pirate?" Was I getting too old myself? I knew even less about what 11-year-olds wanted than I knew about Sonic Assembly's financials, and apparently I knew absolutely nothing about them. Our entire business, and my future along with it, was suddenly disappearing with New Kids On The Block's fall from musical favor. Maybe I would have thought twice about using the phrase "Old Kids On The Clock" with Paul had I known the purchasing power of those 11-year-old girls was the key to my success.

Then I followed the money. It wasn't those 11-year-olds who had the purchasing power. *It was their parents.* Maybe we needed to tap into *their* musical taste? Maybe it wasn't about what was next, but about what had always been. What were people older than me listening to when they were 11? Who did they worship?

"How about The Beatles?" I asked.

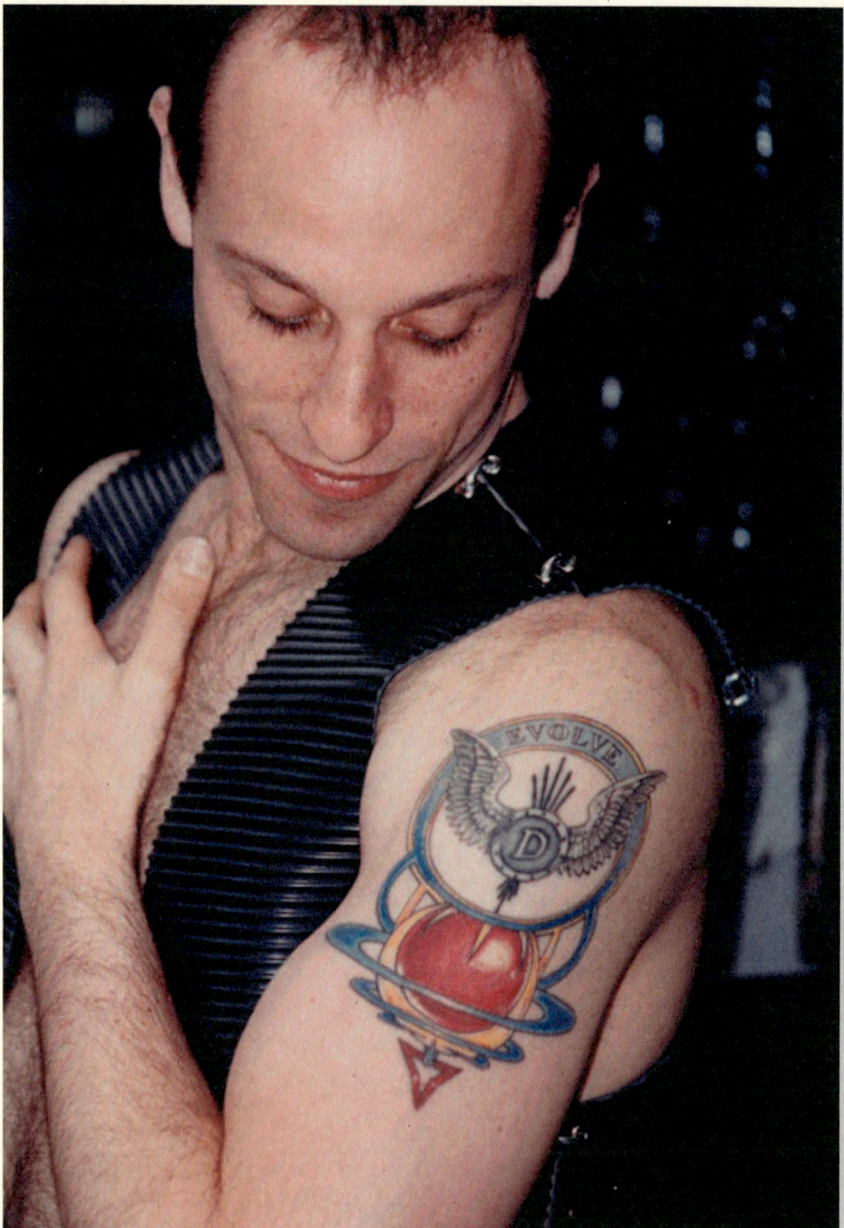
EVOLVE
D

Chapter 15

I had become a total Sound Factory rat. No matter how many Tuesdays I told myself I needed a break from going out the following weekend, I inevitably ended up at the Factory by the following Sunday morning. If Fred and I went out to Roxy on Saturday night, it was understood that it was merely a warm-up for Junior. If Fred wanted to stay in, I would wake up Sunday morning and go by myself. As an annoying morning person, I honestly preferred getting a good night's sleep then showing up fresh to the club at 8 a.m., and I wasn't the only one. There was a changing of the guard that occurred as the sun came up on West 27th Street. The crowd that arrived at 3:30 a.m., the famed "party people" of New York City, would feel their energy winding down and start to filter out, and by 10 a.m. they were basically gone. But in their place, as the morning turned into the day, the club would fill up again with "the children" — the true househeads, the artist collectives, the sex workers who were finally done with their shifts, the Aviances and the Xtravaganzas, and all the "girls" who *really* knew the tea. This was widely considered to be not just the deepest underground club scene in the city, but in the entire world. It was a vortex of culture and creativity and diversity set to a musical soundscape by the hottest DJ alive, and for the life of me, I couldn't stay away no matter how hard I tried.

Still, the one thing that did manage to keep me out of the Factory for two weekends running was the necessary time it took for my and Fred's new tattoos to heal up properly. Getting inked was quite radical back then, an art form that hadn't really made its way past bikers and Marines. But there was a very small subset of queer people, especially gay men, who began to claim it for themselves. In a world where we had no rights, where each sexual encounter meant a game of Russian roulette with AIDS and death, the idea of taking control of our bodies and marking them with ink forever felt like an act of defiant permanence, or at least that's how it felt to me. I got the letter "D" on my left arm with a pair of wings attached to it, symbolic of feeling that my life had taken flight. Fred got a dragon that turned into a Celtic braid, circling the globe, a fusion of art forms that were inspiring him at the time. I absolutely loved mine. It made me feel powerful and rebellious, an outward facing nod to my difference from what was considered acceptable by the world. Fred was, of course, unhappy with his, just as he was with everything he created. He felt like it resembled a hot air balloon. I thought it was truly beautiful.

After a record 20 days without having gone out clubbing, Fred and I were more than ready to debut our new tattoos, and to dance our asses off and do plenty of drugs. While he was healing, Fred made a gorgeous leather vest for himself that was scooped out in the back, perfectly framing his dragon, and he was ready to show that off as well. Actually, I was the one ready to show it off. I was constantly flaunting Fred's talent to just about anyone who encountered his creations. Fred, on the other hand, never spoke about what he made. He wasn't interested in accolades, he was in it for the process. He found joy in learning the details whereas I was obsessed with seeing the big picture. Together, our different ways of approaching creativity were proving to be quite complementary. I wasn't quite sure how, but I felt like Fred and I could take the idea of the Metropolitan Faggot Authority and really turn it into something. We had talked about making posters and wheat-pasting them across the city, an idea I obsessed over, even though no one would know what it stood for. That didn't matter to me, though. I knew once we started putting it in front of people they would take notice, and once I had their attention, I would figure out what to do next to keep it.

We started the night, as usual, at the Roxy, and within minutes of walking in the club our extended group of friends, along with some strangers, were complimenting his vest. I bragged about his talent to everyone who'd listen. I showed off my new tattoo by being shirtless and hairy, newly proud of my furry body, thanks to a combination of the months I had put in at the gym and the approval of Julio and Marcus. I stopped caring so much that I wasn't getting the positive attention my smooth body used to induce from the overly manicured boys at the Roxy. In fact, I liked the negative attention that my body hair generated. It felt comfortable. I was used to it. I expressed my queerness through my distinct, counter-culture sense of style, and my body hair only added to it.

After a few hours of dancing and rolling, I checked my beeper for the time — 3:40 a.m. — and I was all-too-happy to gather the troops and head north for the main sonic course. The Factory was on fire from the moment we walked in the door. Some mornings Junior would make us wait as he played relatively bland beats to clear out the relatively bland crowd that arrived when the doors opened, making room on the floor for his minions before he let loose. But damn, he was giving us *everything* right out the gate.

I wanted to be out on the floor, but it was so packed. I took up a lot of space when I was throwing down, so we found a bit of breathing room under the DJ booth. Standing five feet away from us was Kevin Aviance, the queen in the red dress who blew my mind the fist night I went to Factory. He blew my mind every single time we went as he was *the* diva of the club. He never took the stage because the whole damn place was his theater, and the music never stopped when he performed because his presence was the performance. He glanced over at us, tilted his head and came in our direction. "Girl, that vest is OVAH!" he said to Fred.

Given how obsessed I was with Kevin, I couldn't believe I was getting to talk to the legend himself. He was so different from all the other drag performers who populated New York City. He never wore a wig, he never wore tits or padded his ass to appear more "female." He didn't care about appearing "male" either. Kevin was a complete genderfuck, fearless in his presentation. I admired his fearlessness, and at 6'6" in heels, I found myself looking up to him, both literally and figuratively. We spent that entire night together, and when he wasn't performing, the two of us bonded over our shared love of high fashion, Mugler, house music, and ketamine. From that night on we were fast friends, dancing sisters, and nightlife soulmates.

It took a good three hours for the floor to thin out enough for me to attempt to find a spot spacious enough to accommodate my moves. I took Fred by the hand, and we made our way in, moving toward the opposite end of the club, and I found us some square footage just past the disco ball. My new favorite song, "What Hope Have I," came pumping through the speakers, into my soul and it lit me up from the inside. The only place I ever heard it was at Factory, and despite my deep connections in the record industry, I couldn't land myself a copy. Nobody even knew what track I was talking about. One night it came on as I was dancing with Kevin and I asked him about it. "Girl, it's a Junior exclusive right now. You ain't gonna hear it anywhere but here." Every time Junior played it, I felt transcendent, along with everyone around me. As the song mixed out, Fred leaned in and said to me, "See that guy over there with the big atomic rings on his back? He went to the same artist as I did. I recognize his ink from one of the tattoo magazines." Tattooing was illegal in New York City at the time, so we had to look at people's work in the pages of national tattoo rags, where the shops could openly advertise.

"He's the guy who spins the lights on stage," I replied. Every weekend

he would get on the stage and maneuver himself to the front of the runway, where he would spin three sets of glow sticks from each hand, attached to the ends of what I imagined was rope. It was mesmerizing, otherworldly. I wasn't usually one for light-up gimmicks. I was never a raver. I had seen a few gay guys occasionally spinning flags around on the dancefloor, something Fred told me used to be popular, but this guy had taken it into the future. He was one of the many people who spontaneously performed throughout the night at Factory, and not for the sake of getting paid. Their shows were free. They were more than free. They were gifts for the rest of us, and I needed to thank him.

I tapped him on the shoulder, and he turned around. "Can I help you?" he asked with an Italian accent, and slim, space-age, Geordi La Forge-esque sunglasses wrapped around his bald head.

I leaned in and half shouted in his ear, "I love what you do with spinning the lights for us. I want to say thank you." I pulled back and smiled, awaiting his appreciation for my kind words.

He raised his eyebrow and replied with complete seriousness, "I don't do it for you, darling. I do it for the Gods."

I didn't know what he was talking about, nor was that a problem. I was instantly intrigued. He looked so unique, like some sort of alien or a faggot from the future. I must have just stood there staring at him because he felt the need to say, "Well, I guess I'll start the introductions, darling. I'm Javier."

"Oh my God, sorry. I'm David. This is my boyfriend, Fred. He just got his back tattooed by Emma at Porcupine."

Javier put his hand out and motioned a circle at Fred. "Show me," he stated.

Fred turned around and Javier checked out his dragon, and then I showed off my once major, now petite, D with wings.

"They are both very beautiful." His voice slithered with the dangerous beauty of a diamondback rattlesnake. "This is my boyfriend, Jeff." Javier moved out of the way and there dancing in front of me was one incredibly sexy man. His head was shaved like Javier's. Their bald heads made me question why everyone at the club who was rocking a tight fringe wouldn't do the same. It looked so modern and cool. Jeff's bald head sat upon a thick neck, which sat upon a thick, muscled body, all of which was juxtaposed by a sweet baby face, albeit one covered in stubble. Both his arms were inked up with what looked like Indian Goddesses. His thick legs were wrapped in leather chaps, and beneath them was nothing but a jockstrap. Jeff looked thick down there too.

Javier said to us, "Jeff had his ink done by Emma as well. Turn around Jeff."

As if he couldn't get any hotter, Jeff turned around and spiraling down his back like a tornado was some sort of helix which stopped just above the waistband of his chaps. Jutting out from below were the thickest set of perfect butt cheeks, each one adorned with what looked like a feather from an ancient species of bird curling in upon itself. He looked like a God. They both did — two queer sexual deities — and I was instantly a devotee. Junior began mixing into "Atom Bomb" and Javier took off his sunglasses and handed them to me before getting on the runway to serve up his show, each individual glow stick turning into a spherical orbit around his body, evocative of the interconnecting ellipses on his back. Fearful I would lose them if I tucked them into my jeans pocket, I put his sunglasses on and instantaneously every single light that flashed from the ceiling expanded into its hidden spectrum. Javier's orbits became prismatic. The giant disco ball above our heads shot hundreds of rainbow beams down upon the crowd. I felt like I was tripping on acid without the "14-hours-later-and-I've-gone-fetal-in-my-closet" part. I handed them to Fred and he wore them for a while, barely dancing, looking around and taking in every visual with childlike wonder before handing them back to me. I kept them on until Javier finished his show for the Gods and descended to dance amongst the masses. "These are so fucking cool!" I said as I moved in to put them on his bald head.

"Keep them darling. They look ridiculous on you!" Javier exclaimed. My gut told me that, coming from Javier, it was some sort of compliment. I put them back on, even though I was sure I looked like I had a banana clip across my face.

The four of us spent the rest of the morning dancing together, communicating rhythmically, getting to know each other without words, noon rolled around. "I love dancing with you guys. Can I get your numbers?" I asked.

"Why don't we just close this place and walk to Florent for brunch afterwards?" Jeff asked.

"I'd love to, but we're wiped out. We were at the Roxy before we came-"

"You were at *The Roxy*?" Javier asked with theatrical derision.

"Yeah. We were."

"Well David. I won't hold that against you." He smiled as he said it, both condescendingly and in jest. "And I also won't give you our number. You'll just have to find us back here next weekend for dancing and brunch after a good night's sleep. No Roxy for you. Brunch is on us. And bring me back my glasses. Do we have a deal, darling?"

"We sure the fuck do." I stuck my hand out to shake on it, but Javier wrapped his arms around me instead. He didn't hug me. He held me. I returned his embrace until finally he let go to do the same with Fred.

Jeff locked eyes with me and smirked. "Don't I get some too?" he asked. Without hesitation I grabbed onto his thickness, and I felt his giant arms encasing my body as his dick got hard against mine. "Sleep tight, beautiful boy," he said gently into my ear. "I hope to see you soon."

"Trust me Jeff, you will."

Fred and I left the club and walked to his apartment in the crisp fall air. I didn't say much because my mind was racing. The Factory always left me feeling inspired, but after spending time with Kevin and Javier and Jeff, she felt somehow *important*. Factory was a temple, and that night she revealed to me her high priests and priestesses. I wanted to worship under them, I wanted to worship *with* them. These were my people, the ones dancing for the Gods.

We got to Fred's place, and as I passed the oval mirror by his front door, I caught a glimpse of myself in Javier's glasses. I was right. I did look like I had a banana clip across my eyes. Javier was right too. They looked pretty ridiculous on me. Even though I knew he meant it as a compliment, I had my own strong sense of style, and no matter how enamored I was with the both of them, I wouldn't be returning to The Factory looking like I was on my way to a Star Trek convention. I did fucking love the glasses, though. I just wished the shape was cooler.

"Wouldn't it be sick if these were goggles?" I asked Fred.

Sixteen

"Wouldn't it be sick if these were goggles?" I asked Fred again. And again. And again. "I think then they would be *sick* right!?" I couldn't stop thinking about them. I woke up and my mind raced in a hundred different ways. It was such a rush. I wasn't sure how these would tie together with the M.F.A. I didn't know where to manufacture them, or anything else for that matter. And where the hell would I get the money to put them into production in the first place? Yet, for someone with so many questions, I was lit up like someone who had all the answers.

The only thing that seemed to quiet my brain was jerking off, many times a day, to *The Other Side of Aspen,* a porn made before AIDS showed up and ruined everything. The guys in that porn were so natural and sexy, and none of them used rubbers. Their fucking seemed so spontaneous. So unbothered. Once I saw that porn, I had no desire to watch anything made once the studios moved their actors to using condoms. Of course, safe sex was necessary, but it wasn't nearly as hot as the "unsafe" sex that went down in the late 70s. I wanted so badly to stop using rubbers with Fred, but he had no desire to go to see a doctor, much less get an HIV test. Another one of his weird quirks, like his awkward smile and his empty bank account. I didn't push the issue, but every time he would rub his cock against my hole, I secretly fantasized about him sliding it in unwrapped.

Finally, after about three days and thrice the loads, something clicked in my head. I often made trips to the wholesale district for Sonic Assembly, purchasing blank baseball caps and woolies when we needed to do a quick run of embroidered hats for any act that needed something immediately. At one place, I remembered seeing random beach and pool accessories toward the back of the store. Maybe they sold goggles in bulk and I could get the name of the manufacturer off the packaging? It was the only lead I had, so I followed it to Sunny Day Kim Wholesale on 6th Avenue and 28th Street. There, at the back of the store, in between the water wings and marked down, bootleg MC Hammer shirts, were generic, prepacked, brightly colored by-the-dozen swimming goggles in optic white, generic boxes. The only markings on the outside were a series of Chinese characters and "$36 for Doz." handwritten in red magic marker. I stood there, trying to think of what to do next, and when I came up with nothing, I left to head home to repeat myself to Fred until I whacked off one more time and passed out. But halfway to 7th Avenue, my brain told me to go back and buy a dozen. I think I just needed to start somewhere. Anywhere. I went back into Sunny Day and grabbed a twelve pack: three each of yellow, green, red, and blue.

On my way to Fred's apartment, I had another little breakthrough. Things in my brain were flowing. I opened his door and announced: "You remember when we went down to Canal Street to get my LV wraparounds? There was that store with all the plexiglass and Lucite and stuff."

"They're Louis Vuitton *knockoff* wraparounds, David." He winked at me. "It was called Canal Plastics. I wanted to go down there to see if they sold sheets of latex. I love the latex pieces Mugler has been showing, but I can't figure out how to construct them. It doesn't look like . . . "

"Let's go!" I cut him off. "Maybe they have the right kind of plastic to replace the lenses in the goggles I just bought."

Fred got up off the couch. "We can go, but you're going to have to be patient when I want to look around. I want to take my time and explore."

"But you said you just wanted latex."

"Yes, but that's not how I work. I want to look for latex, but I also just want to look." Fred loved to explore without any real idea of where he was headed. It kind of annoyed me. I was always very focused on pursuing what made me happy. "Besides," he added, "you're going to need to replace more than just the lenses."

"Why?" I asked.

"Because they look cheap. The elastic is cheap. The closures are cheap. They're just cheap swimming goggles. You can do better." I didn't understand why he was being so negative about my project. I had no idea at the time that he wasn't being negative; he was just unafraid to put me in my place, hold me to a higher standard, and be right. Thank the Gods I had him.

We jumped on the 1 Train and got off at Canal Street. I loved that area of the city. From Pearl River Market to the rando jewelry shops where you could make custom grills to the street vendors selling fake designer handbags, everything seemed to be happening all at once at full volume. For a neighborhood that felt so chaotic and loud, there was something about her that whispered in my ear, enticing me to explore her crowded storefronts and find her secrets. I could tell Fred wanted to stop in the first place we passed, but I asked him if we could *please* start at Canal Plastics. I jutted out my lower lip, doing my best to look cute and cherub-like, and I guess it must have worked because he smiled and agreed.

We walked into the store, and I went right to the counter. "Do you sell this type of plastic?" I handed the gentleman Javier's glasses and he said, "Oh yes wait here." I surged with excitement, every neuron in my brain firing as if I had just discovered ice cream that wasn't fattening or the AIDS vaccine. It felt like I was at the beginning of going somewhere. I didn't know exactly where, but that didn't matter. It wasn't about the *where* part, it was about the *going* part. Together, *we* were in motion.

The counter clerk returned and handed me a square of matte black plastic. After a moment of confusion, I realized he was showing me a match to the frames and not the lens itself. "No, no. Put them on." He looked at me confused, as English was clearly not his first language, and I motioned to him to put the glasses on his head. Upon peering through them he said "Ohhh. Very pretty." He swiveled his head back and forth, checking out all the lights in the store now that they revealed their full spectrum. He handed them to the woman standing next to him, who put them on and had the same reaction. "So beautiful!' she exclaimed. While these two weren't the target market for my debut product, I was quite pleased to see that their appeal was broader than just the queer club kids I had in mind as an audience. She handed them back to me. I pointed to the lens and asked, "Do you carry this part?"

"Sorry, we don't have that," he said, shaking his head back and forth to emphasize his reply. I felt my energy drop out from under me.

"Are you sure?" I asked again.

"No, we don't have that. But maybe this?" He pulled out a sample wheel of Lucite strips in just about every color in the rainbow. "Blue? Green?" he suggested.

"No, that's not what I need, but thank you anyway." I looked around and located Fred at the back of the store and wandered over to be consoled. I guess he could see the disappointment on my face because he pulled me in close and said, "Let's keep looking, Angel. There's another place down the block called Canal Rubber. Maybe they will have what both of us need. No latex here for me either. Lots of other cool stuff, though."

"Do you want to keep looking around? I don't want to rush you."

He smiled, grabbing my hand in his. "I really appreciate you saying that. Let's go to the next place."

We walked down the block, Fred bravely holding my hand despite any fears he may have had, and he led me into Canal Rubber. Where Canal Plastics was an explosion of colored Lucite tubes and sheets of 3D lenticular fabrics, Canal Rubber was super industrial and kind of sexy as far as I was concerned. There was a distinct smell that was coming off the rolls of black rubber flooring and yellow ventilation duct hose that hung from the ceiling, available by the foot. It was reminiscent of rubber cement, not quite as strong, but equally intoxicating in its own way. There were large rubber boots in vulcanized green lined up on a shelf, and I was shocked to see they were only $30-40 dollars a pair. A salesman approached me and asked if I needed any help.

"Do these come any taller?" I asked.

"Taller? What the hell you need taller ones than these? Whatchoo do for a living?"

"I'm a professional faggot, and a big pair of these would help me perform my duties fiercely. Do you have any that come up to the knee?" I could tell that the sales guy wasn't amused, but he also wasn't particularly offended. Looking around, I knew that I couldn't possibly be the first gay man who wandered into Canal Rubber for the sole purpose of serving up a look. He asked me to hold on and returned with a catalog. He flipped through the pages until he landed on what I was looking for.

"These here are knee-high rubber boots. You can get 'em in green or black. Perfect for fishing and hunting and shit. But for what you're going for, I'd recommend these." He turned the page and there was a picture of a man wearing rubber boots that came all the way up his thighs. "They're meant to wear if you gotta clean up a chemical spill, but these look pretty fucking gay to me." He looked at me blankly, no wink or a nod, just speaking his truth and trying to do his job. I appreciated his unbothered, New York City stance immensely.

"Can I try a pair in size 9?" I asked.

He laughed. "This ain't Foot Locker, son. I gotta special order these for you. You want em?"

"Fuck yes I want them," I replied.

"You got it. Anything else I can get for you?"

"Well, maybe. I'm trying to find the plastic that these lenses are made from." I handed him the glasses and he looked at them, trying to figure out what I was talking about. I told him to put them on and he did, then he took them off, unfazed by their effect. Maybe I had reached the edge of my market.

"Nah, we don't got nothing like that here. You try Canal Plastics?"

"Yeah, I just came from there. They couldn't help me out."

"Well, neither can I. Not with that. But when you get ready to order the boots just see the old guy at the front counter. I'll leave the catalog with him so he knows what to get you."

I found Fred examining spools of rubber cording in various colors and thicknesses. "No latex. But this stuff is interesting. And the diamond plate rubber flooring over there, I bet I could make a cool vest or something out of that. Maybe use this rubber cord to lace the pieces together." I didn't know what he was talking about, nor did I have any doubts that whatever he was talking about would be incredibly cool.

"Get some. I'm getting boots. Some really big boots."

"I thought you came here looking for that plastic for your goggles," he smirked as he spoke. "Sounds like you found something cool by exploring the place."

"Yeah, well true. Also shut the fuck up," I replied with a smile. "But I still wasn't able to make the goggles happen so be nice to me." I knew I was no longer smiling. I was genuinely feeling defeated. The boots were cute, but they were no substitute for pursuing my new dream.

Fred asked the guy who helped me for two yards of the rubber diamond plate flooring and a hundred feet of rubber cord, which he parsed off and brought up to the front counter as we followed him. I told the older gentleman at the register that I was the one interested in purchasing the chemical clean-up boots. He showed me the catalog page and confirmed my size, then wrote up a bill for them. I instructed him to add Fred's stuff to the bill as well. "My gift to you. I can't wait to see what you make." Fred gave me a kiss and I handed my credit card over to pay for our first Canal Rubber purchase.

"The boots will be here in about three weeks. Give me a call then. My name is Marty." He handed me his card.

"Thanks, Marty. I definitely will."

"Oh, and on the back of the card I wrote down the name and number of a company located in California that makes something like what's in those glasses. My assistant told me you are hunting for the plastic. I don't think it's plastic though. I think it's called prism refraction paper, and I'm pretty sure that company sells it by the sheet."

"You're literally my hero, Marty! If I wasn't with this guy, I'd kiss you." He smiled like a seasoned New Yorker as I gave Fred a huge hug.

"I'm gonna make this happen Fred. It's happening. I can fucking feel it."

* * *

The paper arrived at Fred's apartment about a week after I had ordered it, and for $12, it was exactly what I was looking for. I took apart Javier's glasses and sure enough, the "lens" was nothing more than this thin sheet of paper. The Geordi La Forge aesthetic was done out of necessity. By having a very thin strip of this paper as a lens, the body of the glasses protected it from being punctured. "Form follows function, David. That's the first rule of good design," Fred explained to me.

I popped out the lenses on one of the pairs of goggles and traced out the same shapes onto the paper, then cut them out. Try as I might to hold the cut outs onto the lenses and pop them back in, I failed repeatedly. The paper slid and bent and ultimately tore when exposed to the rigors of my fumbling. But Fred pulled out one of his dozens of creative "kits" that he had stacked up in the apartment and took out a bottle of crazy glue. Gently, delicately, he put the tiniest of drops on each side of the goggle's lens, then affixed the paper cut outs and let them dry. That did the trick. We were able to pop the lenses successfully back in and I ran to the mirror and put them on. There, staring back at me, through the dazzling rainbows that appeared out of nowhere, was me wearing the very first product I had ever made for the Metropolitan Faggot Authority.

"It worked, Fred. It worked! The M.F.A. is born!"

"Can I be honest with you, David?" he asked, and I knew I was about to get schooled. "I don't really see how these connect to the M.F.A." He wasn't wrong. Neither did I. "And they still look cheap. I think you can do better." By "you" he meant "we," because without Fred's help I wouldn't have gotten as far as I did.

"Well, what do you think I should do next? And by *I*, I mean *we*, but that's really more like you because you seem to be the one with all the tricks up his sleeve."

"I think we make a good team, so let's go with we," he replied. I couldn't argue with that.

Fred grabbed a pair of scissors and cut the thin white piece of elastic off the goggles. Using that as a guide, he cut a piece of thick black elastic off a spool he had laying around and handed it to me. "Merrow the edges so they don't unravel." I went to the sewing machine and did just that. I loved being Fred's assistant. He was teaching me so much, and each time I did something right it gave me a rush. It made me feel like I was being a good boy.

Fred took the elastic, threaded it though each side of the goggle frames, and tacked it in place using his straight-stitch machine. From one of his many kits, he produced gold fasteners, which reinforced the elastic closures and made the goggles look a bit cooler. But I wanted them to look a lot cooler, so I ran downstairs to a stationary store on 7th Avenue and grabbed two sheets of stickers marked "Space Age Dreams" for $2. I brought them back home and stuck a flying saucer to the left side and a giant star on the right.

"Those look a lot better than what you started with," Fred said to me. "Form should always follow function, but once you nail the function, make the form count."

Once again, he wasn't wrong. Not only did they work, they looked pretty sick too.

Seventeen

I woke up Sunday morning at 6:49 a.m. without setting an alarm, no problem. I only had the stamina to dance all night and fuck past dawn due to my deep love for both. Without those two things on my agenda, I was usually fast asleep by 10 p.m. and up by six in the morning.

I had picked out my look the night before and moved it to the living room so as not to disturb Fred. He slept hard and I wasn't too worried about waking him, but I also didn't want to take any chances. He was wildly possessive, and even though he knew it was my intention to try out my goggles at Factory, if I poked the bear it would be a whole thing. I crept out of the bedroom and brushed my teeth. I put on the new skintight black tank top I had purchased at Pat Field with my favorite pair of baggy jeans and the vintage, suede Pumas that I had managed to snag in a size 10½. They were too big on me, *but they were fucking suede Pumas* so I didn't care one bit. It was a cute look, good enough for Roxy, but maybe not for Factory, so I added the black batter's helmet Fred had given me as a gift. I had no idea where he found it, but I hadn't seen anyone wearing anything like it, which was why I loved it even more. I took my first pair of M.F.A. goggles and pulled them down over the helmet above the brim. A quick up and down in the mirror — my look was definitely *serving* — and I was out the door.

Walking to Factory as the sun was rising over New York City felt both incredibly cool and incredibly natural. For the vast majority of the world, the idea of walking into a nightclub just as the day was beginning was an absurd notion. To me, it was heaven. I had all my natural energy pent up and ready to be released, and the idea that I was literally holding it down for the city that never slept to maintain her title brought me a lot of joy. The closer I got to 27th Street, the more people I saw who obviously had just left Factory. Even if they weren't dressed like lunatics, their joyous stumbling and laughter gave them away. I was happy for them, and I was happy for me. With each passing Factory rat, I knew there was more space for me on the floor to let loose.

As I walked in, Junior was still delivering some hard progressive beats, and I ran into Kevin under the booth. "These are my girls. This is Cesar. He does all this madness to decorate the club." Kevin waved his hand around the room, pointing out all the fabric and flowers that wrapped around the columns and hung from the bar. "And this is Howie. He paints all the murals over which I'm sure you have thoroughly gagged." He wasn't wrong. "And this is Serenity. She just a Black bitch with a serious tuck." Serenity gave Kevin some major side eye and quipped back, "I'm a fierce Black *queen*, honey. You may have high heels and a half-painted face, but no matter how hard you try, you'll never be anything more than a bald old man in a dress." The whole crew burst out laughing, and I felt safe to join in.

"You got me girl. That was a *read*," Kevin admitted. "You better sleep with one eye open tonight."

"Are you two roommates?" I asked Kevin.

"We're all roommates, girl. We live together, six floors up from where you're standing."

"Wait, what? You live above Sound Factory?" I asked with a mixture of astonishment and excitement.

"Yes, girl. There's a whole collective of us up there. It's real cute. We're the girls who turn this place out."

"Wow, that's so fucking cool! I'm David. I'd love . . . " But before I could finish my sentence, we were suddenly doused in brightness. It was coming from the DJ booth. Junior had a spotlight on us, grabbing our attention.

"Whoops sorry to cut this convo short, girl, but we gotta go," Cesar said as he looked up to the booth. "Miss Junior has something up her sleeve and we gotta hustle."

"Can I come with you Kevin?" I couldn't believe I might actually ascend to meet the legend himself.

"No, girl. Miss Junior don't allow for guests. But make me a dress one day and maybe that will change," Kevin said as he winked at me.

"You got it!" I replied as if I had the skill to pull that off. He gave me a hug and he and Cesar and Howie disappeared into the crowd. I was left there with Serenity, so I asked her to dance, and the two of us carried to "House Is a Feeling" for the next seven minutes until we got caught in the glare of that spotlight again. We looked up at the booth and Kevin was motioning for us to come up. Serenity grabbed my hand to lead the way and a rush of excitement washed over me, but instead she pulled me in close and gave me a kiss. "Looks like I gotta go too. But it was a pleasure to dance with you. Hope we can do it again," she said as she slipped away, along with my opportunity to visit Junior's VIP booth. My dream of hanging out in what was arguably the most exclusive room in all the underground was crushed, twice, within a span of 10 minutes.

But I was there to work on my own dreams, and just as I reached for my goggles, Junior tore into "Can You Party" by Royal House, the track of tracks, and the floor exploded, every voice shouting, every set of hands in the air. I put the goggles over my eyes, amplifying the light show by a hundred, and I put my hands in the air too, feeling a rush like I had never experienced before. I was literally changing the way I saw the world, reshaping it within my own vision. I was manifesting the start of my future, right there, in that moment, until the heat of my skin fogged up the insides of the lenses about 20 seconds later.

I couldn't see a fucking thing. My hands fell from the air and landed at my sides. So much for my grand vision.

* * *

Javier found me in the lounge, wedged between two girls in miniskirts and two boys in miniskirts. "I hope you're not tired from going out to the Roxy, darling," he stated before he even said hello.

"I'm definitely not. Went to bed and got here about an hour ago. That was our deal, right?"

"Well, yes. That and you were to be wearing my glasses. Yet I don't see them. Cosa è successo?"

"I don't have them. They looked ridiculous on me."

"They look ridiculous on everyone darling, present company included."

Hearing that made me laugh, and in turn Javier laughed with me. The skirted boys next to me got up and headed to the dancefloor after inhaling so much ketamine I couldn't fathom how they managed to stand at all. Javier sat down and put his arm around me, and I put my head on his shoulder. I had only met him once, but Javier seemed to have a quality that I wanted. Nothing that I coveted, but something that I wanted to learn. Something I wanted to understand. He and Jeff emanated this energy that felt like it belonged in me as well — or felt like it was already in me just waiting to materialize more fully.

"I promise I'll return them. To be honest I was all excited to show you these." I grabbed my goggles that now drooped around my neck, probably looking as deflated as I felt. "I wanted to make a cooler looking version of yours. Not that yours aren't cool. That's not what I mean." I felt myself stumbling.

"Don't worry, darling. They aren't that cool to look at. They are just cool to look through, and ultimately that's all that counts. It's your world to see, not to be seen in. What other people think of me . . . "

"Is none of my business," I finished his sentence. "It's one of my favorite quotes. And I really don't give a fuck about what other people think of me. I made them for this thing I'm trying to start called the M.F.A."

"And what is the M.F.A., darling?"

That was a well-posed question, because other than what it stood for, I honestly didn't know myself. "It's this thing. It's like my one-man activist organization or something. I'm trying to figure it out. I can't really describe it because it's not really anything yet. I've just got this feeling that I've got some sort of purpose. I guess I feel like all gay people have some sort of purpose, otherwise why would we keep getting made, right? It's not like we are reproducing on our own. Last I checked, my asshole didn't end in a uterus."

"Tell me more," Javier stated as he turned squarely towards me with a gaze both intense and intent. I felt like he was making room for me to share my wild theories, so I made him my first victim.

"Well, yeah. Like we have to have some sort of reason for being born. I'm talking biologically, not philosophically. And it's gonna sound crazy, but I feel like what we are doing here at Factory, well it's something very old. Like we've always danced together to the drums and the lights and done drugs well after everyone else has gone to sleep. We do it for a reason, but we just don't remember why anymore. And most straight people either hate us for this or tolerate us if we don't flaunt our *lifestyle*. This lifestyle. Even the part of society that accepts us wants us to be neutered or sterilized. We can be funny, but we can't be fucking. But I'm not some sort of clown. I'm a full-blown faggot and I'm not okay with being second class for taking it in the ass. I don't want to be tolerated or accepted. I'm necessary to the fabric of society *as I am*. I even feel like what little leadership we have is more concerned with us blending in than being honored for what we are. We're faggots and queens and Leathermen and dykes and everything else that's compressed right here in this place. Put us all together and, I dunno. I feel like we are unstoppable. This energy we create, at least for me, is so powerful." I had found the end of my rant. "So, to answer your question," I kind of chuckled, "I guess that's what the M.F.A. is. It's the Metropolitan Faggot Authority — like the MTA — only it's mine. And, somehow, I'm gonna make it ours."

Javier smiled. "I knew I liked you for a reason, darling. I want to be M.F.A too so let me try these magic goggles."

"That's the thing, the reason I'm sitting here looking so tired that you thought I was out all night. I was all excited to wear them but when I put them on they only lasted for about 20 seconds before they got all fogged up. Kinda bummed me out that they didn't work."

"Well, darling, it sounds like you had *quite a lot* riding on them." We both laughed. It was funny because it was true. "Allow me to give you some clarity, David, something you might be lacking at the moment based upon that white ring around your nostril." He licked his thumb and wiped it off, his presence shifting into something maternal and warm. "Your magic goggles *did* work — for 20 seconds. How did those 20 seconds feel?"

"Powerful." I felt myself nodding as I said it.

"Then be powerful. Be that. And quite frankly, David, based upon all I've heard tonight, it's not like you are going to give up on your — I mean our — M.F.A. so easily, now are we darling?"

"No fucking way." I felt myself nodding as I said that, too.

"Then let's go celebrate your soon-to-be-improved magic goggles." He stood up and put out his hand. I took it in mine, and he lifted me. *It felt like he literally lifted me.* We stepped down off the bleachers and made our way to the dancefloor.

As dawn outside shifted into day, the crowd in the club shifted with it. Those who were left were the truest of the underground, the realest of the househeads, the most glorious mix of New Yorkers assembled under one roof. It felt genderless and raceless to me, and yet filled with every gender and race, all of which I fully embraced. Moving through the crowd, I saw some familiar characters. There was the guy who must have been in a serious accident or had brain surgery because his head was encased in cranial scaffolding. He danced with his skull securely bolted in place to his shoulders, always smiling, with fresh flowers adorning the metallic framework that wrapped around him from the neck up. I passed the older Latin man who zigzagged through the club, looking like a young grandfather, moving as if he was waltzing with the ghost of a lover who had passed on. Fred was always intrigued by him, and a few weeks earlier he introduced himself. "His name is Carlo," Fred told me, "and he's totally Deaf. He comes here so he can feel the bass and dance to it." That made perfect sense as the bass was massive. It rolled beneath our feet. I saw the thick Black queen who always wore plaid pleated miniskirts with polo shirts and equestrian boots. I lived for her femme country club aesthetic, the way it played against her tight afro and her masculine face. She and I would always have a cunty throwdown when we ran into one another. We never really spoke. There was no need. We found something joyous in our anonymity and our shared love of piano tracks, which seemed to magically be playing every time our paths crossed. I'd cross her eyes too, because we also shared a love of K, something she said she was unable to procure herself. I never asked why. I just gave her some of mine, everytime. I saw the tall, svelte Asian gentleman who looked like a businessman from the waist up, dressed in his usual white button-down shirt and tie, paired with a black leather pencil skirt, black tights, and matching pumps. Fred and I once sat across from him in the lounge and we got a glimpse of his business. The tights were actually thigh highs, and he wore them sans panties. We were convinced he was like the CEO of Toyota and flew to The States whenever he could just to live his best life in that room. The hookers were all there too. They had finished working the Meatpacking District, sucking off straight dick for cash while somehow fully concealing their own. They came through to blow off some steam, much the same way most people go to happy hour on Friday at 5 p.m., or at least that was my take on it. They were there carrying and holding their section down, while the Xtravaganzas found Junior's spotlight and turned their runway all the way up, voguing to "Get Your Hands Off My Man" as it tore through the speakers. They worked the house *down*, their bodies doing geometry and bending into shapes. The crowd was truly glorious, a tribe of likeminded urban worshippers congregating beneath the beams of the floor above us, moving between the giant columns that supported the structure of the building itself, each wrapped in painted fabric to animate the concrete. There was nothing but gorgeousness everywhere I looked.

And then there was Jeff, covered in ink, bald and thick, angelic and terrifying, looking like he had materialized from my wettest of dreams. Javier had guided me to their usual spot, to the right of the disco ball toward the edge of the stage and placed me directly in front of him. "Jeff, would you mind entertaining this one while I spin for the Goddess?" He took his tethered glow sticks out of his pocket and gave them a snap, unlocking whatever chemicals they contained, causing them to ignite. Before he got an answer, he took to the stage and whipped up a light show for his Goddess, leaving me there frozen within inches of Jeff, who might as well have been my God. He took the initiative to close the gap between us, pulling me into his arms, and nestling me into his neck with his thick square hand on the back of my head. I breathed him in, and he smelled like pine trees and fresh cut wood and leather and sweat. His smell made my head light and my dick hard as he rocked me back and forth like a child at 128 bpm. He didn't say a word, he just *moved* me for what felt like forever.

Whatever trance I was in snapped as I felt a tap on my shoulder. "May I cut in?" Javier asked. I was quick to let go of Jeff and make space between us, not wanting to overstep my bounds or disrespect their relationship.

"Of course! He's all yours," I said. "You put on a great show up there. I'm sure your Goddess must be happy."

"As if you could see any of it with your face entombed beneath Jeff's. I'm surprised you actually managed to breathe . . . " He stared me down and I knew I had gone too far.

" . . . darling." He finished his sentence after an intentionally dramatic pause, replacing his galvanized stare with a lightness in his eyes. I felt my entire existence exhale. The three of us spent the next few hours vibrating, figuratively and literally, smoking weed and trading bumps as we danced to one big room Factory vocal after another. Junior tried to end his set twice, stopping the music and turning up the lights, but no one was leaving. Each time we stood our ground and stomped our feet, demanding more from the man who, through his music, made our lives feel somehow transcendent. We got three encores out of him that day, the last of which ended with "Living In Ecstasy" by Sister Sledge, a song I hadn't heard since junior high. The music went off and the lights came on, and to make it clear that we had finally overstayed our welcome, security came through and told us to "get the fuck outta here and go home." I thought to myself *this is my home,* a sentiment I knew was shared by just about everyone left shuffling out onto 27th Street at two in the afternoon.

I turned to Javier and Jeff and said, "So if I'm not mistaken you guys are taking me out to brunch, right?"

Jeff raised his thick square hand above his head to hail a cab. "No, honey. We're taking you back to our place."

Eighteen

I sat in the back of that cab, trying to remain collected, but my heart was pounding at the same rate as the kick drums we had danced to all morning. I had no idea what was about to happen. Were they taking me back to their place to fuck me? Fred and I were in a monogamous relationship, but we both knew that he wouldn't be the first and only dick to grace my insides. What was I going to do? What if they wanted to tie me up and torture me or turn me into an offering for these Goddesses they worshipped? No one knew where I was if something happened. But what the hell could *possibly* happen? I had no idea, nor did I care. There was nothing on earth that was going to stop me from doing whatever Javier and Jeff wanted.

We got out on Bethune Street, one of those tiny West Village blocks that didn't need an accompanying cross street when telling a cab driver your destination. If anything, you needed to give them directions because it was such an obscure location. I loved the far West Village with its confusing layout and its proximity to the Piers and the Meatpacking District, two of the most storied gay areas in New York City. But whereas both of those locations were renowned for their crumbling structures and their gritty sensibility, Bethune Street was posh as fuck.

I followed them to their building, a beautiful six-story structure with massive floor-to-ceiling windows on the ground floor. Contiguous horizontal fabric blinds concealed whatever existed behind them. I would have guessed those were empty storefronts had it not been for the lack of doors. The five floors above all had tall narrow windows, reminders of the building's original use as a factory loft, I guessed, but the casings and the glass had been replaced and updated, preserving some character while modernizing the vibe. I had done enough apartment searches in Manhattan to know that whatever Javier and Jeff did for a living must have been very lucrative. We walked through the lobby, past the elevator, and Jeff took his keys out and slid one into the lock of apartment D. *As in Daddy* I thought to myself.

As soon as I stepped foot in their place, I knew it was *beyond.* First came the kitchen on the right. It was about the size of my entire studio apartment, very light and open, with pops of color created by sets of red, blue, and yellow dishes kept behind frosted glass cabinet doors, and a large, intricate tapestry hanging from the wall that matched the dishes beautifully. A small, green bird happily chirped within a black metal cage. To my left was a staircase that went both up and down. A fucking triplex? In NYC? Ahead of me was a wood dining table with four chairs around it, and beyond that was a railing. I walked over to it and looked down. There beneath me was a living room with four intentionally and tastefully mismatched chairs. I looked up again and realized that the giant windows above the living room, eye level with me, were the plates of glass I had noticed outside. I turned around and looked up, and recessed about six feet from where I stood was what I assumed was the top floor. Or maybe it wasn't the top floor. I assumed it was a triplex, but maybe it had four floors. Or five even. I began to realize I shouldn't assume anything about my two new friends.

Javier took me by the hand. "Let me give you a tour, darling." He led me downstairs to "our library," as he put it, and placed me in front of a huge wall of books. The spines indicated the collection was about everything from queer poetry to psychedelic substances to non-western religious practices to sadomasochism. "Wow, I wish I could read every single one of these," I told him.

"Hmm. Then why don't you start with this one?" He pulled out a soft cover called *RE/Search: Modern Primitives* and handed it to me. "Let's get you some context as to why you have chosen to mark your body with ink. Maybe it will help you understand your nature, darling. Now come. Let's move on."

He led me into the living room, which I realized was a level below ground. The large glass windows were now above my head, illuminating the space with a beautiful indirect light. I was able to get a closer look at the chairs. One was a stout, mid-century modern piece upholstered with dark teal fabric, supported by angled wooden legs with metal tips. Next to it sat a sculptural orange leather lounge rocking chair with a separate headrest and individual leg supports, all held together by a black metal frame. A black leather lounge chair faced the orange one, but that one was equal parts stately and whimsical, with its dramatic curved edges and a leopard pillow made of the same fabric that covered my favorite piece of all, a gently contoured sweep of a cushion that held the sleekness and beauty of the jungle cat it represented. All four chairs faced inward, surrounding a cow-skin rug, creating a conversation space flanked by lush plants and flowing curtains that led to an odd subterranean outdoor space, the purpose of which escaped me.

To my left was a large wooden barn door held onto an exposed metal track by brushed steel wheels. Javier pulled it open, and my jaw must have hit the floor. "Close your mouth and stop drooling, darling. It's just our office."

The room was dark with strategically placed red lights along the floor and the ceiling. Centered in the space like some sort of altar was a leather sling that hung from the ceiling with thick metal chains affixed to four oversized eye hooks that looked less like they came from a hardware store than an industrial interiors showroom. Attached to the wall was a black wooden fixture of shelves and clamps that held a collection of sex toys, objects, and instruments, some of which I couldn't begin to understand. There were dildos ranging in size from petite to Fred to elephant. Beautiful leather floggers and single tail whips, all black and red, hung downwards, almost gently, in their resting state. There was rope and handcuffs and a set of metal implements that I assumed were designed to enter some orifice of the human body. A giant leather body bag was laid out on a matching leather table, and a rack of leather and rubber garments and hoods were staged behind them.

"This is your office?" I was dumbfounded.

"Yes darling, we're prostitutes." The only prostitutes I had ever met were the ones who showed up to Sound Factory at 9 a.m. Being a hooker wasn't a thing. At all. It was frowned upon by queer people, let alone by society at large, although I never understood why. It seemed like a perfectly respectable way to make a living, although it came with the risk of dying of AIDS every time you clocked in. Maybe that was why pretty much everyone I knew looked down upon it. Well, everyone but me, and apparently Jeff and Javier, who stated: "It's truly the Lord's work."

"I thought you worshiped the Goddess?" I asked with genuine curiosity as to how this mystical being could invoke such a traditional Christian reference.

"What makes you think they aren't all one in the same?" He smiled with that all-knowing smile. "Let's move on, shall we? There's more to see before Jeff is ready for you." I had no idea what he meant by that, but I felt my dick instantly get hard at the thought of being the subject of their "bring your kid to work" day.

We left the red room, walked past the stairs, and behind them was a bathroom, clad in concrete and marble, with a Jacuzzi in its center. "Are you kidding me?" I exclaimed. I could no longer contain my amazement.

"Do we look like we're kidding, darling?" He raised an eyebrow and gave me a head tilt to emphasize his point. "Our clients come to us to make contact with the God of fire. It is very powerful magic. We must bring them to Oshun and bathe them in the water to create true balance before they leave." I had heard that word before: Oshun. It was printed beneath the name of the India record "Love and Happiness" that I had picked up at Eight Ball a couple of weeks earlier.

"Is Oshun the Goddess of water?" I asked.

"She is the Goddess of the river. Jeff worships her upstairs in his space. We pray that she honors this room as there is no Goddess of the jacuzzi!" Javier broke out into laughter as he took my hand and led me back up the stairs.

Adjacent to the dining room was a simple quiet space that contrasted the tribal-meets-luxe feeling of all the other rooms we had toured. A red futon adorned with a long purple pillow sat on the ground, and a beautiful tatami mat covered the floor. At the far side of the room, behind a pair of wooden blinds, were a set of interior glass windows, allowing for a view of their office below. "This is my space," Javier said in a near whisper. "I purchased this mat when I lived in Japan, teaching Italian to the locals, and the futon was a gift from a client I fisted quite regularly when I lived in Bali. These are my belongings. I don't need much."

"Says the guy with the jacuzzi in his triplex," I said, adding my two cents to his millions of dollars. Javier laughed heartily. "You know what David, you are correct. I say I don't need much but I am quite happy with all the abundance that surrounds me. I deserve it after all."

"You deserve it?" I asked. "How so?"

"Because I'm a fierce fucking queen, darling, and the universe knows it too."

We went upstairs to the third floor, which opened directly onto the primary bedroom. To the left was a railing, which I leaned over, revealing the dining room below, and beyond that, two floors down, was the living room, also within my view. It clicked for me that the apartment was stacked like a capital letter E with each floor longer than the one above it. The walls of the bedroom were painted in shades of teal, and the bed itself, draped in a white comforter with two pillows, sat atop a deep blue, built-in platform. At the base of the bed, notched into the wall itself, was a four-foot-tall, gold-leafed alcove that housed an altar of sorts. A few candles surrounded a statue of an Indian God, with the head of an elephant and the body of a man. This same figure was tattooed on Jeff's arm, and I made a mental note to inquire about its role in all of this well-deserved, abundant, fierce fucking queenery.

Connected to the bedroom was the ensuite bathroom, a beautiful space that matched the vibe of the bottom level jacuzzi temple, all concrete and marble with polished steel fixtures. Across from the bathroom was an imposing, dark wood door with a polished steel knocker that looked like a giant nipple with a ring thrust through it. I couldn't figure out if that was the original design intention or it just took on that appearance in Javier and Jeff's three-story temple of ill repute.

"What's behind door number, like, 19 I guess?"

"That is Jeff's space, David."

"Can I see?" I couldn't begin to imagine what was inside. I wanted to see for myself what Jeff was all about. *I needed to see.*

"That's up to Jeff, darling. Speaking of . . . " Javier went back to the bedroom, and I heard him call out to the floors below "Jeff, are you ready for our guest of honor?"

I could faintly hear him reply, "Yes. Bring him down." Once again, Javier took my hand and led me downstairs. My heart was pounding in my chest and my breathing quickened. My dick was engorged and pressed so hard against my jeans I thought it was going to burst. All I could imagine was Jeff, two floors below me, in his chaps and his tattooed muscles, his face cast devilish from the moody red lighting, one hand holding a chain from their sling, the other waving me forward to climb into it so that he and Javier could do whatever they wanted to my body in order to connect me with the God of fire and the Goddess of the river.

But there on the second floor, standing in the kitchen, wearing a gingham apron, and holding a platter of eggs, was Jeff. "I hope you like huevos rancheros, honey."

* * *

I spent the next three hours in their dining room *learning*. I was taught that my gayness, my queerness, was indeed the gift I knew it to be. Javier and Jeff spoke of non-western cultures, both modern and ancient, where gay people were honored for their identities. Our uniqueness was nurtured. We were raised to fulfill specific roles in society, such as priests and marriage counselors and healers. We were thought of as a third gender and revered for our mystical and balanced perspective that united the masculine and the feminine. We were often considered the closest to the deities themselves. I learned that we were only considered sinners within western Christian societies, a poisonous ideology spread around the world through the relentless and unfair colonization of the planet, all in the name of greed, dressed up and made acceptable under the banner of saving the wicked through accepting Jesus as their holy savior. That afternoon I understood why so many of my religious countrymen allowed my gay ancestors to die of AIDS. They did so in the name of righteousness, and it was vile.

I learned that I could be both man and woman and everything in between. My gayness was a ticket to freedom from the oppression of the binary that had been hoisted upon humanity. I learned that throughout my life I would take on many different roles: the son and the daughter, the father and the mother, the sister and the brother, and that I should allow each energy to course through me without question. It was explained to me that at times I would be called upon to be the protector, and that by selflessly stepping up and doing so without any desire for reciprocation or thanks, when my time came, I would be the protected and not the rejected.

I learned that my body, that Jeff's and Javier's bodies, that everything in their apartment and in New York City and in the entirety of the earth was made of literal stardust. When I looked down upon my hands, I was looking at things that were created in the cores of collapsing stars before being blown out into the universe. I may have been birthed by my mother, but I was born of cosmic energy. I learned that Javier and Jeff worshiped this energy as it manifested itself through the many Goddesses and Gods that were tied to nature and ever present, that some coursed through me more strongly than others, but that all were to be honored and respected in their totality. If I honored them, I too could embody the magic of the universe.

Perhaps most importantly, I learned that all these things were manifesting themselves in my desire to explore sex as something *more*. I told them about the time Fred and Eddie had a bunch of us over after the Roxy, and Eddie threw on a porn to prove to us that he looked like one of the guys in the film, only to land directly in a scene where one guy was getting fisted by another. I told them how everyone in the room was like "eww, that's disgusting!" while I sat there quietly mesmerized by its intensity and connection. I told them I would go into The Noose on 19th Street any chance I could to look at all the harnesses and the chaps and inquire about the restraints and devices that hung from the walls. I wanted to know how anyone could fit some of those toys inside their asses. I told them that I wanted to be blindfolded and tied up and gang banged and humiliated, treated like an object to be used by groups of men in any way they wanted. And in a moment of weakness, I confessed that I wanted to feel another man cum inside me. "I know that's really bad," I said, and I began to cry uncontrollably.

From the moment the three of us met, and up until then, Javier had done almost all the talking within their relationship. But my tears must have triggered something within Jeff because he jumped out of his chair, sat in the empty one next to mine, and as he pulled my body into his, wrapping his thick arms around me, he said:

> *Shush, honey. That's not bad. There is no bad. There is no good or evil. There's only love and fear. These feelings that you're having, that you're letting yourself have, they're signs of your willingness and your courage to question the boundaries and the connections between those two energies. Your tears are signals of strength. Most people happily go through life confined to the box that society puts them in. Hell, most of them don't even realize that anything else even exists outside of their boxes, and those that do, well most of them are too scared to question if they're living in a gift box or an empty one. You, you're questioning everything, honey, and as well you should. You're genuinely trying to figure out your queerness, just like us, and there are plenty of answers that lie within the sex we can have if we choose to honor it with curiosity's approach. This space that you want to explore is tied to everything we've been talking about. It's ritualistic and it's sacred. It's its own form of body modification, and it can modify your mind too. It can disconnect you from reality so you can reconnect with the universe, and you'll come closer to understanding the masculine and the feminine because you'll feel both urges surging through your body as you objectively explore it. It's called sex magic, honey, and It's very, very powerful stuff. So let go of all that good and bad bullshit. It's bullshit! Reframe it all as love and fear and be proud of that fact that you're a fierce fucking faggot who's ready to call everything into question so you can get some real answers.*

Jeff was right. I *was* a fierce fucking faggot. And I was definitely ready.

Nineteen

Fred was exactly as I had expected, seated in the corner of the couch, his legs pulled up to his chest, arms clutched around them, a twister of defiance, defensiveness, and damage in his eyes. Whenever I was gone for too long, and for whatever reason, I always returned to find him in this fetal posture: cowering and coiled, ready to strike. The placid man I knew was replaced by this infuriated entity. It was like I was dating two completely different people, and the one before me I couldn't understand. Had it not been for the consistency of reaction to my absence, even if I was out with my straight friends, I would have chalked it up to jealousy. But it was deeper than that. It was *darker*. With my experience of relationships confined to the one I was in, I didn't yet have any wisdom upon which to draw upon to figure it out, so I settled for jealousy as it came closest to fitting the bill. The first words out of my mouth were: "Nothing happened, so calm down." He reacted by storming into the bedroom and locking the door. I spent the next hour trying to get him to talk about what he was feeling and asking why he didn't trust me, but as poor of a communicator as Fred was when he was in a good mood, he couldn't even find his words when he was in that state. And each time he got like that, the confusion I felt was being eroded, one outsized reaction after another, by anger.

Eventually he let me in and as I opened the door he got back into bed and pulled the covers over his head. I laid down next to him and did my best to meet the moment with some level of empathy instead of losing my shit.

Despite my best efforts, we had a screaming match for the ages, fueled by anger and insecurities, by fears of abandonment and threats of self-harm. His outbursts fluctuated between dramatic and unhinged, with plenty of door slamming to add some percussion to the mix. Eventually, however, we exhausted ourselves and managed to recenter our energies. Rather than rehashing every painful moment or nasty thing said, we sat together in silence. Then we slowly tiptoed into calm communication by talking about a new candle he had purchased. Eventually, Fred found it in himself to ask me about the goggles.

"They didn't work." Then Javier popped into my head. "Actually, they did work, but only for about 20 seconds before they got all fogged up. I guess that's why they need to be glasses, not goggles." I picked them up off the coffee table and went into the kitchen and dropped them in the garbage. Since coming out of the closet, I'd gotten pretty good at being dramatic myself.

"David, stop. No more drama from either of us today." Fred got up and retrieved the goggles from the trash, pulled an implement from one of his many tool kits and sat back down next to me.

"I know you used to go skiing as a kid," he said to me. "Did you wear goggles back then?" I confirmed that I did. "And did they fog up?" he asked. I confirmed that they didn't. "Well, these goggles are made for swimming. So, what's the difference between them?" Any lingering anger I had for him disappeared. The real Fred, or at least the Fred that occupied his body most of the time, was back, challenging me to think, pushing me to be better. It took me a minute, but the lightbulb went off.

"Well, these are made for going under water so they need to be waterproof. I remember my skiing goggles had these little vents on the side. They reminded me of gills. I never thought about it until now but I guess they must have served a purpose because every pair I owned had the same thing by the lenses."

"So, when it's cold outside and you get in your car and the windows fog up, what's the first thing you do?" he asked.

At that point I was putting two and two together and coming up with my answers. "You crack a window." The vents in my skiing goggles were there to basically crack a window on my face.

Fred handed me my goggles back, along with the tool he had put on the cushion next to him, hidden from my sight. It was the hole punch he had shown me how to use when I needed to put a notch in my leather belt, a personal triumph courtesy of my commitment to cardio at the gym. Unlike a hole punch used for paper, this one had multiple prongs on a wheel, each one capable of creating a different size puncture, so I clicked through a couple of options until I found the one best suited for the job. I carefully punched out four holes on each side of the goggles, two on the top and two on the bottom, allowing for air to pass through them.

My excitement came rushing back. "Oh my God! I hope they work now. Maybe I can turn the shower on in the bathroom or something and steam it up in there." My brain was flying again with that same flood of endorphins I got every time I thought about the M.F.A. and everything I wanted it to be. My afternoon with Javier and Jeff had confirmed what my gut had been telling me all along. I didn't need any answers to justify my mission. I was armed with all the questions, and they would hone my vision. By that point I was pacing around the living room, unable to sit still, a tornado of energy and elation, trying to figure out where I could go to confirm that my dreams were about to begin their transformation into my reality. Looking back, my wild fluctuations were just as unhinged as Fred's in their own way.

Fred went into the bedroom and came out fully dressed. "There's only one way you're going to know if they really work, so let's go to the tea dance happening at that club on 17th Street."

"Really Fred?"

"Yes, really. It's the only way you're going to be able to get any sleep later, and if you don't go now, I know I won't be getting any of your attention tonight. You'll be lost in that crazy brain of yours and I'll be talking into the void." He wasn't wrong. "But you have to promise me that we'll only stay for like a half an hour just to test them out. I didn't sleep that well last night and I'm kind of beat."

So that's exactly what we did. We went and we danced, and I wore my goggles and they worked the entire time. I passed them to Fred, and he wore them too. Watching him looking around at all the lights, doing his little signature clap dance, smiling his held-back smile, I just couldn't believe how lucky I was to have met such a good man, even if we did have our moments of homosexual high drama. He wasn't anything like the man of my dreams, because I never could have dreamed up anyone like Fred in the first place. I felt my eyes tear up as my soul became filled with the warmest, most overpowering feeling I had ever experienced. I had to admit it. *I was falling in love.*

We left the club and walked back to his apartment. I ordered us some dinner and we watched *Absolutely Fabulous* before shutting off the lights and heading to bed. I knew I wouldn't be able to sleep without telling him how I felt.

"Fred I really want to thank you for being so supportive of what I've been doing with these goggles and the M.F.A. and all this crazy stuff I talk about. You're so patient with me and you teach me so much."

"Well, what did you learn tonight?" he asked.

I had the answer real quick. "That good design dictates form follows function."

"You already knew that, David." He almost looked disappointed that I didn't even take a moment to think about the actual question before blurting out my words. "I'm kind of worn out, so I'll just tell you what you need to know. It's true that in good design, form follows function. *Good* designers put their work out even when the function isn't that solid because they're so impressed with the form they've created. They admire their work too much." He paused to look deep into my eyes. "*Great* designers, on the other hand, don't stop until they nail the form *and* the function. So, if you want the things you make to be great, you can't just quit when they don't work out. You have to keep pushing or all your creations will end up in the garbage, either because you gave up too soon and put them there yourself, or you put them out too soon and they deserve to be there in the first place."

What a gift his words were. I didn't take them as criticism. I took them as a vote of confidence.

"Fred, I want you to be part of the M.F.A. I want you to be half. I know I call it my one-man activist organization, but it's not. I don't even know what the fuck it is, but it's definitely not a one-man anything. It's only taking shape because I have you. On my own, I know I'm going to settle for good, even when I don't mean to. Together, it can be great."

I waited for his response. He lay there silently for what seemed like forever when matched against my impatience. I began assuming that he was figuring out a way to gently let me down with his refusal, but then he sat up and turned on the lamp by his nightstand so he could look me in the eyes once again.

"David, nothing would make me happier." I could see he was starting to cry. "I don't know what it is that you're doing either, but I see how passionate you are. You have so much drive. I've never told you this, but I really admire that about you. It's inspiring. I've never met anyone like you. My whole life, I've been content to be in the background making things for myself, but I have tried to start my own line. Well not really. I haven't really tried. Not like you try. You're fearless. I love being around that energy. I love being around you. So, whatever it is that you want to do, I want to do it with you."

I sat up and climbed on top of him, straddling his legs with mine as I leaned in and kissed him. I looked into his eyes and said, "Then it's me and you. The founders of the Metropolitan Faggot Authority."

He looked back into mine and said, "But there's just one thing David, and I know you're not going like it. I can't be part of anything that uses the word faggot. I get why you love that word and why you use it to describe yourself.

I know you're reclaiming it so it loses its power and that's fine for you, but it doesn't work for me. It's holds too much darkness in my soul. So if you meant what you said — if this can only function with me and you in it together — then you're going to have to change the form to something we can both believe in."

He was right. I didn't like that one bit. "Reclaiming that word and weaponizing it against the world, Fred, that's at the heart of everything I've learned, from hip-hop to ACT UP. It's the good, the bad, and the ugly neatly packaged into two syllables. It holds my anger and my identity, my power and my community, so it has to be in the name. It has to. I'm taking it back. Faggot is *mine*." I stood my ground.

"It can be yours David." Fred shut off the lights and got back under the covers. "It just can't be ours."

Twenty

Paul called me to his office, and as I walked in, he put on a denim jacket and turned around to show me the back. "Beatles," he said, as did the embroidery on the jacket. "We got The Beatles!" I knew what a big deal that was, because The Beatles were renowned for their unwillingness to do just about anything when it came to licensing. But somehow Paul had managed to pull it off. He always knew how to make shit happen, and I hoped to do the same with my organization (formerly known as the M.F.A.) once it began to take off. I wasn't going to let anything stand in my way. I wasn't going to quit.

"That's amazing Paul! Now we just have to sell it."

"It was your idea David, so you better hope it sells — along with all of these."

There, on his desk, were stacks of albums by Led Zeppelin, The Rolling Stones, The Who, and Pink Floyd. That's another thing I loved about Paul. He embodied the "go big or go home" mentality that I figured one needed to run a business. And he wasn't wrong. For The Beatles merchandise to work they needed to hang with products from these other groups, more of them even. One random classic rock denim jacket in between N.W.A. and Smashing Pumpkins hoodies wouldn't make any sense.

"Holy fuck, Paul. Those are some big names. How did you pull that off?"

"The Norwegians. They're tired of losing money but if they don't lose some more, they will never make any of it back. They paid some big dollars to get these licenses. This is it, David. If these rock bands don't land us this deal I think we're cut off."

"Which deal?"

"HBN. They want to buy us and sell our merchandise on TV to Middle America. The numbers will be huge, David. And they have the money to back the retail expansion as well, but infomercials are the future." I couldn't exactly see a future where Nirvana was okay with their flannel shirts being peddled on cable TV by white ladies wearing too much make up, but I was sure whatever deal Paul struck with the bands gave him full license to sell their product wherever the hell he wanted.

"I need you to take all these records back to your office and tell me how to turn them into clothing. Clothing that is going to sell *a lot* of units."

"I'm on it, Paul."

"And I'm serious David. This is still a longshot so don't get your hopes up and don't quit your day job."

I laughed. It was rare that Paul made a joke that truly landed, but I heard him loud and clear. We were at the start of an all-or-nothing moment for Sonic Assembly and for my future. By the tone of Paul's voice, I could tell he was preparing me for the latter outcome more than the former, so I needed a plan B — as in: "Bitch what the fuck are you gonna do next?"

Then I got serious. B had to stand for "Be your own boss."

Twenty-One

Fred and I got to work on making our first run of goggles out of the eleven pairs remaining from the original dozen I had purchased. Figuring out how to best apply the crazy glue to the lenses cost us two of them, so we ended up with a total of nine units.

"So what are you going to do with them?" Fred asked me.

"I'm going to sell them!" I happily announced.

"What does that have to do with activism? I thought that was the whole point of the M.F.A."

"They don't make sense with the M.F.A. You're right. But you killed that name anyway, so I've been rethinking what this whole thing should be. I have activism in my heart, but whatever this becomes, it doesn't have to be anything traditional. I feel like all the great organizations redefined what activism could be. The music I listen to — my favorite hip-hop artists — they're all activists in their own right. So are graffiti artists like guys at GFS. They make statements through what they make *and* what they sell. So I thought about what you said and I realized we need to let the form take on whatever shape it needs to fulfill the function."

"I can't exactly argue with that," Fred replied with a smirk.

"So, I'm feeling like it shouldn't be an organization. It should be a brand. It should be goggles and fashion and music and anything else — *everything* else that makes sense to queer culture. It should marry creativity and sex and love. The cock and the ass with the heart and the mind. I want to seal it all together and change the way gay people see the world. I want them to see my vision." Fred cocked his head at me, and I corrected myself. "Our vision, honey. It's definitely *our* vision. If I didn't really think that was true, I wouldn't have changed the name."

"Did you change it?" he asked.

"Not yet, but I have an idea that I'd like to run by you. If you think it works, then we will change it."

Fred cupped my face with his strong, talented hands and kissed me, first tenderly, then passionately, then aggressively. "Thank you, Angel. I love you so much." He stripped me of my clothing, put a Magnum on his cock, and fucked me on the floor until he came on my back. We lay there together as

Fred's heavy, quickened breathing slowed into a gentler rhythm. He climbed off me and I shot back up. "Ok let me show you!"

I grabbed my nylon Nervous Records bag, pulled out a manilla envelope and displayed its contents on the coffee table:

1. An 8 ½ x 11-inch sheet of glossy paper printed with the word "re:vision" across the top in Arial Bold, each letter outlined in black, with all the letters filled with a spectrum effect rainbow that ran vertically through them, red on top through violet on the bottom. Under that was Fred's home address. At the bottom of the page was a tagline "change the way you see the world"
2. An 8 ½ x 11-inch sheet of lightweight cardstock printed with two columns of ten rectangles, each containing the word "re:vision" in the same rainbow treatment as the first page. On the left side of each box, next to the "r" was a small black dot.
3. An 8 ½ x 11-inch sheet of paper, one side smooth and one side rough, with "re:vision" in rainbow printed seven inches across, three times top to bottom.

"So, I was thinking about everything that's been going on in my head and Metropolitan Faggot Authority doesn't work. None of it really reflects what I want us to be about. Metropolitan limits us to cities, and I want us to be global. Faggot limits us to gay men, and I want us to be queer. And Authority means I know everything, and I don't. I want to change the way people see the world. I want to reframe. I want to reconsider. I want to reexamine and revamp and remake and release. I landed on revision, but I added the colon because it's all regarding vision. Our vision. It ties in neatly with the goggles. So, I tried a few different graphic treatments."

I spread out my visual pitch. "This is like letterhead, and these can be cut out into hang tags, and this is special paper that you can iron onto fabric and it transfers the ink so we can make shirts or something. I didn't want to go too far in case you hated it. Or even if you just like it. Whatever we do it's important to me that you *love* it."

I could see Fred's eyes get just a little weepy. "I do love it, David. I love it a lot. Now it feels like ours."

Fred used a pair of his good scissors to cut out the hang tags and his hole punch to knock out the little black circle on each. He affixed the tags to the

goggles with a thin strip of black leather, and we repackaged each pair back into the clear polybag it came in. I lined them up in front of us, our very first products, ready for the market. I cut out one of the heat transfer "re:vision" logos, placed it over the chest of a blank three quarter sleeve raglan baseball jersey, and using an iron, pressed the ink from paper to cloth.

"Are you planning on selling that as well?" Fred asked.

"I wouldn't sell anything without your approval." I smiled. "Maybe one day we can sell them. But for now, this is part of my uniform." I got up and went to the bedroom, and returned wearing the goggles, the shirt, a long yellow and red Lycra tube dress, and six-inch platform combat boots I had re-soled on St. Marks Place. I gathered up the goggles and placed them in a pink Hello Kitty knapsack which I slung over my shoulders. I stood there looking and feeling like a 6'4" club kid entrepreneur. Fred was speechless.

"So . . . *ta-da!* What do you think?' I asked.

"Well, you're definitely going to get noticed. And no one is going to think you're working for The Gap."

"That's *exactly* the look I'm going for!" I shouted.

Fred got up and hugged me, and it was so weird being taller than him and looking down into his eyes. In that moment, it felt very appropriate, because even though re:vision was ours, I knew in my heart he was doing this because he believed in me and because, in his own way, he looked up to me. "We're gonna do great things together, Fred. I promise I won't let you down." Fred had been let down enough in his life. I was going to revise that, too. Jeff told me at times I was going to be called upon to be the protector, and I thought to myself I was going to be that for Fred.

A little voice inside my soul finished that thought, and whispered to my heart, *forever*.

Twenty-Two

Other than Sound Factory, I never waited in line to get into a club, and The Limelight was no different. I went on Michael Alig's night, knowing full well there would be the maximum density of my target audience: suburban club kids tripping their faces off courtesy of the money given to them by their unsuspecting parents. As I approached in my platforms, towering over the masses of colorful children with fake IDs, I was quickly spotted by the door person and waved right through.

"What's in the knapsack?" security asked me.

"Goggles. I'm selling them," I replied.

"Is that all you're selling tonight?" We both knew what he was talking about.

"Yup. That's it. But you're welcome to search me, Mister Security Officer," I said flirtatiously.

He was unamused. "I'll pass thanks, but if we catch you dealing, you're landing in a squad car."

The Limelight was originally an Episcopalian Church that was converted to a drug rehabilitation center, but was ultimately transformed into a massive nightclub by Peter Gatien. Along with The Tunnel, The Palladium, and Club USA, Peter was considered by many to be the king of New York City nightlife, but most people who actually lived and partied in NYC would beg to differ. There was no disputing Limelight's status as a truly sick club. When Gatien renovated the space, he was careful to leave much of the church's original detailing intact, including massive stained-glass windows that looked down upon the rather "unholy" shenanigans that took place on the main dancefloor and throughout the club's many passageways and lounges. That night in The Chapel, a separate club inside the club, there was a gay party taking place, complete with a small back room, that I had frequented with Fred on a couple of occasions. As much as I wanted to head to The Chapel and grope dick in the darkness, I was there strictly for business. Besides, looking the way that I did, I probably wouldn't get much action from the Chelsea boys anyway.

I made my way to the main room, throbbing with bass and moving at about 136 bpm. With its four-story-high ceilings, the lighting rig would rise and fall above the dancefloor, and there were additional lights along the walls and behind the balconies, an ideal setting for re:vision goggles to do their thing. I planted myself adjacent to the dancefloor where the music was just low enough that I could pitch my product, but still close enough to the flashing action to show off their efficacy. I saw a group of kids with their pupils nicely dilated and their jaws grinding away, practically to the beat. They were all dressed up like stuffed animal alien kindergarteners, and quite honestly, I loved them. As I approached their little crew of five, I hoped they loved re:vision.

"Check these out," I said, taking the yellow pair off my face and handing them to the porcelain-skin girl who was gnawing on her candy necklace. She held them, looking up at me, and I said, "Trust me. Put them on. You'll love them." She trusted me. She put them on. She loved them.

"Oh my God these are so cool!" She spun around in a slow circle, looking up, mesmerized by the newly augmented light show. Her mouth dropped open, and I considered the positive, medical effect the goggles were having on her clenched jaw.

"Lemme see, lemme see!" all her friends begged. She took them off and they passed them around. The goggles had the same effect on all of them. They were amazed, and most importantly, they were smiling.

"Where did you get these?" a tall white boy with green pigtails and matching green Adidas velour track suit asked me.

"I make them myself," I answered with this feeling of genuine pride.

"Where can we buy them?" the girl asked through the crunching of her necklace.

'Well, I actually have some right here." I took off my knapsack and pulled one out. "They're $20 each."

"*No way!* That's so cheap! I'll take it!" she exclaimed, but the white boy grabbed them out of her hands.

"I want those! They're green and they match my hair!" He reached into his pocket and pulled out a crumpled $20 bill and handed it to me. He ripped open the packaging, dropped it to the floor, and put them on immediately. "Can I leave the tag on?" he asked me.

"Sure. They're yours. You can do whatever you want with them now. I just hope you really enjoy them," I replied with all the sincerity in the world. "I'm David, and you are my very first customer. Thank you so fucking much."

"No way, dude! Can I hug you?"

"Absolutely." He gave me the biggest hug I could imagine getting from a total stranger. I'm sure some of it was the ecstasy he was clearly rolling on, but that didn't make it any less genuine.

"What other colors do you have?"

"I want one too!"

"Do you have one in purple?"

"I want one in red!"

I couldn't keep up with their questions, so I just opened up my knapsack and let them pull out whichever ones they wanted. I was sure to let the girl pick first though. I didn't know much of anything about being a businessman, but I knew I wanted to be fair. She grabbed a red one, as did her friend in the matching outfit, and the remaining two boys in the crew took purple ones. Each one handed me a $20 bill, except the boy with the glitter eyeshadow, who asked me if I could break a hundred. He handed it to me, and using his friend's twenties, I gave him his change. They all put their goggles on. They all thanked me. They all wished me luck with my new venture, and as they turned to head into the thick of the dancefloor to enjoy their new accessories, green pigtail guy shouted out "I'm gonna tell all my friends about you, David!"

I made my way to the bar to get a Gatorade. I took out the hundred and just stared at it. I couldn't believe that in a matter of minutes I had doubled my $50 investment. But even more majorly, people actually paid for what Fred and I had created. That group of kids could have spent their twenties on drugs or shots or the overpriced candy that was for sale in the bathrooms. But they chose to spend it on re:vision. I was so overcome with joy that I began to cry.

"You ok buddy? You need help?" the bartender asked me.

"No, no I'm good. I'm great, actually. Can I have a Gatorade?" I replied.

"Sure, what color?"

"Yellow I guess" . . . *to match my goggles* I thought to myself.

He brought me my drink and I handed him the $100 bill, but before he could get to the register, I shouted after him. He turned around and came back to me. I took off my knapsack and pulled a $10 bill out of the side pocket. I handed that to him instead, and he gave me my hundred back. *That's not your money, David. That's company money,* I thought to myself. I put the hundred into the side pocket and he returned with my change, five singles, all of which I left for him on the bar. "Thanks man," he said to me. "Half these kids forget to leave me anything."

I replied, "Guess I'm just helping to balance a couple of them out." When it came to money, Fred had loosened me up just a little bit. I was learning that it was actually good to spread some of it around. I heard his voice in my head: *"You can't hoard money, David. If you hold onto it too tightly it will never circulate back to you."* I uncapped my Gatorade, took a few gulps, and someone tapped me on the shoulder. I turned around and there was another group of adorable swirled-out Limelight kids.

"Are you the guy with the goggles?"

* * *

I walked into Fred's apartment about an hour after I had left, sat down on the couch, and started unlacing my giant combat boots. Fred came out of the bedroom and sat down next to me.

"That was quick. What happened?" he asked.

I unzipped my Hello Kitty knapsack, turned it upside down and shook it. The goggles were gone, but five singles, three fives, two tens, and four twenties fell out, landing on the coffee table, a display of our success, dramatically capped off when the $100 bill, as if on cue, fell out last and landed perfectly on top of the rest.

"I sold out of them without even trying," I replied, "so we started a business tonight, Fred. That's what happened."

Twenty-Three

Laying out the artworks for the Sonic Assembly classic rock collection was pretty simple. The bands we signed all had incredible iconography, so it was just a matter of photocopying the album covers, cutting out the parts I liked, and pinning them to the silhouettes that I felt best suited the aesthetic of the group. It wasn't that hard to figure out that a black denim jacket with the Led Zeppelin logo on the back and the symbols from their fourth album on the front left chest would be an easy sell. When I was finished, I made my presentation to Paul, holding each garment up and explaining the thinking behind it, and he seemed pleased with the work I had done. I handed him back the stack of albums but asked if I could keep *The Wall* by Pink Floyd. "I'm surprised you want to listen to something without any *flava*," he joked, innocently, not realizing that his words were totally inappropriate, as he honored my request.

The Wall came out when I was in fifth grade, its lead single "Another Brick in The Wall (Part 2)" dominating the radio as it climbed to number one on the *Billboard Hot 100* charts. Like just about everyone else in the world, I couldn't get the hook out of my head, and the lyrics were a rallying cry for students everywhere:

We don't need no education
We don't need no thought control
No dark sarcasm in the classroom
Teachers leave those kids alone

As a young queer kid who was outcast, labeled a faggot, and bullied nearly every day, I channeled my desire to be left alone by *everyone* when I screamed those words in my pillow.

Returning to my office, I laid *The Wall* out on my desk, removing the records and their inner sleeves so I could see all the art together. The Mugler book that Fred had given me for my birthday had made its way to work with me, so I took it out of my filing cabinet and flipped to my favorite pages: Two images of Iman in a gold metallic dress and oversized accessories, standing in the Sahara casually presiding over every single goddamn grain of sand in the desert. On my sample rack was a GFS "Krylon" long sleeve shirt that I brought over to my desk and folded neatly into a rectangle. From Pink Floyd to Mugler to GFS, I stood back and looked at the work and the worlds these artists created, and I *knew* I could join their ranks. But it wouldn't be right at that moment, because it was almost 2 p.m. and I was hungry. I put on my Tommy Boy Carhartt and went to grab lunch.

* * *

I walked over to Broadway Italian, one of my favorite spots in the neighborhood, and ordered a baked ziti to go. As I waited for it to be prepared, the two-liter bottle of Diet Coke I had polished off between breakfast and lunch was ready to make its exit from my body. I went to the bathroom. I pulled out my dick and began to piss, trying to glance at the guy three spots over, a practice I had perfected over many closeted years of hanging out in public men's rooms. As I stood there though, I got the feeling he was kind of doing the same thing. I turned my head slightly toward his direction, and he did the same, only his came with a quick nod of his head. I nodded back. Without zipping his pants up, he stepped back, showing off his thick, meaty cock and parked himself at the urinal next to mine. I could tell he was stroking as he stared straight ahead to the wall. He was some serious trade in his Mets shirt and Dickies pants, both of which were covered in drywall dust and paint splatter. He had some in his beard and on his rugged face as well. It wasn't long before I was stroking my cock, too.

"You got someplace we could go?" he asked with his raspy deep voice. My apartment was clear across town and down 30 blocks, too far away to get off and come back to work on time. Besides, Fred and I were in a monogamous relationship, and I knew better than to bring random men home anyway.

So I brought him to my office.

I walked past Rich at the front desk reading the newest issue of *High Times*. "Yo," I tried to get his attention so he could get a look at the guy I had with me, but he didn't even look up. I led him past Carl, whose head was buried in *The Economist*. "I'm back," I announced, smiling like a kid in a candy store. He looked up just as I paraded my crazy hot trick by his door. I was thrilled I would have someone who could testify to what was about to go down. We got to my office, I closed the door behind us, and I sucked his dick until he came on my face, almost, but not quite, silently. He pulled up his pants and said, "I can see my way out. You might wanna wipe off or something." He exited my office, without giving me his name or even saying thank you, and I couldn't have been happier. I grabbed an Alice In Chains crew neck and ran it across my well-used face.

There was a hard knock on my office door. Before I could answer Paul let himself in, his face knotted up and his pale Scandinavian skin looking like he had been out in the sun all day. I had no idea what had happened to him, but whatever it was, I knew I could change his state of mind with the tale of my sordid lunchtime encounter.

"Are you okay, Paul?" I asked.

"Not exactly, David. Are you?"

"I'm so very okay, Paul. I just met the hottest guy when I went to get lunch. Total contractor or painter or something. He cruised me at the urinals at Broadway Italian and I brought him back here and blew him right where you're standing. It was so fucking hot! Shit, it looks like he left his sandwich there so you can totally have it if you're hungry."

"What the hell is wrong with you, David?!?!" I could tell my story didn't cheer him up one bit.

"Were we too loud? I wasn't really thinking. If it's any consolation, I can assure you the noise wasn't coming from me. My mouth was *very* occupied," I shared gleefully, still very much not reading the room.

"David, you cannot bring guys to your office and have sex with them!" He held the volume of his voice down, but that didn't take away from the fact that I knew I was being screamed at. Paul was furious. It never even dawned on me that I had done something apparently wrong, but I was very much reading the room by that point. "I'm really sorry, Paul. It won't happen again. You have my word. Please don't fire me."

"You have cum on your neck." He left without giving me an answer.

Rich came in two minutes later. "Dude, what the fuck just happened? Paul just took off and he was *pissed*."

"I must have really fucked up, Rich. I brought a guy back to the office and had sex with him."

"You did *what?!*"

"Well not exactly sex. I only blew him."

"Oh well that's *way* better," Rich said sarcastically. "I gotta tell you, dude, I love you like a brother but you can be really self-centered and fucking clueless sometimes. I mean who the fuck thinks it's okay to just go and get laid at work in the middle of the fucking day? Don't you see anything wrong with that?" I lied and said I did. He walked out and said, "It's like you live in your own little world."

I sat down at my desk, terrified my career was over. I replayed what I'd just done and my dick got raging hard again just thinking about it. I got up and locked my office door, jerked off as fast as I could, and ate the evidence.

Looking at everything I had spread out on my desk before lunch, I thought about how amazing the lives of those artists must be. It was like there were no barriers between their passions and their paychecks. I knew the GFS guys were making money doing what they loved. I could only imagine what it must have been like for a huge band like Pink Floyd to have the freedom and the talent to build their massive Wall and encircle tens of millions of screaming fans within it. Or to be Mugler, traveling the globe on a continuous quest to wrap up women in his wildest dreams, all in the name of making them feel gorgeous and powerful. All the artists I most admired, the artists who consumed me, were world builders.

I took my goggles out of my Nervous bag, along with a piece of our re:vision letterhead, and placed them down on my desk among the creations of my idols. Maybe Rich was right. Maybe I did live in my own little world. But maybe instead of leaving it behind, I just needed to fully enter it.

Twenty-Four

Fred and I reinvested every dime of our $180 in sales back into re:vision. I wanted to be careful to keep that money separate from ours. We picked up another three dozen goggles at a cost of $108, and being that we had plenty of refraction paper, elastic, stickers, and crazy glue on hand, we were able to produce 34 more units, two shy of my target of 36. We lost two thanks to my insistence that I help out with the glue application. One pair ended up stuck to itself. The other pair ended up stuck to me. Fred insisted that he handle that part of the process moving forward. I apologized for costing us $40 worth of sales. "No, you didn't. You cost us $6 worth of goggles and about 50 cents worth of paper. That's how inventory works. And trust me, you'll always lose something in production."

We used the balance of the money to buy some fabric from Spandex House on 37th Street, a hotspot for fashion students, costume designers, and DIY folks who needed to make things that had to stretch. I let Fred take the lead in narrowing down the options, as his knowledge of sewing meant he understood what fabrics worked well, not to mention what his portable Singer straight stitch and overlock machines could handle. "Don't even think about leather," he told me as I eyed the black hides lustily.

We ended up choosing two yards of silver spandex, along with two yards of "wet look," two yards of "slinky," and two yards of a rubberized material that almost looked like latex, all in black. We went up to the register with the bolts of fabric and told the gentleman how much we needed of each. He rang it up and the total came out to $61.29. I handed him $72 and asked, "Can I get a yard of red rubber and a yard of yellow with the change?"

"No, my friend. Rubber is expensive. You have $85?" he asked. "I'll give you everything for $85. Very good deal for you, my friend."

"No, I only have $72, unfortunately. So don't cut any of it. Fred, can you help me put these rolls back?" I had learned from Paul that unless you're buying retail, an asking price is just the opening bid in any negotiation.

"My friend, my friend," the gentleman said as he placed his hands on the bolts before we could move them. "You break my balls, but I'll give you red *or* yellow with everything else for $72. That's a very good deal my friend. Special for you and your brother."

His offer was fair, but when I held the black, yellow, and red rubbers together, they just looked so sick. That color combination felt fast. Very NASCAR. Very superhero. I read his name tag and said, "Ok, Khalid, so how about a half a yard of red and a half a yard of yellow, along with everything else for $72 and we have a deal."

"We only sell by the yard, my friend. Ask your brother for more money and you'll get everything you want."

"He's not my brother. He's my boyfriend. And we all know you can cut whatever length you want. You cut swatches for people all the time right off the rolls and there's a dig bin in the back where you sell the leftover scraps. So, I'll get everything I want when you pick up those big scissors and start cutting my order. Two yards each of these four rolls, and a half a yard each of the red and yellow rubber, which my boyfriend is going to go get and bring up here. Honey, can you do that for me?" Fred looked at me questioningly, as Khalid hadn't yet agreed to my terms, but I nodded at him confidently, and Fred pulled the rolls and laid them on the counter. Khalid did nothing. "Pick up those scissors, Khalid. Take my money and don't break my balls." Still nothing. "My friend," I closed with, and I got him to smile. He cut our order and sent us on our way.

"Come back to Spandex House next time, my friends. I'll take care of you. We get new fabrics every day, so bring more money." Khalid did right by us, and we ended up loyal Spandex House customers, shopping there every week for the next few years.

* * *

Fred had a collection of soft paper patterns that he had used in the past to make himself some tight-fitting shirts and tank tops. He told me they would be a good starting point for the fabrics we had purchased. I was eager to start with the rubber, but he told me that would probably come last. "I have some ideas for that material that I want to sketch out, and I'll need to experiment with the tension on the sewing machine so that the stitches don't pop when I sew it. I want to do that when you aren't around, David. You won't have the patience for it." He wasn't wrong. "Besides, before we even start cutting up the other stuff, I want to cut a sample out of this old blue spandex I have somewhere in one of these boxes. This way we can make a sample and fit it and adjust the pattern before we get to the good stuff." I *still* wanted to start with the rubber. Patience wasn't my strong suit.

Fred laid out the blue spandex on the floor, placed the paper pattern pieces over it, and using tailor's chalk, traced out the front and back panels and three long strips for the binding. "It's important that you do this very carefully, David. You can't rush. If you trace it out sloppily then it's not going to fit well. Same goes for when you cut it. You have to use good sharp scissors and cut right along the lines. And you can't forget the notches. You have to clip the notches."

"What do they do?" I asked.

"When it gets sewn, the notches tell the sewer what parts go where. See this stripe?" He pointed to a sewn in panel that ran across the front of his shirt. "When the sewer gets the panels, they might not know which side of the stripe goes up. So you'd put one notch on the top edge and two notches on the bottom edge. You'd do the same with the panels above and below it. The notches also help when you're sewing stretchy fabric or long seams, like in pants. They can mark a halfway point, so you don't end up with a bunch of fabric left over on one side at the end."

"So, if you don't put any notches the sewing will get all fucked up, right?" I asked.

"No. If you don't put any notches in the sewer will give it back to you. It wastes time. Just don't forget them."

"Ok I won't. Mental note. Don't forget notches."

"Good. Now cut this all out." Fred handed me his good scissors, the heavy ones that were three times the size of any scissors I had ever used, and I carefully cut out all the pieces. I did a good job with the front and back panels, and I remembered all the notches, but the binding strips were a bit wobbly. I brought all the pieces to him at his sewing machine, and upon inspection, he handed me two of the strips back. "These won't work. Retrace them and cut them out *carefully* and don't forget the notches."

"What do I do with these strips then?"

"You're going to have to throw them away and thank me for not letting you start with the rubber."

He sewed up the sample tank top in blue, put it on himself and using tailor's chalk and pins, he made his corrections directly onto the garment itself. He took out his roll of pattern paper, cut a yard off, laid the original pattern pieces onto the blank sheet, and using a number two pencil, he traced them all out. He then used a curved ruler to draw his corrections onto the shapes, erasing what was no longer relevant, and then cut them all out again, marking the pieces like "Front Panel" and "Armhole Binding" and adding straight lines to indicate in what direction they needed to go. He handed them all to me. "Lay out the black slinky and trace them out. And make sure that you . . . "

"I know, I know. That I'm careful."

"No, that you make sure you lay the fabric out very straight and line the pieces up with the vertical knit of the fabric."

"Ok Fred. I got it."

"And make sure that you're careful," he said with his Fred smile.

I cut the tank top out of the slinky, and after my work passed his inspection, he started to sew it. As he pushed the fabric through the merrow machine, I laid out the silver spandex and the black wet look, and cut a tank top out of each, carefully. Throwing away those blue Lycra strips wasn't an issue. Wasting re:vision fabric, on the other hand, was not going to happen. Not on my watch. Once I finished I went into the bedroom, put on my club kid uniform, and after checking myself out in the mirror, I took the re:vision baseball jersey off, traced a line across the center, and cut it into a crop top. I put it back on over my tube dress and said to Fred, "That's much better."

"Why did you change it?" he asked.

"I may not know much about construction yet, but I definitely know about proportions, and this just works better for me." I looked at what he was wearing. "One day I'll get you to ditch those high-waisted jeans. They don't do you any favors, honey. *Love you!*"

I grabbed my pink knapsack and headed to the Limelight, quickly converting all 18 units I brought with me into cash from satisfied customers. Making money was fun, but helping people *have* fun felt incredible. The money was a byproduct of the experience I was giving them. Their reactions and their gratitude filled me with a sense of joy and satisfaction. It made me feel purposeful. I returned to Fred's apartment, excited to share with him both my experience and our coins, but when I opened the door, my thunder was stolen for all the right reasons. Fred had sewn up all three tank tops, and on the back neck of each one was a small printed "re:vision" label, tacked into place. "We've got this printer at work that we use to make labels for samples, so I got them to make us a bunch for our line," he said.

I couldn't believe it. Those were *officially* our designs. My own little world got a tiny bit bigger.

* * *

Selling re:vision goggles out at nightclubs made perfect sense. Approaching people with a one-size-fits-all product that they could quickly put on, instantly appreciate, and easily pay for was effortless. Selling clothing, on the other hand, was a totally different beast. We needed to design enough individual styles to make an impact as a small collection when combined with one another. We'd then need to make samples of each style to show our line to retail stores that might be a good fit for our collection, and should they then place an order, produce whatever styles and size ranges they wanted. All the upfront costs would be on us, and from the time we delivered the product, the stores would get terms of 30 days to pay. While I wasn't involved with the wholesale division at Sonic Assembly, our accountant was very vocal about what a nightmare it was to get boutiques to pay on time. Being that our "line" consisted of three tank tops, and we only had enough fabric to make about two more of each, I knew we had to approach things differently. Jeff had talked about how most people lived their lives happily in their boxes, but I already realized that boxes weren't for me, so thinking outside of them came naturally.

"We're going to put on a fashion show, Fred," I announced to him as if it didn't sound insane. He didn't even bother to ask me what the hell I was talking about. He just looked at me, shrugged his shoulders, and put out his hands, palms up, letting his body language say to me "And?"

"I want to make up a cool flier and print it at work. We'll give it out to our friends and invite them to your apartment one night. We'll use some of the re:vision money to buy weed and ketamine, play some house, and once everyone arrives I'll go into the bedroom, put one of the tank tops, come out and give a little runway, then go back and change and do the same thing again. Twice. I'll wear the goggles and we can have them for sale, and we can take orders on the tanks. We'll only have to make what they actually want. I think we could definitely get $40 for each."

"That's not a fashion show, Angel. That's just us getting people high and you walking around in three tank tops."

"Sounds like a fashion show to me!"

The next day, I stayed late at work to design the flier. I landed on a black and white outer space vibe with the following messaging:

calling all homosexuals

you are invited to the launch of

re:vision

a new line of products

designed with your needs in mind

friday, april 22nd

170 west 23rd street

apartment fourgy

10 p.m. until the drugs we supply run out

change the way you see the world

I printed one out and showed it to Fred. He hated it. Fred was more conservative when it came to talking about sex and drugs. That bugged the shit out of me. I was daring. I wanted to push people's boundaries and get in their faces. There was nothing wrong with what I had written, other than that it was right there, out in the open, available to be read.

"I don't understand why, Fred. It's funny and people will laugh. It will get people's attention. And it's not like we're running an ad in the *Times*. We're just handing it out to friends."

"I just don't like the idea that we're telling people to come and get high. This is supposed to be about selling clothing. The first thing they see coming from re:vision shouldn't be 'hey let's do a bunch of drugs.' It makes me uncomfortable."

"Fred, if talking about doing drugs makes you uncomfortable, you sure don't seem to have an issue with actually doing them. I get why you didn't want to call us the M.F.A. You couldn't relate to the word faggot. You said it was dark so I changed it, even though I loved it, because it was important *to you*. You need to understand that if we're going to do this, it's important to me that we reflect our culture back honestly. I told you from the beginning it needs to be about the good, the bad, and the ugly. There's nothing wrong with who we are or what we do, and re:vision needs to lead with that. When it comes to the brand and the messaging, I need you to be on board with the fact that if there's something we ourselves do behind closed doors, it's fair game for us to put it out there in public. I'm not ashamed of anything I do, and if there's anything you do that you're ashamed of, you either need to stop doing it or start owning it." I put my foot down squarely on the truth, and Fred agreed to let me print up the announcements. I went around the city hand-delivering them to our friends in my black batter's helmet and my platform boots.

* * *

The launch was a success. We had about 15 people show up, all of whom commented about the messaging on the flier. "Until the drugs run out? Bitch, you are too crazy!" Axel said to me. "'Calling all homosexuals' is *so* good," William exclaimed.

"Do me a favor," I replied to all of them, "tell Fred."

I put out two black plates, one with a handful of joints that I had twisted up in rainbow rolling papers. The second plate featured a sizable pile of ketamine and a bevy of different colored straws. My friend had gotten me a tape of one of Merritt's sets at the Roxy, so between the beats and the favors, I had set the mood. At 11 p.m., just when people were feeling good but before they couldn't see straight, I went into the bedroom and put on my first look. Fred shut the lights, and much like what went down at Factory, he turned on a couple of high-powered flashlights, pointed them directly onto me, and I strutted out into the living room, serving up some runway with just the right amount of camp. Everyone applauded. I repeated that show two more times, then Fred turned on the lights and I took a bow as if I was mother fucking Jean Paul Gauliter.

"That's it, girl?" Axel asked defiantly.

"That's it, girl!" I answered defiantly.

"You better work, bitch!" he exclaimed. The room exploded with laughter. I gathered up the three tank tops, put them on hangers and brought them into the living room for everyone to see and feel, along with a display of goggles that I wedged between the party plates. Axel put on the wet look tank and a pink pair of goggles. "Oh, honey," he said as he felt himself up and down, "this fits me like a glove. And these goggles are insane. How the fuck do you make them?"

"Good news, bitch! You don't need to know how we make them, cuz that pair right there on your face can be yours for $20. And I'll give you a deal if you buy the whole look. Sixty dollars gets you everything."

"Girl, the price tag on this tank top is $40. How is charging me $60 for the look giving me a deal?"

"Cuz if things go well tonight we will definitely be raising our prices!"

Axel bought them both. Javier wanted the same shirt in medium, but Axel handed me his cash and said to Javier, *"Mine!"* Javier placed an order for a medium for himself. Jeff ordered a silver spandex shirt in large, as did Dominic. The medium silver went to Randy. We sold the slinky shirt to Jason, and his boyfriend put in an order for a matching one in small. Eleven pairs of goggles found new homes. There was so much excitement in that room. Watching people try things on, fighting for the mirror, talking about how good our stuff made them feel, that was the reward. Axel shut the lights out and made an announcement. "Ok ladies, let's take this show on the road to hear some Frankie Knuckles at Sound Factory Bar" — an amazing midsized club on West 21st Street, not to be confused with Sound Factory on West 27th.

NEW
YORK
The Big Apple

Friday nights were packed, as Frankie always delivered. We made our way inside and took over a spot on the dancefloor. Watching everybody carrying in their goggles and Axel and Randy and Jason rocking their newly purchased re:vision tank tops, it literally brought me to tears. I grabbed hold of Fred and held him as tight as I could without breaking him.

Before I could fully gather my composure, a short, stylish gentleman approached me and said, "Excuse me, but I was talking to your friend over there about these goggles and he showed me what they can do. He said that you guys made them."

"Yes, we do! We have a brand called re:vision. Normally I have them out with me to sell but I forgot to bring them tonight. Do you want a pair?" I asked.

"Well, yes. I work for a magazine called *Paper,* and I'd love to list them in our A-Z guide to New York for our next issue. My name is Mickey." He handed me his business card. Mickey Boardman — from *Paper Magazine!* — just about the coolest publication out there. I was *gagged.*

"I love Paper Magazine!" I screamed so loudly I could see him take a step back, but I couldn't contain my excitement. I took the pair I was wearing off my head. "Here . . . take mine!'

Four weeks later, re:vision got its first piece of press.

chicest
design-
ew bou-
and toys
outfits —
gners —
runway
purses
or adults
irts and
461 W.

ose East
erienced
kery, run,
Avenue,
biggest
cookies,
and Rice
u suffer a
style. **175**
St.; 228
4-9501.
jewelry
now has
rner Bros.
buckles,
nd loony
57th St.,

ps of real
obsessed
Florent
ild. These
complex
and fanta-
th at the
vies & Co.
***raphies* at**

Barbarian — blazes, pings and ka-pows to life at the Alexander Gallery with a collection of his comic and fantasy illustrations, spanning a 50-year career. **980 Madison Ave., 472-1636. Through Dec. 23.**

QUEER MIX It's time for Mix 94, the eighth annual N.Y. **lesbian and gay experimental film and video festival**, featuring over 200 films and videos from around the world, with programs ranging from queer Jewish sexuality to drag queen feminism. Also featured will be Cyberqueer, the first installation of interactive media. **Anthology Film Archives, 32 Second Ave., 505-5181. Nov. 10-20. $7.**

RE:VISIONISTS Throw away your rose-colored glasses and pick up a pair of **hologram goggles** from Re:vision, the most stylishly mind-scrambling fashion accessories to hit the scene in ages. Available in a rainbow of colors at only $15-$18, these specs are real eyepoppers. **Re:vision, 807-1213.**

SMOKE GETS IN YOUR EYES 150 live goldfish, 70 full-size trees and two cigarettes are some of the stars in a new piece by German choreographer/director Pina Bausch. ***Two Cigarettes in the Dark*** promises to be one of the most surreal trips you'll take this month. **BAM, 30 Lafayette Ave., Brooklyn. Nov. 17-19, 22-23. $20-$45. (718) 636-4100.**

TEA *TIMES* Tête à Tête, a new series in Henri Bendel's Salon de Thé, lets you **sip and spin with *New York***

Just imagine Do
ing his inner se
International
Photography,
Americas. Throu
WALL OF DIST
earplugs and h
Kitchen for th
Ensemble's Sym
10, where the for
eardrum-shatter
you. **512 W. 19**
Nov. 16-20, 8 p.r
XXX INDEX Hav
know what Joh
was? Curious ak
sics? Then chec
Videotape Star
Books, $22.95),
blowing 80,000
performers, alt
graphical data a
tions. Mmmmm
YOUNG THIN
adults? Sounded
I wasn't disapp
Won't Grow U
lovely Judy Gar
for $10, and a
family for $6.50
get doesn't hav
265A W. 19th S
ZIP ME UP, D.
incredible handiv
the woman behi
and pleats of c
Vionnet creatic
Institute at the
of Art this montl

KUCZYNSKI, VICTORIA PEDERSEN, HUGO SAUER AND RICKY SPEA

Twenty-Five

"We're driving to Cherry Hill on Thursday to meet the team at HBN. They're putting us up for the night in Philly, and then on Friday they have a realtor lined up to show us apartments. It's me, you, and Carl. Just us." Paul looked me up and down. "And wear something a little *less* urban to the meeting. These guys won't take you seriously looking like that. I sold you on your street smarts, not your street style, so look like you're about to be paid a $100,000 a year." He looked me up and down again. "Not like you're about to steal it."

Paul did most of the pitching, laying out the business plan as Carl walked the team at HBN through the numbers. When they gave me the floor, I presented our strategy to deliver a line of products that would directly target the tastes of the audience they already had and handed out samples of denim jackets with The Beatles licensed artwork on the back, along with crew neck Rolling Stones sweatshirts and Pink Floyd Hoodies. But it wasn't until I pitched the HBN execs on the chance to reach a whole new demographic — American teenagers — that we truly sealed the deal. They were so stuck on selling merchandise to adults, that they never saw the magnitude of the opportunity we were offering them: the opportunity *to be cool* and cash in along the way. Recognizing that Sonic Assembly could make them twice as much money as they had originally thought, HBN made an offer to buy our company.

The experience of taking my skill set to the next level was thrilling. I loved everything about the idea of merging with HBN and bringing my talents to a bigger operation with unlimited potential. Paul shook on the deal before we left their offices, and after viewing a few incredible apartments the following day that were half the price of Fred's place and three times as nice, it seemed the next stop on my journey was going to be the City of Brotherly Love: Philadelphia.

* * *

The three of us drove home triumphantly, and when we arrived in Manhattan I had Paul bring me to my studio instead of dropping me off at Fred's place. My adrenaline was flying, and I needed to calm myself down before facing Fred. I needed to calm myself down period. The past 48 hours had been some of the most exciting in my life, and when I got excited, I was *a lot*. I was a lot even when I wasn't excited, so I knew I had to get to my apartment, shut off all the lights, sit down on my couch, smoke a joint, and be still in the silence and the darkness and just think. Before I got out of the car, Paul asked me if I had one hundred percent made up my mind to move with the company. I told him I was close. I wanted to say yes very badly, but I needed to think through what leaving New York, the city that I loved, would actually *feel* like. I understood what the move would be affording me, but I really needed to consider what it would be costing me.

After a good 45 minutes of quiet in my studio with some equally good weed, I managed to clear my head of most of its racing thoughts, and I ordered Chinese food. I got out a pen and paper to organize the choice I was facing into a simple, digestible list of pros and cons. But before I got started, I picked up the phone to give Fred a call. I couldn't leave him just waiting there to hear from me, but I had no idea what to say to him. I wanted more than anything to share my excitement with my boyfriend, but doing so would have the opposite effect on him. When he answered and asked me how everything went, I spoke in generalities, commenting on Paul's incredible performance at the meeting, and describing a couple of the "cute" apartments I had seen. I kept the details, along with my enthusiasm, to a minimum. He asked me if I wanted to come sleep over, but I told him I had just ordered dinner, that I was really exhausted and didn't want to get off the couch. I could hear the disappointment in his voice. Other than the nights I spent travelling for Sonic Assembly, I had slept at Fred's apartment every night since about three weeks after we met.

He knew something was up. I knew that he knew. We said our goodbyes, almost cordially. It was the best we could muster in our shared avoidance of discussing a future we suddenly might not be sharing.

* * *

I assumed making my pros and cons list would gain me the last bit of clarity I needed to say with complete certainty that I was accepting the incredible opportunity being offered to me by Paul and HBN. Looking down at it, however, only caused me more confusion. The list of pros for taking the job was lengthy. I would be living in a sick apartment and driving a company car while I continued in the A&R role that I loved. I would have a serious career at a big company while gaining loads of experience for my future. I would be traveling more. I'd have an expense account. And most importantly of all, I'd be getting rich. The column for staying put, however, was very concise. It contained only three items: New York City, re:vision, and Fred. I drew a circle around them to emphasize their brevity to myself.

fred
re:vision
NYC

That should have closed the deal for me. I picked up the phone half a dozen times to call Paul with my yes, but not once could I bring my fingers to dial his number. I was mentally and physically paralyzed. Fortunately, my doorman buzzed to let me know my food had arrived and was on its way up. I put my list to the side, gorged my way through a huge meal, finishing it off with some cookies and ice cream. After smoking joint number two, I put on *Golden Girls* reruns and passed out.

* * *

I woke up the next morning and gave Fred a call. I could hear in his voice that he was still sleeping. He sounded groggy, like he had been up way too late, probably losing sleep over me. "Go back to bed, honey." I said. "I'm going to the gym, and I'll call you when I'm done."

"I miss you," he said in his half-awake voice.

"Not for long," I reassured him. I hung up and felt sick to my stomach. It wasn't due to the near-Roman-level gorging I had committed upon myself the night before. I felt sick over the decision I knew I had to make. Moving to Philadelphia meant getting everything I used to think I wanted in a man, only now I had the chance to get it for myself. *I* would be the upwardly-mobile one. *I* would bank the six-figure salary. *I* would have the career that was acceptable to my straight friends and family. But moving to Philadelphia meant I would have to give up on New York City and on my plans for re:vision. That sickness in my stomach was my gut telling me that if I moved to Philadelphia, even if I tried not to, I would be giving up on Fred as well.

I was a mess. I picked up the phone and called Jeff, praying he would answer and provide me with some clarity before I had to see Fred. I thought my prayers were answered when I heard him say "hello" in his sweet Texas accent.

"Hey Jeff. It's David. Am I disturbing you?" I asked.

"Not at all, honey. What's going on?" I proceeded to spill my guts to him, messy as they were, while attempting to keep my thoughts in order. I read him my pros and cons list, trying to provide him the necessary structure to play back my dilemma to the Gods and Goddesses. I hoped in turn they would channel back through him the true path I should follow. Once I got it all out, I waited patiently for him to divine me some answers. All I got was silence.

"You still there?" I asked him.

"Of course, honey. Where else would I go?"

"I don't know. When you stopped talking to me, I thought maybe we got disconnected or you went into some sort of trance."

Jeff burst out into laughter. "A trance? Who would have put me in a trance?"

"I don't know. I thought maybe you had like closed your eyes and you were calling upon a deity to provide me with some insight."

"Oh, honey. It doesn't work like that. I wasn't calling upon anyone or anything. I'm not Miss Cleo," he chuckled. "I was just processing what you told me. Sounds like you've got a very big decision to make, a life-changing decision. When do you need to give your answer to your boss?"

"On Monday, ideally sooner."

"Well from what I can gather, you probably already have the answer. Giving it sound, saying it out loud, that's the hard part. Once you give it sound, you take the first step toward your destiny."

"So, you really think I have the answer, Jeff?"

"Of course you do. You're just not ready to speak it."

"It doesn't feel that way to me."

"Well how *do* you feel, honey?"

"I feel like I should take the job. It's the smart thing to do. It's the right thing to do. It's also the obvious thing to do. I feel like I was given this incredible opportunity with Sonic Assembly. I'm insanely lucky to be in this position right now. Passing this up would be ludicrous. I owe it to Paul and I owe it to my family and I owe it to my future to take it."

"So why are we on this call, honey?"

"Because taking this job means leaving New York City. I know it will be the end of me and Fred. And I know it will be the end of re:vision. I really love those things."

"I know you love New York and I know you love re:vision. I see what you are manifesting, honey. But I didn't know you loved Fred. Have you told him yet?"

"I haven't, because honestly, Jeff, I don't know how I can be sure. He's the very first guy I've ever dated and he's amazing. He's got the biggest heart and he's so creative and inspiring. But he's changing me, Jeff. He makes me question my priorities. When I'm with him, I feel like the goals I had for my future are slipping away, and they're being replaced by his live-in-the-present outlook. And there are things about him that just seem *off* sometimes. They make me question whether I really know who he is in the first place. He can get so possessive, and he snaps over the smallest things. And when he smiles, it's like he's hiding something, Jeff. Honestly, sometimes I wonder if he's crazy."

"We're all crazy in one way or another, honey. We all come with plenty of baggage, so I suggest you get used to that."

"So you're saying I'm wrong? Are you telling me I really do love him?"

"I'm not telling you anything of the sort, honey. You've got to figure out for yourself what you love and what you fear. My advice to you would be to forget the pros and cons. That's just another way of saying good and bad or right and wrong. Look down both paths and ask yourself what energies are pushing you in what directions. What parts are fear? What parts are love? You'll figure it out, because like I said, you've already made your decision."

"I thought I was going to call you and you were going to tell me to follow my heart and stay here in New York."

"You are such an adorable boy," he said sweetly. Jeff calling me boy made everything I was feeling disappear in an instant.

"Thanks for listening, Jeff. I've got another call coming through. Will I see you at the Factory tomorrow morning?"

"Yes, you will. I'll be there with my goggles on honey."

"I love you, Jeff." I hung up the phone with him and picked up the other line. "Hello?"

"Hey David, it's Carl. I'm sorry to bother you on a Saturday but I have some bad news. You know my friend Josh, Paul's friend?"

"Yes, of course. He's the tall blond guy who was at Paul's last house party," I replied, but it wasn't his height or his coloring that left an impression on me. Josh was the first guy I knew that was positive. Carl had told me himself, and I never could get past it.

"He died this morning," Carl explained.

"Holy shit what happened?" I asked ignorantly.

"David, he died of AIDS."

My heart sank so hard I felt it plummet through my body. "But he was fine, Carl. Paul's party wasn't that long ago. How is that even possible? He didn't look sick."

"David, sometimes it happens quickly. I've seen friends change almost right before my eyes. They go from being strong and gorgeous and . . . they're just so beautiful. Then the next time you see them, they're just . . . they're just not." Carl began choking up. I probably would have too had I not been in such complete shock. Someone I knew had died from AIDS. Someone was gone. Josh was gone.

"I'm so sorry Carl. Is there anything I can do? Should I call Paul?"

"Thanks, but there's nothing you can do. And don't call Paul. I know that you were maybe going to give him an answer about Philly before Monday so that's why I'm calling you. He's a wreck and he needs some space. He's on his way to Josh's place right now to get there before his parents show up. Josh asked Paul to be his person to handle things when he passed."

"What do you mean? The arrangements?" I was confused, heartbroken, dumbfounded.

"No, David. Josh's parents weren't very good to him. They didn't approve of him being gay, and when they found out he was positive, they cut him off completely. But Josh did okay for himself, and they know he has some money. They're on the way to take whatever they can find. Whatever they can steal. Josh gave Paul his instructions and a key to his place. He wants to make sure his belongings and his money go to Gods Love We Deliver." Carl's crying eased a bit.

"I can't believe that Carl. No one's parents would just go and steal their kid's stuff like that. Their son just died for God's sake." My voice was trembling. "Doesn't he have a will or something?"

"Doesn't matter. This is what happens, David. It happens a lot. They'll go to his apartment, take whatever they want and head back to Long Island. They won't follow his will. They won't go to the morgue to identity his body. They won't attend his funeral. Josh stopped existing to them a while ago, so nothing's fucking changed for them. It's like their revenge." Carl was sobbing again.

"I'm so sorry Carl. I really am. Thank you for giving me the heads-up about Paul. Send him my condolences, please."

"I will, David. And listen, there's something else I want to say to you. I've been telling myself I should keep my mouth shut but I just can't. Not anymore. You need to take this job David. Life doesn't give you that many big breaks. Most people don't get any. But you got one when Paul hired you and now you're lucky enough to get a second. I know you have your re:vision thing and you love it so keep it as a hobby or something. Do it in Philly, But please David, don't pass this up because of Fred. I know he means a lot to you. He's a really good guy. But something's not adding up David. The possessive behavior you talk to me about, it's not normal. It's controlling. He doesn't have your ambition and from what you've told me he just kind of lives paycheck to paycheck. And this thing where he won't go to the doctor. *He's hiding something from you* and I'm scared you're gonna get your heart broken. Maybe something worse."

There it was. Carl had given it sound. He might not have said it exactly, but that didn't make a lick of difference. We both knew what he was saying. "I'm sorry if this was harsh or out of line, but I wouldn't be able to sleep with myself if I didn't bring it up."

"No, Carl, I really appreciate it. And before you even called I already knew what I had to do. I'm going with you guys to Philly. I'm taking the job.

Twenty-Six

I didn't call Fred after I hung up with Carl. I just got dressed, put on my rollerblades, and raced to his apartment, crying the entire way over. I showed up at his door, let myself in, and climbed into bed with him. I buried my face in his chest, and the remainder of my tears emptied from my eyes, leaving his body hair damp with my sorrow. He rubbed my head, asking me questions and trying to get to the source of my pain.

"What happened, David? Did the job offer fall through? Did you decide to take it? If you want to take it you don't have to feel bad. I would never hold you back. Can you tell me what's going on, Angel?"

I lifted my head, looked into his murky green eyes and whimpered, "You know Paul's friend Josh? He died this morning. Of AIDS." Fred nestled my head back into his chest, held me in both his arms, and we cried together under the unfinished canopy, surrounded by his jungle. But something had changed. Fred's bedroom didn't look the same anymore. It was as if all that crying had done something to stain my vision. All the queer magic that had kept me spellbound was gone, and in its place was a new secular reality where unfinished projects felt more like signs of problems than promise. His jungle was just a bunch of houseplants we were doing our best to keep alive. We weren't shamans in the Amazon, we were just two guys in a room in Chelsea, a neighborhood where lots of gay people lived, and lots of gay people died.

"I can't believe he's gone Fred. I just saw him. He was fine."

"He wasn't fine David. He had HIV. He even might have had AIDS by then, only you couldn't tell or he was hiding it. But he wasn't fine. It's never fine, David. It's always so awful."

"Have you known a lot of people who have died?" I asked.

Fred nodded his head, and his eyes began to water again. "I have, Angel."

With Josh gone, with the magic of Fred's bedroom gone, I felt like the AIDS monster was suddenly gone too. AIDS was no longer a cadaverous troll living under the Brooklyn Bridge, or a boogeyman haunting the gutted remains of the West Side Piers. It was all too real, and its reality was sitting *right there* in bed with me and my man. AIDS wasn't some mythical creature. It was a fucking real-life serial killer coming for us all. I had no choice but to stare it in its sunken face now, and in doing so, I knew it was time to face Fred and get real with him as well.

"You need to tell me why you've never gotten an HIV test, Fred. I don't understand why you won't even go see a doctor. I can't keep ignoring this like it doesn't exist for me."

"Are you taking the job?" he asked.

"What does that have to do with anything, Fred. Don't try to change the subject."

"I'm not trying to change the subject. I just feel like you're going to leave and I want to know if getting an HIV test would mean you'll stay with me because I don't want to lose you Angel. I've lost so many people in my life and I can't lose you. You have no idea how much I love you. You're my whole world." His heart broke open and all of his love, his fear, his hope, and his trauma flooded his bedroom. I watched as he sank beneath its weight, drowning before my eyes. Without hesitation I reached out for my man and grabbed hold of his being, yanking him up. I wouldn't let go.

Eventually, he regained his composure and explained himself to me. "I don't like going to the doctor because I've never liked going to the doctor. And I never really had to go because I never got sick as a kid. I mean, literally, I never got sick. When AIDS started to happen, I was still living in Jersey and we would hear talk about people in the city getting sick, but it wasn't even AIDS then. It didn't have a name. It wasn't on the news or anything like that. My friends and I talked about it almost like it was a rumor. By the time things started to get bad I was already with my first boyfriend, and we were monogamous. I kind of went from one long term relationship to another, so I was never part of the wild gay sex scene happening in Manhattan. The reason I never got tested was because even though I came out in 1980, I was always pretty safe."

He paused for a moment and took a deep breath. I could see that giving this sound was also setting it free. "The other big reason is that I just didn't want to know. I never saw the point. What good would it be knowing that there's this virus living inside you that's going to kill you one day. There's no cure. There's no treatment. If I had HIV, knowing about it would only cause me stress, and that would just kill me faster." I didn't have a response for him. I had nothing to say. His logic had silenced me because it was sound.

"You need to know, Angel, that I would never hurt you. If anything ever happened to you I'd . . . I just don't know what I would do. So, I will always keep you safe. And if getting tested means that you'll stay with me in New York, then I'll go get tested."

I had to ask, "But what if the test comes back positive?"

"Then I'd lose you, I know that. I'd never expect you to stay with me. I'd never even let you stay. That's how much I love you. But if not getting tested means one hundred percent that I'll lose you then I'll do it. We can go today."

Fred had finally let me into his past, just a little bit, and I began to understand the choices he had made in his life, just a little bit, too. Losing Josh that morning, a man I had barely known, had shaken my world so hard that I lost my innocence. I could only imagine what it must have been like for Fred to have gone through that, over and over again. The scars he built up. The trauma he dealt with. The pain that he felt. I always had suspected that Fred was just trying to ignore reality. I began to realize that perhaps I was wrong. Maybe he was actually facing it head on. Maybe had I lived his experience; I wouldn't be all that keen to get tested either.

"Definitely not today, Fred. Not today. Honestly, I'm not so sure I want to find out anymore."

Fred and I got back under the covers, and as he spooned me close, it dawned on me that AIDS was a both serial killer and a monstrous apparition, hell bent on stalking and haunting me until the day I died.

Twenty-Seven

Fred took the news of me accepting the job as best he could and I assured him my decision had nothing to do with his unknown HIV status or his desire to keep it that way. Jeff was right all along: Even as I was asking him for advice as to what I should do, I had already made up my mind. I knew I had to go. There was never really a choice. I was being offered a once-in-a-lifetime opportunity and I had to make it a reality, even if it meant letting go of my dreams for re:vision.

But I didn't want to let go of Fred. The conversation he and I had about his status ended up solidifying my desire to have a long-distance relationship with him, and I told him as much. I admitted that Josh's death had all but convinced me it was time to start a new professional and personal life in Philly, but his willingness to get tested, for me, had changed that. No matter his status, I one hundred percent trusted Fred to keep me safe, and that was the best level of protection I had against contracting AIDS, hands down. No matter how badly I wanted to stop using rubbers, the fact of the matter was that anyone could tell me they were negative. Anyone could show me a test result, then go behind my back and do a bunch of risky things that would get passed along to me. "We're all crazy in one way or another," Jeff had told me. I was sure there were men out there crazy enough to get burned by the heat of the moment, and in doing so, risk their own lives, along with mine. Fred would never burn me.

He and I spent all the time we had left, before I had to relocate, together. He offered to come visit me every single weekend after I moved so we could decorate my new place together. I knew he could help me make it great. But Fred had a life in New York. He had his friends and his own creative projects, and as much as I loved the idea of saying yes to his offer, I knew it would be selfish. I'd need to come to NYC as much as he came to Philly, and as soon as I got more settled in, I could certainly do that. Working at HBN was going to be exciting, but it was also going to be a shit ton of work, so I didn't feel comfortable really committing either of us to anything until I knew exactly what I was getting myself into.

As the move got closer and closer, I found myself less inclined to discuss the specifics of how our long-distance relationship was going to work. My behavior toward Fred began to grow erratic. I went from being unbearably clingy to unnecessarily distant. I'd pack my mental baggage and be ready to leave, only to turn around and empty it back out all over the floor. Mostly, though, it emptied out onto Fred, who eventually hit his limit with my manic inconsistencies.

"You're driving me crazy, David. I don't know how to handle you. One minute you can't stop talking about your future in Philly and the next you're sitting on the couch and staring down at the floor in despair. I can't deal with you."

"Well I'm sorry you can't deal with me Fred. Maybe you should try dealing with picking up *your* entire life and moving it!" I raised my voice at Fred. He didn't like when I did that.

"Don't fucking yell at me David. I'm doing my best to keep you calm and be supportive but you're all over the place. I feel like you're mad at me or something." The volume of his voice upped the ante on mine.

"Why the fuck would I be mad at you?" I screamed.

"I don't know. Maybe you don't want to be with me anymore. Maybe this long-distance relationship sounded great a few weeks ago but now that it's getting close to happening you want to go do your own thing." He screamed back.

"You're fucking crazy Fred. I'm already stressed out and I don't understand why you're coming for me. This is the opposite of what I need." I felt myself turning red. I was furious that he was throwing his shit all over my fan.

"How am I supposed to know what you need? You haven't said a word to me since we got home. I'm not a fucking mind reader David, and even if I was I wouldn't be able to keep up with your brain. I can't take it anymore!" Fred stood up enraged and grabbed his jacket.

"Oh, so what are you going to do . . . leave me? *I'm* the one who has to leave!" And as those words came violently flying out of my mouth, I lost it. All of it. I crumbled apart into a million little terrified pieces, none of which wanted to leave New York behind. Fred took off his jacket and sat down next to me to unpack his own baggage. All his million little terrified pieces came unglued as well. We sat there in two million little pieces with no idea how to put us back together.

I had tried my best to be sure of myself regarding my decision to move to Philly. I *was* sure about it. Turned out that didn't make a lick of a difference, though. Turned out I wanted to stay right where I was, more than anything. It had nothing to do with pros and cons or good and bad. It wasn't about my past or my present or my future. The obligations I felt I had to honor were nothing but illusions I had made up to keep me on track down the predictable pathway of life. In the end, it turned out everything I needed to know was on that piece of paper that I had crumpled up and thrown away with my takeout the night I got back from Philly. With that simple illustration, my gut was showing me the shape of my own little world, and inside were the only three things that mattered because those were the things that ignited my passion.

I was about to trade all of that in for a corporate life I had squarely rejected when I dedicated both my major and my soul to poetry. Sitting there with Fred, among his million little pieces, wearing the blue spandex tank top he made as a prototype for re:vison, listening to the sounds of the city beneath our labored sobbing, I knew I had trapped myself in a nightmare of my own making. I was so focused on being a fully licensed adult, planted firmly in life's driver's seat, that I didn't even realize I was asleep at the wheel of my own happiness. But there was no turning back. I had signed on the dotted line. I was headed to Philly, like it or not.

Eventually Fred promised me that everything was going to be okay. He took me by the hand and brought me to the bedroom. I looked around: it *was* truly magical. Everything about my queerness was magic, and not even AIDS could take that away. The only thing that could destroy it was me if I chose to stop listening to my heart. I *had* to believe all the magic was real, for a life without magic, at least for me, felt really, really bleak.

Before I fell asleep I prayed to whatever powers would listen. I vowed to live a life honoring love, never fear. I would stand up against AIDS and fight for our identity. I reaffirmed my commitment to spending my life making my community feel sexy and empowered. I asked in return for their guidance.

I begged them to allow me to remain with Fred right there in our garden of eden on West 23rd Street.

Whoever they were, my personal Gods heard my prayers that night. Four days later Paul called me into my office and informed me that HBN had pulled the plug on the deal. I pretended to be devastated, and asked if I could take the rest of the day off to process the "terrible" news.

"Sure, David. Go home."

So I did, to Fred's apartment. Fred was my home. When I got to his place, I hugged him with every atom in my body. Then said "I love you" for the very first time. I gave it sound, and it felt so fucking right. Everything I truly needed was in that little circle I had drawn. Two weeks later I moved into Fred's place, and we officially started our life together. Two weeks after that, we adopted a Jack Russell Terrier, named her Piggy, and the two of us became three.

From that day forward, I prayed. Not to Oshun, certainly not to Jesus, and not even to the magic of the Universe. I prayed to the Gods that moved me to tears on the floor of Factory and blessed me with the understanding that I was reenacting a sacred ritual my queer ancestors participated in long before AIDS, long before America, long before any history that I had learned about in school. They were the same gods that had delivered me a chosen family of likeminded queers who intrinsically knew — like I knew — that despite having lost it to time, we had real purpose on the earth. They were the same gods I felt coursing through my existence as Fred made love to me, filling my body with his while filling my soul with truth — our truth — that what society had told us was evil our entire lives wasn't evil at all. It wasn't blasphemous or sinful or wrong. It was right. It was light. It was love. It was divine.

My gods were the Sodomy Gods, and from that day forward I would live in their service forever.

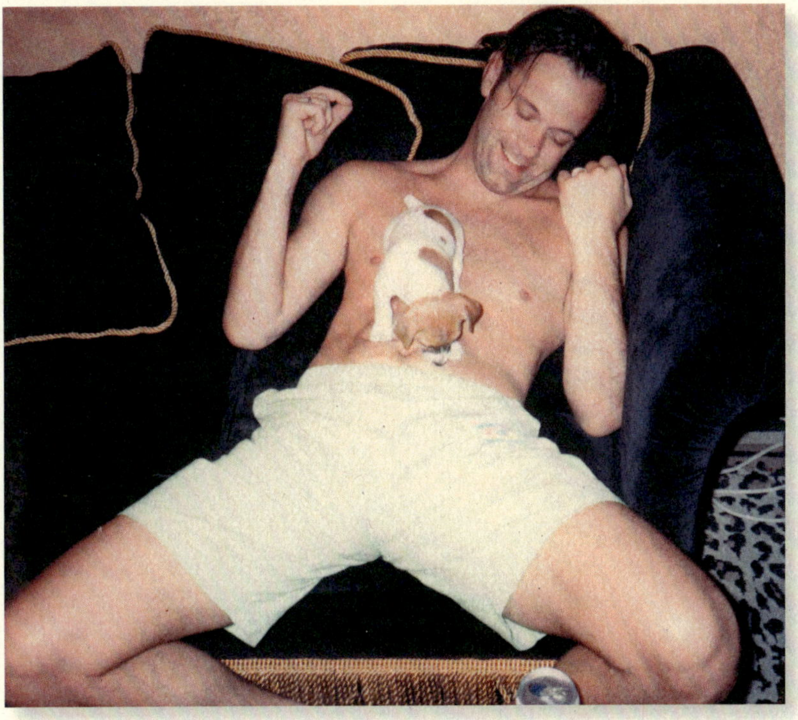

Twenty-Eight

"I have an announcement! We're renting a house in The Pines and we're all going to the Morning Party." Upon issuing this decree, Louis raised his Bloody Mary in a toast, but other than Eddie, who lifted his mimosa, no one else at our table of 12 for brunch met the moment with such confirmatory enthusiasm. The rest of us chimed in with excuses like: "I'm not sure I can afford that"... "My boss won't let me schedule a vacation without two-months' notice"... and "Depends on the DJ, girl!"

Louis put his Bloody Mary down before putting both his hands on the table and pushing himself up dramatically. It was *full* Alexis Carrington Colby realness.

"Perhaps there's been a misunderstanding. I wasn't floating an idea in the hopes of getting your feedback. We won't be taking a vote after a spirited debate. We *are* renting a house in The Pines and we *are* going to the Morning Party. This is happening if it's the last thing I do. So, follow along, ladies." Louis picked up his Bloody Mary once again and held it to the center of the table. "A toast! To our future selves high as fuck on the beach and dancing this summer." Fred stood up along with Lucy, Leslie, and William.

Louis wasn't done. "May I remind you all that this party is a benefit for GMHC, the *Gay* Men's Health Crisis. So, if these two biological ladies can pull it together and raise a glass in the name of helping our community then none of you ladies has any excuse not to do the same." I didn't know it was a fundraiser, but upon learning that, I stood up too, along with Stephan, Gay Bob, and Cody.

Looking at the stragglers, Louis barked, *"Now!"* and they all got up from their seats and raised their glasses. Louis was incredible at getting what he wanted, another reason I had grown to like him so much.

"That's more like it. A toast to ..." But before he could finish, I offered up, "... to sunshine, sand, and sodomy!' The table went quiet because interrupting one of Louis's moments was a dangerous bet to place, but Louis and I both loved a quick wit as much as we both loved Fred. He blessed my alliteration with a genuine "Here, here, queers!" We all clinked our glasses and the deal, as if Louis had any doubts about it, was sealed.

"Oh, and one more thing," he added, "Fred and David are going to be

making our house looks. The theme will be *Silver in the Sun*. So, everyone take $10 out of your wallets or your purses or your pussies and fork it over so they can get started on buying the fabric. When faggots ask us 'Who are you wearing?' we are all going to proudly say *re:vision!*"

I looked at Fred and Fred looked at me. Neither one of us knew any of that was coming, but one by one, all our friends passed their cash down the table toward us. I collected the money and put it in my pocket.

"I want a silver bra top!" Leslie exclaimed.

"Ooh, me too! We can be twins," Lucy chimed in.

Eddie hunched his shoulders forward, placed his hands on the sides of his chest, and pushed his tits together. "Triplets!" he squealed.

Everyone broke into laughter, including me, but I took that moment in with all the seriousness it deserved. I wasn't sure whether Louis's entire Morning Party plan was merely a ruse to book us the biggest order we had to date, but either way, we had just been commissioned to make a dozen looks at once, and I had the down payment in my pocket to prove it. I looked over at Louis and mouthed the words "I love you." He blew me a kiss and mouthed back "I know." I had the waiter bring over a pen and a piece of paper, passed them to William on my left, and told everyone to write down what they wanted to wear to the party so Fred and I could get started on 12 new pieces from re:vision.

* * *

I woke up to what could not have been a more perfect day for a beach party. The sky above The Pines was so blue it felt saturated, unlike the air which lacked even a hint of humidity. As the resident annoying morning person of our house, I made breakfast for our crew and insisted that everyone eat *something*. "Consider it your anchor meal for the day. Once that first pill hits none of you are gonna want to eat a thing until tomorrow, so I expect to see your plates as clean as your asses. That's an order."

"Get her," Eddie quipped. "Not even 25 and already she's a Daddy."

"I'm just being sensible, girl, unlike those silver heels you plan on wearing to the beach. I am so looking forward to finding you face down in the sand."

"I can handle myself in heels *everywhere* Daddy, so when you find me face down it's because of the kitty and *not* my legendary pumps." Kitty was code for Ketamine, and legendary lost all meaning when used as an adjective to describe Eddie's bargain bin shoe choice.

"Girl, you don't get legendary for $29.99 at Payless, so pipe down and eat your eggs before I decide to fertilize them." Eddie's eyes lit up. "Not with my dick, honey." I turned around, pulled down my shorts, and flashed him my butthole. "That kind of fertilizer. Now *eat!*"

"Yes, Daddy," Eddie said with a grin. We all had breakfast together outside, my queer family fueling up before a long day of carrying that would turn into a long night of the same. Once we were done, we adjourned to our respective rooms to shower, hose out, and get dressed for the party. I put on my silver y-front briefs, along with a white, ribbed tank top adorned with a silver star, both custom pieces by re:vision. I sat on the back deck by myself, in the warmth of the shining summer sun. I couldn't believe how lucky I was to be right there, in that house, with the man I loved and our amazing group of friends. But my luck didn't stop there. I was fortunate enough to be living in New York City, and to be vacationing in The Pines. I was getting ready to go to a party on one of the most beautiful beaches in the world where I would dance and openly kiss my boyfriend and embrace the men I loved. I began to realize I had been blessed with tremendous privilege. There were queer people living in abject poverty, literally afraid of having walls toppled in on them by their own families, as punishment for being themselves. By nothing more than a cosmic roll of the dice, I got to have *this* life.

The enormity of my good fortune crashed over me like the Atlantic Ocean waves I could hear from where I sat. I looked up to the Sodomy Gods, thanked them for all their blessings, and reiterated my promise to live my life in their service forever. One by one, my friends joined me outside on the deck, each in their custom silver re:vision looks. Once we were all ready and accounted for, we headed from our bayside house to the party of the summer.

* * *

Standing atop the stairs to the beach, my re:vision look now included a jaw that had literally dropped. Like a massive open-air temple packed with sun worshippers, surrounded by speakers and steel structures that climbed into the sky, draped in silver fabric that seemed to vibrate as it rippled in the wind, was the Morning Party. I had never seen anything like it. Before me was a true spectacle that had risen from the very same sand I had played in as a child with my sister and my cousin. The Pines felt like magic to me back then, and it felt just as magical before me on that breathtaking, sun-drenched afternoon. Everything, even the music, shimmered like mercury against the backdrop of a sky so perfectly blue it felt unreal in its uniformity. Had Fred not tugged me onward, I probably could have stood there all day, mesmerized by the sprawling, glorious harmony of nature and technology that dazzled before me.

We made our way to the entrance of the party and traded in our tickets for silver wristbands that security affixed to our wrists. "Good guess with the silver outfits," he said with a big smile. "Looks like you're part of the show. You guys definitely won today."

"It wasn't a guess," Louis replied. "I knew it would all about silver. I can see the future. That's one of my superpowers."

"Well maybe you can tell me next week's winning lottery numbers," he said.

"Doesn't work like that. But if you want to make some money you should invest in these two." Louis pointed at me and Fred. "They made our looks. They have a clothing line called re:vision, and it's going to be big one day."

"I'll keep an eye out for it. Good luck guys and enjoy the party." He motioned for the next group of queens to step up and get their wristbands as we made our way in.

We went to one of the bars and Tom bought us a round of Gatorades. Lucy took a bag of pills out from the pocket of her Daisy Dukes and dispensed them to us all. We raised our bottles and Louis said, "To sunshine, sand, and sodomy."

"That's what I'm talkin' about, bitch!" We dropped our pills simultaneously and guzzled down the entirety of our Gatorades to combat the August heat. "Stay hydrated" was rule number one of going out clubbing, and that was with a roof over your head and air conditioning on your skin. We were outside under the blazing summer sun, so doubling down on rule number one was rule number two for the day. Tom took out his vial and sent it around the group for bumps, and with that, we made our way into the crowd of shirtless revelers.

Then, as if he had materialized from the very air itself, Jeff appeared spontaneously and stood between me and the masses. "Hi, honey," he said to me. "Hey Fred. It's so good to see you guys." He hugged and kissed us both. "You guys all look adorable in your silver outfits. Did you make these, Fred?"

"He did!" I interjected enthusiastically. "They're all from re:vision!"

"I didn't ask you, David. I was talking to Fred. Settle down." He put me in my place. I very much liked being there. Fred normally liked me being there as well, but I could sense his slight discomfort when I was put there by Jeff. "So, you made these Fred?" he asked again.

"Well, actually, we made them together. It was both of us. David did the cutting and some of the sewing. He's learning."

"Yes. He's got a lot to learn, doesn't he?" Jeff replied, but he did so with an energy of commiseration, and the two of them had a good laugh at my expense. It didn't bother me at all to be the butt of their jokes. Looking at them looking back at me, nodding their heads in agreement at my rambunctious immaturity, I was ready to exit the party and be the butt of anything they wanted. I started to fantasize about Fred saying "we're leaving" and the two of them taking me back to Jeff's place and spending the rest of the day doing all sorts of things to my body. I wondered if he and Javier kept an office in The Pines fully equipped with a sling and a wall full of dildos and floggers just like the one they had in their apartment. I was fully imagining what it would feel like to have both of their dicks inside me at once when Fred snapped his fingers in front of my face. "Hello? Where did you just go?" he asked me.

"Oh sorry, I zoned out. Got a second wave from that pill." I lied, then quickly pivoted. "Where's Javier?"

"Oh, he doesn't like to come to parties like this. It's not his thing. I came alone." More for me, I thought to myself.

Fred and Jeff continued to make small talk as my pill really started to hit me. I suggested we head to the dancefloor so I could roll and get lost in the music. But we only made it a few feet before a gentleman stopped us to offer his praise for our custom re:vision looks. "Thank you! I really appreciate the kind words. We made them ourselves — me and my boyfriend," I stated proudly, holding Fred's hand in mine.

"You actually made these?" he asked. "That's amazing. They look so professional. I was going to ask who designed them, but I guess that's you. I'm Eric."

We shook hands. "I'm David. This is my man, Fred. He's the designer. We have a line called re:vision."

"I haven't heard of that. Where are you guys selling?" he asked.

"Okay, to be honest, it's not exactly a line. I mean I guess it is. It's really just me and Fred making things for our friends. Stuff like what we're wearing.

And these goggles too. It's just a hobby. Calling it a line . . . I guess I'm getting a little carried away with myself."

"Well, for what it's worth, I started out just like you guys, making stuff for my friends as a hobby. Eventually I turned it into a successful business. Don't sell yourself short so quickly."

"Do you mind if I ask what you do?" Fred inquired.

"I make a line of socks, kind of like the ones you're wearing," he replied.

"You own E.G, Smith?" Fred and I both asked, practically in unison.

"Yes, that's me," he laughed. "It always surprises me when people know my brand by name. It amazes me to be honest."

"Who wouldn't know your brand?" I asked. "Everyone I grew up with wore your socks. We still wear them. Lots of our friends, too."

"I love them," Fred added. "The quality is amazing."

"Now I'm the one appreciating you guys. You're making me smile. It never gets old hearing from happy customers. Maybe one day I'll be a customer of yours. You guys should definitely build out your line. From what I can see, you've got the makings of something special."

I turned to Fred. "See, honey. He gets it too and he's actually in the industry! We have to turn this into a business — now!"

"You're quite a firecracker, David," Eric said with a smile.

"You have no idea," Fred replied. "He's a handful."

"Well, I have news for you David, if you're making and selling products, you already have a business. It may feel like a hobby, but if you want my advice, that's a good thing. Loving what you do is worth more than you can imagine. Keep it enjoyable and let the rest fall into place."

"Can I give you a hug?" I asked Eric.

"Of course," he replied with a smile.

I put my arms around him and thanked him for *seeing* us. When I let go, Fred shook Eric's hand then took mine and pulled me away.

"You okay Angel? You were kind of slurring your words and you look a bit twisted." He wasn't wrong. I was a bit twisted. I put on a pair of goggles to conceal what I imagined were my very crossed eyes.

"I'm great . . . but it's best you lead the way." Listening to the words come out of my mouth was confirmation that Fred wasn't wrong about my kitty induced speech impediment either.

Fred successfully guided me out to our crew, and there, surrounded by the people I loved, I closed my eyes and let the ketamine wash over me in waves that seemed perfectly timed with those from the wind and the sea. My reality began to fold in and out of itself like origami. Everything swayed in different dimensions, and each dimension arranged itself geometrically. Geometry became kaleidoscope. Kaleidoscope became fractals. I traveled to places without even moving, until eventually I came back down on the earth and her simplified three dimensions. Things began to make sense again. I was happy to have landed. "That was some trip," I said to Fred and Louis as their faces began to make sense again.

Louis looked at me and said, "We need to take a walk young lady. Are you capable of doing that, you cute little mess?" Louis turned to Fred and told him he needed to bring me to the ocean to "do some schooling." Fred consented without hesitation. "Good luck with that!" Fred said to Louis as he looked directly at me.

The thump of the music subsided as Louis and I gained some distance from the speakers, and the sounds of the wind and the water took over my ears. The sun was getting lower in the sky, and as we headed west along the beach, it gave our skin the most beautiful glow. Louis stopped our walk somewhere west of the co-ops and asked me to sit down with him in the sand.

"Does this mean school is in session?" I asked.

Staring out toward the ocean, he nodded, and then began to speak. "David, I've known Fred for a while now. He's become my best friend and I love him — a lot." He turned back toward the waves and continued. "He's been through so much in his life, and despite all the shit he had to swim through growing up, despite a bunch of shitty men who took advantage of his incredibly kind nature, nothing diminishes his ability to stay so beautiful. It's like he's got this soul that can't be corrupted."

He paused and I took it upon myself to express my agreement. "I see that."

Louis continued, "Okay, so here's the thing. Since Fred met you, I've never seen him so happy. He's in love with you. Like *so* in love. Head over heels kind of love. When he talks about you, it's like you make his spirit soar. You're everything he deserved all along, and now he finally has it. He's all in on you." Louis put his hand on my hairy back. "You overgrown orangutan."

"I see that too Louis, and I really appreciate you telling me all of this. Fred loves you so much, as much as you love him, and I'm glad he has a friend like you who sees him the way I do. Since we met, me and you, I've seen how protective you are toward him. So I'm guessing you brought me out here to tell me not to break his heart and I promise you . . . "

"Hold up," Louis cut me off. "I didn't pull you out of that party and walk you halfway to The Grove so you can make me some drug-kissed promise that you may not even remember, let alone actually keep. And to be clear, I'm certainly not here as Fred's protector. He's the strongest man I know, and he can protect himself just fine. I'm not here to ask you to be good to my best friend or not to break his heart. I'm not here to ask you *anything,* girl." Louis paused again. "I'm here to *tell* you something. Are you listening?"

"I'm all ears, Louis."

"David, men like Fred, truly great men, practically don't exist. We go through so much hardship as kids, only to grow up and come out of the closet and face a whole new batch of hardships. Being gay is amazing, don't get me wrong. But gay life takes its toll. It causes a lot of damage. Doesn't make us bad people, it just makes us . . . it makes us hurt people. We get good at building walls around our hearts, so we don't have to hurt anymore. And those walls do a great job of keeping the pain out, but they also keep out people. Fred is that incredibly rare man who goes through life without any walls up."

Louis placed his hand beneath my chin, turned my head toward his so he could look at me — through me — past my eyes and into my soul.

"David, you landed a lifer. I'm here to tell you: *don't* fuck it up."

It felt like the entire world had stopped. The only things that existed in that moment were me, Louis, and the message he was sending out on that sacred strip of sand. "I don't want to fuck it up, Louis. I really don't. I promise I'll try to keep my head screwed on straight."

Louis cracked a smile and said, "It's not your head I'm worried about, child. It's your greedy ass, your 25-year-old hole. That's never gonna be on straight, and I know you're gonna keep it well screwed. That's the fucking problem." We both laughed.

"Since you're Fred's best friend, I guess that means I landed a lifer with you, too, Louis. So do me a favor and promise to keep me in line," I asked, my tone bordered on pleading. "Please, Louis. I'm gonna need your help. Like I'm *always* gonna need your help."

He shook his head. "That's a big ask girl, and as much as I'd love to say yes, always is a long fucking time. Way more time than I have to give," he replied.

"I'll take whatever I can get, Louis. I love you so much. Thank you for this." I put both my arms around him and held him as close to me as I could. "You're like my guardian angel."

Louis began to whimper. He whispered meekly into my ear. "More than you know. David . . . I'm . . . I . . . I need to tell you . . . I'm positive. I have HIV."

Everything shifted. I pulled back and let go.

"What?" I asked, but that wasn't a question.

"You're gonna make me say it twice?" he replied with the best smile he could muster up.

The sun had gotten low enough that the breeze coming off the ocean no longer cooled me down. My surroundings had darkened, and a chill ran through me. My head was no longer spinning. It felt like my brain had hit a wall and abruptly stopped. The world had stopped its spinning too. Everything I knew just froze.

And then came my tears.

It felt awful that Louis had to be the one comforting me, but I couldn't control my emotions. I heaved with sobs. That beautiful August day — the sand, the sun, the silver — it was just a mirage. No matter how hard I tried, there was only one reality. It was inescapable. It was omnipresent. AIDS was the ugliest of all the four-letter words. It had us truly cursed.

Eventually I was able to compose myself enough to speak. "I'm sorry, Louis. I'm so sorry. I didn't mean to lose it like that."

"It's totally understandable, David. I mean it. It's fine."

"No, it's not. It's not fine. Nothing is fine. You're the one who's positive and I'm here bawling like a fucking baby on your chest."

"I think you got some snot on there too, girl," he said.

I laughed, just for a moment, and said, "It's not funny Louis. You can't just joke about it and make it go away."

"Oh, really, girl? Well thank you for that breaking news. You know people say that laughter is the best medicine, but I've watched every fucking episode of *Absolutely Fabulous* and still my T-cell count keeps dropping and dropping, *sweetie darling.*" We both laughed. He grabbed my hand and held it tight. "David, there's *nothing* I can do to make it go away. Nothing your tears can do either. Maybe one day scientists will find a cure or concoct some magic pill to stop it in its tracks, or at least slow it down. But in the meantime, there's only one thing I can do, and you're gonna do it with me. We're gonna *live*, ok? I'm not going anywhere just yet." He stood up, his hand still connected to mine, and asked, "Am I clear?"

I stood up as well, and without missing a beat, I met *his* moment and through my broken heart I replied, "Clear? Girl, you're the most transparent

bitch I know. So yes, you're clear." We grabbed hold of each other, like brothers, like sisters, and we didn't let go until our world began to warm up once again.

"Come on," he said, "let's go back to the party. It's for me after all! You're looking at *the definition* of a Gay Men's Health Crisis."

We found our crew on the dancefloor. Fred must have seen something in my eyes because he asked me if I was okay. I said I was, and maybe I wasn't lying. Maybe things were okay, or at least they were okay at that moment, and that moment was all we truly had. We spent the rest of the evening dancing and laughing and holding onto each other. All of us. I closed my eyes and gave myself over to the music. I let it fill me up. With each song my soul was lifted higher, until I found myself carried back into a place of joy and celebration. I promised myself to always choose love over fear. And what Louis needed from me was a lifetime's worth of love. I prayed to the Sodomy Gods to give me the strength to deliver that to him, unconditionally.

We danced all night and all through the morning, and after getting some sleep, we went out and did it all over again. And again. That entire week we danced, defiantly, in the face of AIDS. We met the specter of death that loomed over us by reaffirming our lives together and living them with hope. No fear. Just love.

Twenty-Nine

Fred was not at all pleased when I told him I wanted to have sex with Jeff. He asked if he had a say in the matter, and I did my best to soften the blow of *no*, but it didn't help. I found myself on the receiving end of one of Fred's worst possessive spells, but I wasn't going to let that stop me. We both knew he wasn't going to be the last guy I had sex with, and he was okay with that. But the idea of having any form of an open relationship where we had sex separately from each other was off the table for him. For me, it was very much on the table. It was the main course, actually.

I informed Fred that Jeff and I had set a play date for the following week, and over the next seven days Fred barely spoke to me. It was awful, but I dealt. Fred's silence may have been deafening, but the relentless waves of anticipation crashing through my psyche and into my libido drowned it out as I counted down to my ensuing encounter on Bethune Street.

Seven days later, it was time — and I was ready. Jeff buzzed me into the lobby of his building, and attached to the door of his apartment, which was slightly ajar, was a note: "Come in. Lock the door behind you. Take off all your clothes. Come upstairs to my room." I did as instructed and proceeded. The hallway was a bit chilly, and that made me feel exposed, vulnerable. Goosebumps crawled across my skin, and I wondered if the cold was intentional. I wondered if Jeff was capable of that level of control over me without even being in the room. I began to question whether I was out of my league. Maybe I wasn't ready. As I climbed the stairs to Jeff's room my heartbeat quickened, and I felt both flush and freezing simultaneously. The tingle of nervousness I experienced downstairs as I stripped myself naked had all but been erased. By the time I reached Jeff's door I was downright scared. My dick, however, was fearless. It pointed straight up, throbbing so hard it almost hurt. I knocked on his door and Jeff told me to come in.

"Hello, boy." Jeff was seated in an imposing black leather chair. He confidently leaned back into it, commanding in his posture, stroking his chest beneath a black leather bar vest that made his tattooed biceps, strapped into black leather armbands, look twice as massive. He wore matching black leather chaps, a white jockstrap and motorcycle boots. The room was dimly lit by a floor lamp that sat adjacent to his chair, its faint glow concealing more than it revealed. It all felt so restrained, so purposeful and daunting. And everything smelled like sex. The air reeked of it. My quickening breath rapidly pulled that scent up through my nose and it flooded my brain, leaving me spellbound and lightheaded.

"Get down on all fours and come to me," he stated firmly, and I dutifully obeyed. I got down on my hands and knees and made my way toward him. I tried to feign some confidence, lifting my head to meet his gaze with a devilish smirk on my face, but we both knew it was a lie. "Stop," he ordered. "Don't do that. Don't look at me right now," and I dropped my eyes to the ground. "Don't talk to me unless I tell you to talk. Don't move unless I tell you to move. And don't bullshit me like you just did. It won't do. I can see right through you and if you bluff again, I'll call it. You'll be sent away and I won't ever have you back here. You'll always be welcome in my home, but you'll never come back *to this place.* Am I clear?" he asked. Without lifting my head, and without question, I said yes.

"Good. Now come to me." I just proceeded toward him until I found myself between his legs. He crouched forward, put his thick hand on my head, and rubbed it softly before pushing it down to the vamp of his left boot. "Start cleaning." My eyes darted back and forth along the floor, looking for a rag or some shoe polish, but I saw nothing. I didn't dare feel around because I was just told not to move without permission, and I didn't dare ask because I wasn't told I could speak. I didn't know what the fuck to do. I was powerless, trapped, and a sense of panic washed over me. I wanted to get it right. I *wanted to be a good boy.*

I had no idea how long Jeff left me down there in my confusion, but eventually he said, "With your tongue." His guidance relieved my anxiety and I began licking his boot before I could even think about what I was doing. Feet had never turned me on, and when I had seen guys groveling over someone else's shoes in porn I didn't really get it. But none of that mattered, because I was doing what *Jeff* wanted and that was driving me wild. As my tongue moved across the skin of his Wesco's, the taste of leather in my mouth paired with the smell in my nose got me so fucking turned on and high. I licked every inch of his boot, going back for seconds and thirds, until he instructed me to move on to the right one, which I attended to with equal fervor.

"That's enough," he said. I took my mouth off his boot, and held my head between his legs, eyes pointed downward, waiting for him to tell me I had done a good job, but he didn't say anything. His silence confused me. I wanted his approval so desperately. I wanted to know if he was happy. I had no idea how he just sat in his chair, ominous above me, leaving me to my own racing thoughts. The longer I was down there, though, the more my mind began to quiet, and I realized none of this was about what *I* wanted. This was about what *Jeff* wanted — and what he wanted was for me to follow his rules. He had made that abundantly clear. I let go of everything, and lowered my forehead to the ground between his feet. I didn't talk, I didn't move, and with my eyes an inch above the wood floor, I didn't look at him, nor did I look for his approval any longer. My gesture was quiet and sincere, and I put my faith in his words. If he could truly see right through me, he would see I wasn't bullshitting.

I was submitting.

"That's a good boy," he said in a tone that had changed ever so slightly from before. It was the tiniest bit softer, and that was all I needed to hear. I didn't talk. I didn't move. I didn't look up at him. Despite my best attempt to keep my face locked in stillness, I couldn't help but smile just the tiniest bit. Maybe he could tell though, because he said, "Lift your head and look at me." I got control of my expression fast and raised my head to face him without any sign of self-gratification. I lost my composure when he came fully into my view. Jeff had moved his jock to the side and pulled out his fat cock and his heavy, pierced balls. He was jerking off, slowly, stroking his shaft and twisting at the head. I knew my mouth had opened, instinctively, and I felt a drop of my own saliva fall from my lower lip, landing on my hand. That made Jeff smile, and I did nothing but uncontrollably drool a bit more.

Jeff reached into his bar vest and pulled out a perfectly rolled joint and a chrome Zippo lighter. He put the joint in his mouth and handed me the lighter. I knew what was expected of me and I flicked the flint three times before the wick caught flame. The smell of lighter fluid danced with the scent of his leather before both intermingled with the smoke off his joint. It was all so powerful and dizzying. Jeff put his hand beneath my chin and moved my face closer to his. He took a big hit of weed and shot-gunned it into my mouth, his lips barely brushing mine. Twice more he fed me his smoke, getting me even higher, before he slid his tongue into my mouth and kissed me. His energy shot through me and I vibrated. I was no longer even the slightest bit cold. I was done with my shivering. I was heated up and shaking with desire.

"Lick my balls, boy." I buried my face between his legs, inhaling the scent of his crotch before going to work on his heavy set. I licked them every which way, taking one in my mouth, then the other, back and forth between them, then both at the same time. Jeff kept one hand on the back of my head, keeping me firmly in place, as stroked his dick up and down. I could feel his nuts moving around in his sack as his groin pulsated against my face. "Now suck my dick, boy. Suck me off." I took his cock into my mouth and worked it up with one hand while my other hand played with his balls. He held my head in place and pushed himself past the back of my throat, thrusting inside me and bringing up that thick, slippery spit that made his cock slide even deeper into me. My eyes were watering. I could barely breathe but I was determined to do a good job and whatever limits my throat may have had before were obliterated. "Oh fuck . . . oh fuck! *I'm gonna cum!*" Jeff pulled my mouth off him and he shot a huge thick load all over my face. I was drenched in his sweat and his cum, overwhelmed by his energy, barely able to remain upright as I knelt between his legs, watching his chest heave and shudder in the aftermath of his orgasm.

He opened his eyes and looked down on me. "Good boy. Now get over my knee. Show me that ass." I jumped at his command. I laid my body down over him and arched my back in anticipation. He moved his hand gently across my butt cheeks, tickling the skin and heightening the sensation, sending me into near uncontrollable gyrations as his fingers made their way toward my aching hole. And just as he was about to finally stroke it, he pulled his hand out and spanked my ass so fucking hard I screamed. I felt my skin heat up, furious at the pain he inflicted, and while the gentle stroke of his fingertips on my right butt cheek helped to soothe the burning sensation, it didn't feel as good as getting fingered or fucked. This wasn't what I wanted to happen. I just wanted to fucking leave. But after a couple of minutes telling myself that, it dawned on me that I wasn't being held captive. I could leave at any time, and yet I stayed bent over and naked, not moving, not talking, not looking at him.

I felt my energy settling down. Jeff must have felt it too and he told me, "Now breathe with me, boy. Breathe." He inhaled and exhaled steadily, intently, until my rhythm synchronized with his. We found each other's energies again and reconnected. My butt cheek was cooling down and I noticed it started to feel all lit up, ignited. And while I may not have wanted to be spanked anymore, that didn't mean I was done. I was ready for more. Ready, willing, ass up, and able.

Jeff leaned down and whispered to me, "I'm going to beat your ass some more, boy. If you want me to stop, at any time, just say the word *banana* and it ends. That's our safe word. Am I clear?"

"Yes, you are Jeff, but I have a question. Is it okay to ask?"

"Go ahead, boy"

"Why do we need a special word to shut it down? I mean *banana* of all things? I don't get it."

Jeff laughed deeply, and he bounced his thick legs up and down beneath me. I felt like a child on Daddy's lap. "Because you're gonna be begging me to stop, boy, and I just need to know when you really, really mean it." He raised his hand and spanked my right cheek harder than he did my left. I screamed even louder. Again, he took to stroking the skin to cool it down, but after only a few moments *whack* he tore into the left one. I shouted at him: "Fuck, you're hurting me." He replied, "I told you no talking unless I tell you to talk." *Whack!* he spanked me again. And again. Back and forth, barely a moment in between each truckload of pain. It was almost unbearable, then finally, thankfully, he stopped to light up again and take a few more hits off his joint. He blew the smoke toward my face and I tried to breathe in every molecule of THC possible to help with the pain.

"Reach into the outside of my left boot, boy. There's something in there I need you to take out." My hand was shaking so badly, but I managed to slide in three fingers. I latched onto some sort of object and with what little strength I had left, I pulled it loose and held it out for Jeff. He took it from me and hovered it beneath my face. Through my watering eyes I saw a black, rectangular, paddle-like object, about a foot long, with three different sized holes cut through it.

"I bet you're wondering what that is," he said. I couldn't be sure if he was asking me a question or just making a statement, so I played it safe and kept my mouth shut. I had not been told to talk.

"I'm asking you if you know what it is."

Reassured by the clarity of his language, I took a deep breath and focused myself enough to properly say the word "no" through my moans and whimpers.

"It's what I'm going to finish you off with." I saw the implement disappear from my blurry field of vision, and waited for the pain. It arrived with a blazing burn on my already tortured skin. Spittle flew from my mouth and my eyes went from watering to full blown tears. He hit me with it three more times, until I finally broke.

"Banana . . . banana . . . "

Jeff stopped immediately. He placed something blissfully cool and damp and soft on whatever was left of my ass, shifted his legs a bit, and slid a towel down around my waist to hold the soothing compress in place against my ruptured skin. Then, with the strength of a god and the tenderness of a father, he moved his arms beneath my body and slowly rolled me over. With one forearm behind my knees and the other supporting my shoulders, he vaulted us both from his chair, and proceeded to rock me in his arms. And much like a terrified, lost child who had just found his Daddy, I lost it and cried, uncontrollably, for God knows how long, until I passed out in his embrace.

* * *

"Hi, honey," Jeff whispered. "You're safe, and I'm right here. You let me know if you need anything."

It took me a few minutes more to pull myself together enough to speak, and eventually I managed to ask him, "What just happened, Jeff?"

"Well, honey, we did some traveling together. We danced in the fire of power exchange and conjured up some serious sex magic. Maybe even shook out a couple of demons with those tears of yours." He kissed me on the forehead. He looked like an angel.

"Is it always like that?" I asked him.

He laughed, gently. "It's never the same thing twice, honey. All depends on where you're at in life and who you're with, not to mention what the Gods have in store for you. Ultimately, it all rests with them. We can show up with expectations or questions or intentions, and sometimes we may get exactly what we want, but in the end we're always gonna get what they feel we truly need."

"Can I ask what you got from it, Jeff?"

He looked into my eyes and stroked my face with the outside of his wide beautiful fingers. "I got to connect with you, boy, and I enjoyed it very much." Then his face changed, "But goddamn that was intense, way more intense than even I expected! We conjured up some things, honey. *Major* things. May I ask how it was for you?"

I tried to find some words to describe what had transpired for me over the course of the afternoon and evening, but it was just too immense. There was way too much to process, and it was way too soon. Maybe, eventually, the words would come, maybe in a poem or maybe in a conversation. But at that moment, the Sodomy Gods had left me uncharacteristically speechless. "It was a lot, Jeff. That's all I have right now. It was a lot."

"Well, honey, that's plenty. It was a lot indeed." He pulled me in close to him, holding my head up against his chest, and the two of us just lay there in our shared state of quiet bliss and disbelief. I could have stayed there forever, but I could tell the sun was getting low in the sky, and I needed to get home to Fred. Despite facing a whole bunch of fears that afternoon, nothing was as terrifying as what was to come next. I had no idea what was in store for me, but I knew it wasn't going to be fun.

I extracted myself from the safety of Jeff's energy and told him I had to head out. He went downstairs, gathered up my clothes and brought them to me. As I put on my underwear, I got a very sharp and painful reminder of the traveling I had done with Jeff. I still wasn't sure where we had gone exactly, but I knew that my ass was some serious roadkill from wherever we had traveled. I managed to pull my jeans up over my undies, wincing with every tug, and I waddled behind Jeff as we headed downstairs. Before I left, he kissed me and then deconstructed everything he represented to me, the God and the father, and allowed himself to be vulnerable and human. "Listen, boy, I know you said today was a lot, but I hope I wasn't too much for you."

"It was kinda major, Jeff. And it was perfect." I kissed him one last time and headed back toward reality.

* * *

While Jeff wasn't too much for me that afternoon, Fred sure the fuck was that evening. As soon as I walked into the apartment and said "hello" he got up out of bed and slammed the bedroom door in my face. My ass had been slammed all afternoon to the point of me blacking out, but none of that compared to the force with which Fred hurled the door into its frame. He locked it behind him, ensuring that whatever terrible communication was to come would be both unproductive and loud. I took it upon myself to knock gently, and with an equally gentle tone I asked him, "Baby, can I come in please? Let's talk."

The door flew open, but there was no talking. There was plenty of screaming though. Plenty of wild threats and nonsensical logic. He stormed out of the apartment, fury across his face.

When he came back home, shaking, eyes swollen from crying, he ran past me on the couch and locked himself in our room once again. I slept on the couch for three nights in the dead silence of our home. Finally, on the morning of day four, Fred said, "David, we need to talk."

"I'm listening, baby. Let me in to your feelings," I said.

It took him a few minutes to say, "I'm not stupid, David. I know you're young and I'm your first boyfriend and I'm not gonna be the only guy you have sex with. That's scary for me but I don't want to deny you those experiences. I just love you so much that I don't want to lose you. I get so confused." He took a sip of orange juice and drifted back off into a silent void.

"Keep going, baby. I'm here. Find your words."

"I see how you are with Javier and Jeff. I know you look up to them. You want what they have. You want to just run around and have sex whenever you want and then come home to me, and I'm supposed to smile and serve you dinner like a Stepford Wife. But I can't be that, Angel. I can't. That's who I was for all my boyfriends before you. If you want to have a totally open relationship, you can have it. But you can't have it with me. If you need time to explore what it feels like to be single, I understand." He started to cry again. "But you're going to be single."

I held him as he let out a lifetime's worth of fear of abandonment. I cried too. I knew I wasn't done with Jeff. I knew I wanted to discover parts of my sexuality on my own. But I also knew I didn't want to lose Fred. I told him I understood and that we could make what he wanted work. It was a lie, and I hated him for putting me in that position. Still, I had to respect him for standing up to me. Knowing he was ready to walk away from me, the love of his life, out of love and respect for himself, came as a huge surprise to me — and not an unpleasant one.

I knew Fred had a big dick. But that night, I learned he had a big set of balls to match.

Thirty

Fred and I stood on the north side of 22nd Street, a couple hundred feet in from the corner of 8th Avenue heading east. I was staring at a glass door covered in newspaper directly across the street from us. "That's it, baby," I said to him, lacing my fingers between his. "That's it."

I took him by the hand, led him between the parked cars, past an oncoming cab, and planted us in front of 268 West 22nd Street, quite possibly the smallest storefront in all of New York City. The paper was peeling away on the left side of its one and only window, and I asked Fred to look inside.

"That's it?" he asked.

"That's it," I replied.

"Is there a bathroom?" he asked.

"Nope. That's literally it, baby. We don't need a bathroom. I'll piss at the Big Cup or just run home. I can go in the street if I have to, but this is it."

The store was, at most, 8 feet wide by 8 feet deep. It had a front door, a small glass window, and 64 square feet of selling space. It was basically the size of a modest walk-in closet, right in the heart of Chelsea. Most importantly, it had a "Store For Rent" sign angling from the second-floor fire escape above it.

"How much is the rent?" he asked.

"No idea, but how much could it be?" I couldn't contain my excitement. "I didn't want to call and ask without showing you first but it's the coolest little spot I've ever seen, and I really want to find out." I gave him my poutiest face. "Please let's just find out."

"Ok, but you have to promise me that you won't get all crazy and just start signing things. You get something in your head, and before you know it . . . "

"I promise, I promise! Wait here. I'm gonna run to the deli and borrow a pen." I returned and wrote the name and the number of the landlord on the palm of my hand, and started practically sprinting home so I could call.

But Fred put a stop to that. "David! You're doing it already. Return the pen. Then we can go home." I sprinted back to the deli, handed the pen over, and bought a couple of ice cream sandwiches for us to eat as we walked the one block between the store and our apartment. I did my best to stroll at a casual pace, and while my feet did a fairly good job of obeying, my mind was racing.

I leapt into our apartment, landing on the couch right next to the phone. I could feel my heart pounding as I dialed, and after three rings a man picked up. "Dunn Partners. This is Michael Dunn. How can I help you?"

"Hi, my name's David Lauterstein and I make clothing and these goggles and things are like *happening* for us. Like really happening. People are buying it, and we even got a write up in *Paper Magazine!*"

"May I ask what this is in reference to?"

"Oh, right. Sorry. I get all excited. I'm calling about the store you have for rent at 268 West 22nd Street. The little, tiny one. I'm wondering what the rent is per month."

"Mr. Lauterstein, did you say?"

"Yes, that's me but you can call me David. Or Mr. Lauterstein. Or whatever. I'm easy."

Fred sat down next to me and mouthed the words, *Calm down.*

"Okay, Mr. Lauterstein, may I ask you what type of business you'd like to open in the space?"

"Yes. Our business. Yes. We'd like to open a clothing boutique for our line. It's called re:vision."

"And how long have you been in business, Mr. Lauterstein?"

I had no idea how to answer. I didn't know if we were even *in* business. I had sold my first pair of goggles three months prior, which wasn't much of a track record, so I told him, "Two years. It's been very successful."

"You sound like a good candidate for the space. The rent is $500 per month. We require first, last, and a four-month security deposit at signing. There's a two-year minimum on the lease, and just to be clear, it doesn't come with a bathroom." I scribbled everything down on a piece of paper so that Fred could have the details. He shook his head back and forth at me and whispered, "No David. No way. It's too much money. Hang up." He was right. We only had about $900 in the re:vision account. We had other debts and couldn't scrape together the $3000 if we tried.

"Are you still there, Mr. Lauterstein?" Michael asked.

"My apologies. Yes, I am. I was just discussing the details with my business partner. We'll take it," I replied. Fred looked at me, eyes open wide with shock, and he threw his palms up in a *what the fuck are you doing* gesture. I made the same gesture back only mine meant *I don't know what the fuck I'm doing either, but I'm doing it.* I put the phone on speaker so that Fred could hear the rest.

"It sounds like we have a deal! I'll need to run a personal credit check on you and your partner, along with a check on the corporation before we can proceed. Is there a fax number where I can send the forms?"

"Oh, uh, yes. Just put the cover page to my attention. But I'm not at my office right now. Would you mind sending them through tomorrow morning at 10 a.m?" *when I get to Sonic Assembly.* I gave him the fax number.

"That's fine, Mr. Lauterstein. You'll have them tomorrow. Please fill them out and fax them back as quickly as possible. Chelsea is one of the hottest neighborhoods in the city, and I wouldn't want you to lose the space."

"I'll get right on it, Mr. Dunn. And don't worry, that space is mine."

I hung up the phone, jumped up off the couch and screamed in unrestrained and unrealistic excitement, *"We got the fucking space! We got the fucking space!"* That we didn't have the money, or the credit, or the corporation, left me completely unfazed. I got what I wanted, and I would figure out the rest one way or another.

* * *

"I need to talk to you about something. It's important. Can we get lunch today?" I asked Rich.

"Dude you already came out of the closet to me. You kinda filled your quota for the 90s," he said without even looking up from his copy of *The Source.*

"Rich, you might want to get your facts straight. You got to hear me say I'm gay, but I got you this motherfucking job, so be ready for lunch at 1 o'clock. And don't forget your Amex — you're buying." Before I headed back to my office, I snatched the magazine out of his hand to get his full attention.

With the collapse of the HBN deal, work was pretty slow, so when 12:30 came around I went back to Rich's desk and told him I was heading out to lunch early. "Thank God. I'm so fucking bored," he practically announced as he grabbed his Tommy Boy Jacket.

"Make sure you have your wallet too," I reminded him.

We headed over to Riverside Grill and ordered up two plates of chicken-fried-chicken. I tagged on a couple of Dos Equis to lubricate the conversation. Rich looked at me quizically and said, "Dude, we can't drink at work. And it's not even 1 o'clock. What are you doing?"

"I get that sucking dick at the office is off limits, but a couple of beers won't nail either of our coffins. Even if they did, the office feels like a fucking cemetery anyway, so who's gonna notice?" The waitress brought us our bottles.

"Okay. What's so important that I'm here buying you lunch, homo?" Rich asked.

"I need some business advice." He knew that I was making stuff and selling it, but I handed him a piece of paper with some basic numbers so he could see my sales and get an understanding of my cost of goods. I told him about the little store, and my need for a corporation filing and some cash. I shared with him my vision to make an in-your-face queer culture brand that harnessed the energy of streetwear and translated it for my community. I even talked about wanting to mix it up with kinky stuff like rubber and leather to signal sex positivity.

I could tell Rich was listening, but he kept his head down and engaged with his chicken cutlet more than he did with me. Something wasn't right.

"Look, Rich, just so you know, I'm not asking you for a loan or anything. That's not why I'm here. I just feel like Fred and I are onto something, and I know you majored in economics or money or some shit like that so I wanted to run it by you. I don't know shit about business."

Rich put his silverware down and took a swig off his Dos Equis. "Alright Dave, here's the good news. First off, you do know shit about business. Probably more than I do. I mean, you were always making necklaces and shit in college and putting rhinestones on baseball caps and selling them all over campus. That's like the *definition* of a business. Make something, sell it, turn a profit. Sounds like you're actually running your second or third one right now."

"As far as the store goes," he continued, "yeah you're gonna need some sort of legal business to grab a commercial space I'd imagine, but that's nothing. There's like 1-800 numbers you can call and they'll do that shit for you right over the phone. Me and Matt set one up in college and I think it cost like two hundred dollars or something."

"Raising three grand — that's not a ton of money. Maybe ask your parents for a loan or Paul or someone. And if you can't get the money then move on. Keep making stuff and selling it and build up some cash so you're ready the next time." Rich took a couple of bites of his chicken, then a few more.

"Okay, okay. Now for the bad news? Just lemme have it," I said.

Rich put down his fork and swallowed the last of his lunch. "The part that doesn't make sense to me — and I'm gonna try to say this the right way — is that there's such a small market for what you wanna do."

"What do you mean? Like the square footage of the store, because I can't even afford this one let alone some Barneys-level shit."

"No, you idiot. Market is like the total of all the buyers and all the sellers in a specific region. So, like the market for men's clothing is huge since there are billions of guys on the planet and they all buy clothing. But that's not your market. You're not selling to every guy on earth. You're selling to guys in New York City, and that's only a few million. But you wanna sell just to gay guys. When you took me to that Roxy place, I saw more homos in one night than in my entire life, but there's just not that many of you. Or at least the ones who wanna dress super gay." He wasn't wrong. Most gay people still lived in the closet, and those who came out usually worked overtime to look as un-gay as possible.

"What I don't get at all is that shit about leather and rubber. Like the Village People. What the fuck is that all about? We both grew up in New York City and I'm sure you remember seeing those guys all over the news getting arrested for spreading AIDS at sex clubs in the Meatpacking District. You really wanna sell to *them?*"

"I don't know. Maybe."

Rich shook his head back and forth. "I love you dude, but this sounds like business suicide. I gotta be honest."

"You're right." Everything he said made perfect sense. "So how do I get the number for that 1-800-INCORPORATEMYSHIT company?"

The waitress brought us the check and I picked up the tab. I thanked Rich for his help, and we headed back to the office. Right before we crossed Broadway at 57th Street, Rich stopped me to check his beeper. "Sorry Dave, but Tommy D is blowing my shit up with 911s. I don't know what the fuck that clown wants but let me call him. You got a quarter?" I dug out two from my pocket, handed them to Rich, and he found a payphone that actually worked and dialed our junior-year roommate.

"What the fuck do you want asshole?" Tommy aggravated Rich, and that aggravation was all over his face. But then Rich got quiet. He went from mouthing off to listening intently. Then, as if Tommy had reached through the phone and smacked some sense into Rich, all the aggravation disappeared from his face as his eyes lit up wildly and the biggest smile wrapped itself around his head. *"Are you fucking kidding me? Are you kidding me?!"* They spoke for another minute before Rich hung up the phone, turned around, put his hands on my shoulders, and basically shook me.

A year or so prior, Rich and I took some of our Sonic Assembly bonus money and gave it to Tommy D to invest in a technology company he was getting involved with. I had kicked in about $200 and had long since forgotten about it, so I was overjoyed when Rich told me that the company blew up big and was sold for a lot of money.

* * *

I bolted into our apartment and handed a folded check to Fred. Tommy had stopped by Sonic Assembly at the end of the day and delivered it to me. "Read it out loud!'

"Pay To The Order Of Mr. David Lauterstein Twenty Three Hundred Eight Dollars and Nineteen Cents" Fred stared down at the check for a moment before looking up at me. "Are you sure this is real, Angel? They're not playing a joke on you or something right?"

"It's definitely one hundred percent real fucking money and it's ours!" I did a little dance. "We can get the store! It's like it was meant to be. The Sodomy Gods are listening and they're telling us, *'Here's some coin bitches, now get to fucking work!'"*

Fred laughed. "I had no idea the Sodomy Gods were such big queens. They talk just like you."

* * *

In bed, our puppy Piggy nuzzled in between us, I put the phone on speaker and dialed the number Rich had left on my pager.

"Good evening, this is Susan with Fifty States Incorporators. With whom am I speaking?"

"My name is David Lauterstein and I'm here with my boyfr . . . business partner, Fred Kearney. We're calling you from New York City and we want to start a company."

"Well you've reached the right gal to help you with that! Setting up a corporation is easy as pie, so if you and your business partner are ready, and one of you has a valid credit card, we can get started!"

Her overworked enthusiasm would have annoyed me at any other time, but in that moment, I was as giddy as she was. "Yes ma'am! We're ready to rock and roll!" I shouted. That might have been the corniest thing I had ever said, but Susan had me all worked up. My excitement must have been contagious, because Piggy latched onto my leg and began humping. Fred hated when she did that.

"Don't let her do that David. Get her off of you. It's gross," he said.

"Forgive me gentleman, is everything ok?" Susan chimed in.

"Yes, we're fine Susan. We're still here. What do you need from us first?" I asked.

"Well let's start with the name of your corporation," she replied. "What are you going to call it?"

"Cut it out Piggy!" Fred barked and went to pull her off me.

"Leave her alone Fred! She's not doing it to you, and I feel like she's blessing the moment." I threw him a look "I won't start our company while you're slut shaming our dog!" That may have sounded unhinged, even to me, but I wasn't joking one bit.

"She can hump your leg all she wants, David, but you better train her not to do that to me," Fred spit back. "It's so nasty."

I shot Fred a look and continued. "Apologies, Susan. To answer your question about the name of our company: We're calling it Nasty Pig Incorporated."

"You're gonna call it what?" I could practically hear the sound of her pearls grinding against her neck.

"Nasty. Pig. Incorporated. Would you like me to spell that out for you, honey?"

* * *

Michael Dunn was probably sick of me, as I called him so often with progress reports about our embryonic business entity. I explained it would take four to six weeks before we received our official Certificate of Incorporation, then we could open a bank account and sign the lease. I'd then proceed to ask him questions about pretty much anything just to keep him on the phone. I didn't want anyone else to get through to him and steal our space from under us. He eventually told me I should just make contact when we were ready to sign the contracts. It was his way of asking me to stop bothering him. I played my hand.

"Listen Mr. Dunn, we both know I'm a pain in the ass. I call you every day, because I'm determined to get that lease. I walk by 268 all the time because it's all I can think about, but each time I look up at that FOR RENT sign I lose my shit. I have nightmares about it. It makes me feel like I have to stay on your radar just in case someone else sees it and tries to come for my space."

There was silence, just enough to scare me, but not enough to make me crack and apologize for sounding like a prick. I'd come to realize that I was blessed with blind confidence in myself, and I was unafraid to embody it. I also knew there was a very fine line between confident and cocky, and my ability to walk it got better with each passing day.

"You're quite a character, Mr. Lauterstein," he said.

"Please Michael, call me David."

"Okay David, so now that we're on a first name basis, how the fuck do I get you to leave me alone? My secretary thinks we're having an affair."

"Then let's put a stop to this. You call the super at 268 and have him take down that unnecessary FOR RENT sign. I think we'll both rest a lot easier once it's gone. Don't you, Michael?" I'd always considered my eyes to be the best set of weapons I had, but I was starting to realize my balls were giving them a run for their money.

The next afternoon I walked by the little store to find the sign had been removed, but that didn't stop me from standing beneath the fire escape and looking up at its absence. I fixed my gaze upon the sky, once blocked by the FOR RENT sign, and thanked the Sodomy Gods for keeping an eye on me. I then pressed my hands against the door of the little store and prayed it would soon house our clothing line re:vision and be the headquarters of Nasty Pig Incorporated.

Thirty-One

"You sure you don't want to come with me Fred?" He had already said no a few times, and it wasn't like I was desperate to have him accompany me to The Lure, the new leather bar Jeff and Javier told me about that had opened on West 13th Street. I loved the idea of walking down to the Meatpacking District by myself, cruising strangers along the way, and ending up at a gritty, underground bar where all the men looked like they had materialized from the pages of a *Tom Of Finland* artbook. I fantasized about what all those men would be doing to each other, what they'd be doing to me, pressed up in dark corners and bathroom stalls, lost in our shared physicality. I was hungry for those experiences. I wanted to hunt.

Fred wanted none of that, and with good reason. Where I was free to fantasize about those leather-clad encounters, Fred was burdened by the reality of his experience. I knew leather bars and sex clubs existed in the 80s because I watched news reports of them being shuttered as the city began cracking down on the HIV epidemic. I was 15 and safely on my couch in Staten Island. Fred was 23, and he didn't need to watch TV to get updates on the ravages of AIDS. He watched it in real time, and for him those leather bars and sex clubs weren't filled with fantasy characters, they were filled with the ghosts of men weighing 86 pounds, covered in lesions, cast out as pariahs for their natural desires.

"You can go, David."

"You sure?"

"Yeah, I don't want to."

"I promise I won't do anything."

"If you're gonna wear *that* I don't think they'll let you in anyway." I was wearing a Bike swimmers jock, my favorite baggy jeans that hung low off my butt, the leather armband that Marcus had given me, my signature black batter's helmet, and a sick pair of vintage suede Pumas. I was young and horny as fuck, and from everything I had learned about the leather scene, those two qualities alone would grant me entrance.

"We'll see," I assuredly replied. I put on a three-quarter crop top and grabbed my wallet and my keys. "I won't be home too late." I kissed Piggy on the head, and I kissed Fred as well, but he didn't really kiss me back. "I love you, baby."

I got the feeling I'd be coming home to a set of cold shoulders, and I wasn't exactly okay with that, but I wasn't going to let it stop me either. I headed out the door and into the night, walking west on 22nd Street so I could pass by our little store and say my prayers to the Sodomy Gods before hitting 8th Avenue for some New York City cruising. I prayed religiously to get that space. I felt like it was my destiny.

The boys were out in droves, working their way up and down the avenue, hanging out on stoops, eye-fucking each other in the hope it would lead to more. I *loved* cruising. There was something so simple and primal about wandering around the concrete jungle hunting for dick. It was unspoken, understood, and unnoticed by the straight people as it happened all around them in plain sight. It felt so subversive, my favorite lane to run in, and I got plenty of attention, most of it wanted. Other than a car of scared little men who threw a bottle at me and shouted *fucking faggot* from the safety of their Cadillac Seville, the general consensus among the men I passed was that I was one very hot piece of 25-year-old ass.

"Fucking losers," I said to myself as I watched them drive away. I was smiling from ear to ear. I loved being called a faggot. That word had so much power over me as a kid, but I took it back and owned it, making its power mine. My jock may have come from Sports Authority, but my attitude was one hundred percent Metropolitan Faggot Authority, head to toe.

As the concrete beneath my feet turned to cobblestone, I felt the dark pull of the Meatpacking District in my bones. It smelled like animal carcasses. The hookers flagged down cars, trying to get a date for the next 20 minutes. The only businesses open were a smattering of bars, the sex clubs that survived the 80s, Florent, the famous French restaurant that was the late night turn up for the creatures of the underground — and now The Lure.

The facade was painted black except for a six-foot-tall boot print graphic on the door. A tall man clad in a black leather motorcycle jacket, blue jeans beneath a pair of black leather chaps, and black leather gloves, stood guard. He was the man Fred warned me about. He looked very serious about his role, and I knew he'd have the power to turn me away. "He doesn't know who he's up against," I thought to myself.

"Sorry, boy. No sneakers," he stated firmly. "And those baggy jeans aren't doing you any favors, either."

I was up for the challenge. "We both know you're making a mistake sexy man, so how about you bend those rules for me. I'll make sure your patrons won't regret your discretion on this one."

"Then you don't know shit about this place or the guys inside. We've got a strict dress code for a reason. Keeps kids like you from fucking with the vibe. It's a no. Walk home and put on some boots and maybe I'll reconsider."

"So let me get this straight," I replied. "I could walk up to you with zero personality, zero sexy, and zero desire to be a nasty pig, and as long as I was wearing the right pair of shoes I'd get in?"

"That's right. Lose the look. This is a leather bar, not a Lil' Kim concert. We set the rules."

"Your rules are fucking stupid," I told him as I walked away. I couldn't believe it, but Fred was right. I didn't get in because I didn't look the part. I finally understood what it was like for all the people who got turned away from the clubs I so easily entered. And on top of it all, I wasn't going to be getting any dick when I got home. Knowing Fred, I was destined for his unique brand of a hard time, but it turned out I didn't know Fred quite as well as I thought. Before the night was done, he gave me his hard cock instead—and a couple others to boot.

Thirty-Two

“You were right Fred. They didn’t let me in.” I fully expected him to take some pleasure from my night of defeat. I figured I’d get a combination of gloating and distance. Maybe he saw the disappointment in my eyes though, or maybe he wasn’t used to seeing me defeated. Maybe he was just happy to have me home by his side, far away from my fantasies that translated to his fears. Rather than berate me, he got up off the couch and encircled me in his embrace. “That’s their loss, Angel. Those rules are dumb. You’re the hottest boy in New York City and they may not know it, but I do.”

He was doing his best to lift my spirits, but it wasn’t working. “I know how to cheer you up,” Fred said. “I’m getting dressed and we’re going on an adventure.” He was in and out of the bedroom in no time, having changed into a look that felt pretty casual for a night out dancing. Jeans and a tee shirt could be super cute, but it appeared as if Fred had grabbed whatever was at arm's length. Suddenly I felt overdressed and asked, “Should I change? I mean we don’t exactly look like a couple right now.” Fred grabbed my hand, and he replied, “Angel, I don’t want you to ever change. C’mon.”

We walked out of our building and to my surprise we headed east. I couldn’t tell where we were going, so I let Fred take the lead. It all turned me on so much, him secretly determining where I was headed. Fred was an amazing top in bed and knew damn well how to put me in my place when I needed it, but I was more of the leader when it came to our relationship and social life. I savored every moment as he took control of the night, guiding me into the unknown.

We headed toward the chaos at the entrance to Limelight, and for a moment I wondered if a Saturday night somewhere other than the Roxy or Sound Factory might be Fred’s idea of an adventure. It certainly wasn’t mine. If anything, Limelight on a Saturday was work, since it was where I sold most of my goggles. But we walked past all the club kids and the wannabes and made a left on 20th Street. Just ahead of us, snaking out of a nondescript office building, was a line of gay boys quietly waiting to get in the door to go up a set of stairs. No one was saying much. Some of them had knapsacks. Others were grinding their teeth so hard I thought sparks were gonna shoot out their mouths. I had no idea what the fuck was going on, and I was totally excited.

"Where are you taking me, honey?"

"You'll see," he smirked. Fred was giving me some major Daddy vibes, and everything about him was making my ass hungry and wet. I sincerely hoped this adventure was going to include me bent over. Between my fantasies about my night at The Lure and the reality of Fred owning me so fucking hard, I could feel my hole throbbing with the physical need to get destroyed. For as horny as my dick could get, my ass put it to shame, no contest. By the time we made it past the lobby and were half-way up the stairs, I felt like my hole was going to devour the entire building.

We finally got to the entrance, a glass window with people scurrying about behind it. The lighting was dark, and while my sense of smell was pretty weak, there was no covering up the odor of chlorine that hung in the air. "Welcome to the Westside Club," the attend said to us. "Are you members?"

"No, we're just here for tonight. One room and one locker please." Whatever was going on, Fred had clearly done it before. Unlike me, Fred had a past, one that he didn't often speak about. I knew he had some ex-boyfriends, and he told me stories about how he used to cruise around on his bike in college and hook up with strangers in parks, but there was so much about Fred I didn't know, including his knowledge of both this place and how the hell it worked.

"That'll be $46 dollars. ID's please." Fred took out his wallet and slid his driver's license through a hole in the glass along with some cash. "Give him your license, David." The attendant called out a couple of numbers to the guys working behind him. One guy returned with a lock box and two keys, each attached to a rubberized cord. The attendant slid us the keys and opened the box. "You wanna put anything in here?"

"Give me your wallet David, and your keys." I did what I was told. Fred but both mine and his into the lockbox and the attendant slid us two white towels. "You got six hours. Check out is at 6:10. If you wanna renew you gotta come here before then. Don't make us come get you." He pressed a button to his right, and I heard the door next to us buzz. Fred led me through it, and the smell of chlorine amplified in my nostrils as the sound of house music filled my ears.

"What is this place, Fred?"

"It's a bathhouse. Follow me." I followed him into this maze of doors, each about eight feet apart and identical except for the numbers on them. There was something about the walls and the doors that felt . . . temporary. They lacked sturdiness. But that clearly wasn't the case, because down each twist of the labyrinth were men, clad only in towels, some visibly hard, leaning against them. They stood there in the glow of the blue lights, waiting, hunting. Others walked the halls, their cocks swinging back and forth like a hypnotist's charm. Music pulsed from speakers above my head, but it was the sound from behind the doors that flooded my ears and sent me spinning: the primal, brutal, unmistakable noise of men wildly fucking each other in the ass. The air thundered with it, and had it not been for Fred holding my hand and pulling me forward, I would have stood still in hedonistic abandon.

Fred found our room and opened the door. Inside was a thin single mattress covered in a threadbare sheet along with a pillow in similar condition. The mattress sat on a raised Formica platform and a single light was affixed to the wall, controlled by a dimmer switch which was perhaps the most expensive amenity in the place. And that smell of chlorine hung ever-present in the air, reminding me of the locker rooms that were the source of so much of my jerking off in junior high school.

"Earth to David. Are you with me?" Fred asked. I realized I had barely said a word since we first got in line to enter this grungy wonderland.

"I'm sorry. I'm just — wow — you weren't kidding. This is definitely an adventure." My heart was racing, for as exciting as this place was, it was also terrifying. In the pit of my stomach, I felt that nauseating push and pull of my desires, wanting to give in, frightened by the consequences. I had done some exploring, but it all had come with a sense of security that allowed me to let go for a moment. I could let go with Fred. I could let go with Jeff. I fantasized about letting go at The Lure. But in this space, in the possibility of giving in to my desire for the anonymous, sexual unknown, I was fucking scared. I had felt myself becoming a fierce champion of sexual positivity, a proud bottom despite the bullshit shame that came with it. I was so fucking good at walking the walk, at the hunt, but when faced with the actual kill, I was terrified at what would come if I actually pulled the trigger.

"David, what's going on? Are you okay?" Fred asked me. I lied, quickly. "Fuck yes." My heart was racing, but the terror only provided half the adrenaline. The other half came from raw desire. I wasn't about to leave. "So, what do we do now?"

"We get naked and put on towels and walk around." Fred began getting undressed, removing a bag of rubbers and a bottle of lube from the pocket of his jacket and placing them on the little shelf by the bed. He took all his clothes off, slid them under the bed, and wrapped himself in his towel, his soft cock thrusting forward from beneath it. I did the same and went to dim the lights. My hand trembled wildly. That tug of war between fear and desire wracked through every inch of my body.

"David, are you sure you're ok? Your dick is saying one thing but your face is saying another."

I came clean. "I'm so happy that you brought me here. It's such a Daddy move and I love you so much for doing this. But it's also a lot. I don't know why I'm so nervous." That was a lie. I knew why. I just didn't want to say the word AIDS. I was so fucking tired of AIDS. I wanted to get lost in the moment. Let go of the fear. But sex and death were inextricably linked like an old married couple who hated each other but couldn't live apart. They just rocked back and forth together, sometimes ignoring each other, grateful for a little silence, but mostly screaming at each other bitterly about their miserable union.

"I get it, Angel," Fred said knowingly. After all, he had lived with them rocking for a dozen years longer than I had. "Let's loosen you up." Fred reached under the bed, grabbed his jeans, and pulled a vial of K out of the pocket. My eyes lit up, because a little dissociation was exactly what I needed. That, and some dick. Fred gave me a powerful serving of both, shoving a bump up my nose and his cock down my hole. Normally, he wasn't particularly verbal, and maybe it was the energy of the grunting and moaning that rumbled through a space completely free from straight societal norms, but Fred got so fucking mouthy with me. He pulled his cock out of my ass and said to me "Is this what you want? You like these Daddy moves?"

"I fucking love them. I love your big cock so fucking much."

"Then beg for this Daddy cock."

"Please give it to me, Daddy. Please. I need it so fucking bad." I begged for it, and he gave it to me, again and again, our grunts and moans and foul-mouthed banter joining the debaucherous chorus of the men who surrounded us in their tiny dark rooms, losing themselves in each other's bodies. Fred wrecked me for a solid 30 minutes before he climbed off me to catch his breath. I wiped him down with my towel and laid my head on his chest, listening to his heart as it slowed from a racing pace. His breathing slowed as well, steadying and quieting, until he came to a state of rest. I looked up and said, "Thank you, Daddy."

He laughed and said, "OK I don't know how I feel about this Daddy stuff now. How about I let you call me Daddy for tonight and we'll take it from there."

"That sounds amazing, Daddy."

He laughed and said, "Yeah ok we can try it tonight but don't get used to it" and that was enough for me. "How about we do another bump and put on our towels and walk around."

"If that's what you want, Daddy," I said coyly.

"I know that's what *you* want so let's go." We put on our towels, Fred put our room key around his bicep, and we headed out hunting. With each passing moment, I felt my pulse quicken. Desire and fear, desire and fear. They rocked back and forth in my head. But being there with Fred, holding his hand, *Daddy leading the way,* it made things okay. It made me feel safe. Clearly Fred couldn't protect me from HIV, but Daddy could protect me from harm. It was a false sense of security, and I knew it, but that was okay for tonight. Nothing else about sex being deadly made sense, so not being afraid for a night because I had a Daddy watching over me was a lie I gladly embraced and allowed to wash over me as truth.

We walked past a tall muscular guy, who stared at us both and smiled, but Fred kept walking, holding my hand and bringing me with him as we turned a corner and went down another hallway.

"Why didn't we stop, Daddy? He was so hot."

"Because we're stopping here. He's gonna come walk by us in a second. Trust me." Fred was right, as usual, and a moment later the tall stranger made his way toward us. He nodded as he passed us, walking another five feet before stopping and leaning against a wall. Daddy took my hand and led me to him.

"What's up?" Fred asked.

"Hablas Español?" he replied. I reached back to my high school years and grasped for what little Spanish I could recall from my four years of classes.

"Me llamo David. Y esta mi novio, Fred. Tu eres muy fuego."

He flashed a mischievous smile at my broken attempt at Spanish. "Gracias, maricón."

I knew enough Spanish to know what that meant, but I had just about exhausted my bilingual capabilities to come up with a witty retort. Luckily he grabbed my hand and put it under his towel so I could feel his thick, uncut dick. He reached around and grabbed my ass. I looked back at Fred and asked, "Are you okay with this, Daddy?"

"That all depends. I wanna feel it too." Fred reached under his towel, and

I handed over his meat, which had grown even thicker from my groping it. "Yeah," Fred said, "I'm definitely okay with it." I found one more bit of Spanish with which to close the deal. "Vamos," I said to the incredibly sexy stranger. He nodded. "Let's go, Daddy."

Fred led the way, holding my hand, our nameless, uncut Latin trick trailing behind us, grabbing my ass the entire way. We got to our room, Daddy unlocked the door, and we all dropped our towels as we entered. Daddy stood up on the bed so I could suck his dick, and our trick dropped to his knees and devoured my ass. I was so riled up, so turned on, and with Daddy there to protect me, I let myself go. The trick ate me hard and when he stood up and began stroking the head of his dick against my hole, Daddy climbed down off the bed, grabbed two rubbers, and put one on himself and one on the trick. They took turns using my ass, back and forth, one cock in me then the other.

"You like that uncut cock, boy?" Daddy asked me.

"So fucking much, Daddy. But not as much as yours."

"That's the right answer. That's a good boy." I was so wound up and turned on that my dick was leaking precum like never before.

"Sí niño. Take it, maricón." His broken English was driving me wild. I could feel his thrusting getting faster. I knew he was getting ready to cum.

"No leche en mi culo," I told him, and just before he blew his load he pulled out and took the rubber off and shot all over my back, covering my skin with his seed. He collapsed on top of me, his body heaving, winding down with every breath until he found his strength again and stood up. He was all smiles, as was I, and as was Daddy.

"Gracias, chicos," the trick said as he put on his towel and left our little room.

Daddy grabbed a towel and wiped the cum off my back. I laid down on the mattress and looked up at him. "Was that okay for you?" I asked.

"It was more than okay. I love making you happy."

"You're making me very, very happy tonight, Daddy."

Fred laughed and said, "Remember this Daddy thing might not be sticking around so don't get used to it."

I nodded in agreement, knowing full well that I'd be calling him Daddy for the rest of his life. "Whatever you say, Daddy. You're in charge. So now what do you want to do?"

"I'm ready to go home," he said. I was most certainly not. I got all quiet. I didn't want to leave at all, but I had just told Fred that he was in charge. I suddenly realized this whole Daddy thing was a double-edged sword upon which I had thrown myself with careless abandon. There was no way I would get everything I wanted, but I thought about my time spent with Jeff, and the importance of power dynamics in a Dom/sub scene. I wanted Fred to be this sexed up Daddy for me, but that wasn't going to happen unless I was willing to assume my place. He wasn't the type to take my submission, so I had to offer it up and let him know it was his.

"If that's what you want Daddy . . . " I paused to see if he would interject, hoping he would surprise me and tell me we could stay, but he didn't, so I finished, " . . . then I guess we should get dressed." I got down on my knees and pulled our clothing out from under the bed. We silently changed into our street clothes, and I prepared myself to leave behind all the nameless, beautiful, terrifying men, their bodies obscured by the darkness, their hungers left for other bottoms to serve. I opened the door to exit our room, and Fred slammed it closed in front of me.

"I'm impressed," he said with a smile. "I thought I was going to have to drag you out of here kicking and screaming."

"Yeah, I kinda thought the same but I can't expect you to be my Daddy if I call the shots all the time." I shrugged, a bit defeatedly, to show him my submission with a hint of adorable Jewish guilt thrown in for good measure.

"I don't know how comfortable I am with you calling me Daddy all the time. Daddy makes me feel even older."

I looked into his eyes and said, "For what it's worth, Daddy, guys my age don't do it for me at all." I kissed him. "You do it for me, Daddy."

We had the best night, hunting the hallways as a team, bringing strangers back to our room to enjoy together. Sometimes the chemistry wasn't there, and Daddy was quick to say, "I think we are going to take a break," which was bathhouse code for "this isn't working and it's time for you to go." Other times it was incredible: no talking, no names, just immediate, uninhibited pleasure for its own perfect sake. I lost count of how many men we hooked up with, but after a few hours of going at it, I could tell that Daddy was winding down.

"I'm getting kind of tired, Angel. I think I'm really ready to leave this time."

"Can we please just have one more, Daddy? Then I promise we can leave, and I'll walk Piggy when we get home and get you some ice cream and feed it to you in bed." I put on my best puppy dog face in the hopes he would oblige, and he did.

"Okay, just one more then we are definitely leaving."

“Deal, Daddy!” I shouted like a little kid. We put our towels back on and walked out into the darkness. We passed a tall, tattooed guy who looked vaguely familiar to me. He nodded at us, and we stopped. I tried to place his face. I couldn’t figure it out, but I didn’t fucking care. He was hot and I was only getting one more, so we took him back to our room and ended the night with a bang. The timing was perfect, because just as we finished, we heard over the loudspeakers, “Room 170, it’s time to check out or renew.” He thanked us in a heavy accent, put on his towel, and left us to get dressed.

“He was so hot, Daddy,” I said triumphantly.

Looking astonished, Fred asked, “Do you even know who that was?”

Thirty-Three

"I'm taking you to Suzanne Bartsch's Halloween party at The Palladium," Fred told me at the beginning of October. Halloween was Fred's favorite holiday as it gave him an opportunity to flex his creativity a hundred different ways. He had shown me pictures of all the incredible costumes he had made over the years. Some were scary. Others were whimsical. All of them were original. When he asked me what I wanted to be for Halloween, without even thinking about it I shouted out, "A sex demon!"

"That's not a costume for you, David," Fred said unironically. "How about we dress up for real?"

"But I want to be a sex demon with that Fred Kearney twist. And I want to try wearing a pair of chaps. I really want to show off my ass."

"Again, not a costume David," only this time he said it with a bit of levity.

"Please, Daddy, can we be sex demons?"

"Oh, now I'm part of this little show?"

"Well yeah of course. You're my man. It won't be any fun being a sex demon by myself."

"Nice try, Angel," he laughed. "Okay, we can be sex demons."

"Oh my God! Yay! Thank you, Daddy."

"Okay you've used up your 'Daddy' quota for today. Go get dressed and take *Fred* to shop for fabrics."

"Sounds like a plan, Fred!" We were overdue for a visit to the garment center anyway. Fred had sketched out a couple of cool ideas for new styles and we needed some fabric so he could experiment. Up until then most everything we had made were custom pieces for our friends, but as the possibility of opening our little store grew, we knew we had to put together a small line that we could make ourselves and sell off the rack. I didn't think it was prudent to wait until we got the lease to get moving, and sales of our custom pieces left us with a few hundred dollars to invest in our future. We bought a couple of yards of eight different fabrics, and we doubled up on this cool synthetic matte rubber along with some leather for our Halloween costumes. Fred mentioned that we were starting to use company money for personal expenses, something I had repeatedly stated I was fiercely against. "This is different. It's a write off." I didn't exactly know if that was true because I had no idea what a write off really meant. But we were buying fabric and making clothing, and my gut told me that if the IRS ever came digging around Nasty Pig Incorporated, they wouldn't unearth our little Halloween secret.

Over the next couple of weeks, Fred and I worked side by side, alternating between making styles for the potential shop and experimenting with ideas for our costumes. Being creative with Fred brought me a level of joy and satisfaction that I didn't know was in me. I was his apprentice, constantly learning how to do new things while getting better and better at the skills he had taught me along the way. He would joke around about how unsexy he felt when he was at the sewing machine, but I found it insanely hot. I could watch him work for hours at a time, happy to just be next to him. I marveled at his talent. I got into the habit of telling people he was *creatively hung.*

When it came time to make my chaps, he measured me to ensure that his first pattern was as close to perfect as possible. I appreciated that a lot as the matte rubber he would use to make them was the most expensive material we owned. Fred was surprised that I didn't want a pair of "real leather chaps" for my look, a comment that I found quite odd. I didn't understand why chaps had to be made of leather to be real. "It's the whole Leatherman code thing. They only want you in leather or latex. You couldn't get into The Lure in sneakers and baggy jeans so I figured you'd want a pair that would get you in the door."

"Honestly, Daddy, rules don't really interest me unless I'm breaking them." I thought that a pair of synthetic matte rubber chaps would be sick, and the fact that I had never seen that done before made the idea of them even cooler. Once he finished his pattern, I carefully laid the material out on the floor of our living room and placed each pattern piece on top of it. Moving the different pieces around to ensure they used up as little material as possible was like a game, and once I felt I had minimized the waste, I traced out each piece with tailor's chalk. I was learning to identify the different parts of a pattern just by their shapes. Front legs looked different than back legs. Sleeves had a certain slope to their caps. Certain pieces, like back pockets, were always cut in twos. I always took my time, careful not to rush and make mistakes. And just as Fred had drilled into me, I never forgot the notches. Each time I finished cutting out a garment I would put all the pieces into a poly bag and tape it shut so that none would go missing. And I made sure that every single paper pattern piece made it back into its manilla envelope.

Making patterns took a lot of Fred's concentration. It was a complex process, like solving a puzzle in three dimensions, and losing a piece would be disrespectful of his time and talent. His perfect patterns were the foundation of everything we were building. I had thoughts of buying a fireproof box to store them in. "Just in case," I thought to myself.

As I saw Fred was getting close to finishing my chaps, I put on combat boots and a jock strap in preparation of my fitting. I sat on the couch next to him until he handed them off to me so I could punch holes in the waistband and apply snaps and the grommets with a set of handheld tools. I did this with more patience than just about anything in my life. I wanted my first pair of chaps to be perfect. I had asked Jeff about wearing chaps the second time I saw him in a pair at Factory, thinking I would get a description of how it felt to let your ass hang out in public. But in typical Jeff fashion, the first thing he did was to educate me. "Chaps are great, honey, they would suit you well. But you can't just pull them on like a pair of pants. You *must* unzip the legs, put them around your waist and snap them in place, then reach below your balls and zip each leg down along the line of the seam of your jeans. But you have to be careful, honey. You don't want to get your skin caught in the zipper. Learn from my mistakes. Pinching that baby skin down there hurts like nobody's business." I followed his directions to the letter. I wrapped the waistband around me, snapped it up, and had Fred tighten the rubber cord in the back that laced the two separate legs together. I then reached between my thighs and carefully worked the male end of the zipper into the pull, sliding the closure down my left leg first, then my right. Putting on chaps felt almost ritualistic, like I was baptizing myself in rubber in preparation of worship at the altar of the Sodomy Gods. I walked to the full-length mirror to see my reflection. I couldn't believe what was reflected back. It was as if I had been transformed into this sexual superhero. I felt truly powerful. I turned to Fred and said, "These are fucking incredible, Daddy. I love them so much."

"They look hot on you. The rubber works. I think I want to make a pair for myself now."

Before he could object, I began unzipping the legs so he could try mine on. I wanted to see him in them, badly. I took them off, stripped him of all his clothes, then put them around him, loosening up the rubber cord in the back to properly accommodate his waist. Fred had gorgeous legs, much thicker than mine, so I didn't think he would be able to get them zipped over his thighs. Much to my surprise and delight, he did so with ease. He zipped them closed, put on his motorcycle boots, and stood in front of me, decked out in custom gear with his cock hanging between his legs. I stood him to the mirror.

"I want to change a few things to make them better." True to form, he was unsatisfied with his work. I did notice his dick was starting to swell, so clearly something about those chaps were satisfying him on a subconscious level.

"They look better on you then they do on me, Daddy."

"You know you look hot in them," he commented.

"You look even hotter." I paused for a moment and added, "We should make these be part of our line. Leather chaps are so fucking expensive, and we can make these affordable for everyone."

"I don't know about off-the-rack chaps, David."

"Well I do. These are so sellable. I want to have stuff like this in our line. Like streetwear meets club kid meets Tom of Finland. I feel like that's our vibe. I mean what do you think? I think it could really work." I knew it could.

I saw him processing the idea as he admired himself in the mirror. Fred then surprised me and agreed, "You're right. These work."

He was rock hard at that point. "Clearly," I replied confidently as I started stroking him. He brought me into the bedroom, and we tested out those chaps for functionality and endurance. They held up spectacularly well to Nasty Pig's unique version of quality control. The next day I called Spandex House to ask them how to clean synthetic laminates because by the time we were through product testing they needed some kind of maintenance.

"Wash on cold. Dryer no heat," I was told. I added the chaps to our dirty laundry and did a load in the basement of our building while Fred took a nap. When I returned to the apartment he got out of bed and asked me how they held up.

I put them on to show him. "So far so good, but I think we need to test them again." So we tested them again. And again. And again. And no matter what we threw at them, they came back ready for more, kind of like me.

Thirty-Four

We didn't make much more progress on our costumes, other than that one pair of chaps. As the Halloween party was officially two days away, Fred's anxiety began to spike. He was prone to leaving things to the last minute then freaking out about having to get them done in a hurry. He told me he had been doing this since middle school, never studying for a test until the evening before, then staying up all night, learning everything at once in a mad dash to the finish line. It was frustrating for me, having to watch the days slip away unproductively, knowing full well that I would bear the brunt of his stress as he sewed well past the time we had planned to go out. Even worse though, I felt powerless to do anything about it. It was Sunday afternoon, the party was Monday night, and my only solution was to order an extra bottle of K to keep me occupied as I watched TV. Then I had an idea.

"Honey, why don't we call in sick tomorrow, so you'll have more time to finish. We already took Tuesday off so let's just make it a four-day weekend." Fred *hated* his job, so it didn't take any arm twisting to get him on board. His supervisors wouldn't think twice about it, and Paul would just assume that I was on a low-key bender. Sonic Assembly was falling apart anyway, so what could he do?

We went to work on the remaining pieces of our looks. Fred had me cutting out strips of leather at different widths and he coated the suede sides with barge cement. Once they dried, Fred folded the leather back in upon itself so that the edges met and ran down the center of each strip. Then he'd pass the strip to me so I could bang it with a rubber mallet and get it nice and flat. When we finished all the strips, I assumed we would start cutting them down and making our harnesses, but Fred gathered them up and brought them to the sewing machine. He swapped out the needle and began sewing a straight stitch down the edge of each strip. "I'm just trying to help, Daddy, but don't you think it's a waste of time to sew all these pieces when we just glued them into place?"

He stopped what he was doing and insisted, "Glued leather looks cheap, David. I'm sewing mine. If you don't want yours sewn, then that's fine but don't tell anyone I made it." I loved to brag about Fred's creations, so I kept my mouth shut and let him finish the job correctly for both of us.

"There's something else I want to make us before I start on your chaps." I could feel the anger building inside my body, knowing full well that despite taking a day off from work I was going to find myself on the couch at 2 a.m., irritated by the sound of Fred pushing his merrow machine while the rest of New York raged to the sound of progressive house beats on West 14th Street.

"You said you wanted us to be sex demons, so I bought these a couple of days ago." From an unbranded blue plastic bag, he pulled out two sets of real animal horns. "I want to make us leather head cages and sew these into them. What do you think?" I thought I was going to need a a lot more patience because his idea was so fucking sick, and I was fully on board. My patience may have been in short supply, but fortunately my ketamine wasn't, so I settled into the couch and kept myself entertained until he was finished.

Finally, he handed me a head cage. It *was* fucking sick. "I think you're amazing," I said as I held the horns and felt the ridges glide beneath my fingers. I knew what he was going for, and it held that Fred Kearney touch I had requested in the first place. But I also knew there was no way he was going to get everything else done in time. Fred was ambitious, but his time management skills were non-existent. I had to come up with a solution in real time.

"Tell you what. Let's make the head cages, but I want you to wear the chaps and the codpiece. They look better on you anyway."

"No, I want us both to wear chaps and I can finish all of it in time, David."

"You literally can't, Daddy, and the chaps looked *so* good on you. I want you to wear them. So finish the head cages and let's go to the party."

"What are you going to wear then?" he asked. "This whole sex demon thing is your idea."

"My harness, the codpiece I bought at The Noose, and the horns. That's plenty sex demon for me."

"No, I meant for pants," he replied.

"Have we met? I'm not gonna wear any pants at all, Daddy."

Thirty-Five

The Palladium was a massive club on East 14th Street and Third Avenue. Originally designed to be a deluxe movie palace, it was converted into a concert hall before Ian Schrager and Steve Rubell, owners of the legendary Studio 54, purchased it and turned it into one of New York City's hot spots in 1985. Over time, it lost that reputation, and by the time Peter Gatien bought it in 1992, The Palladium might as well have been The Tunnel, only taller.

Still, there was no denying the magnificence of the space itself. It was gigantic with four-story ceilings and walls made of light installations that surrounded the dancefloor. There was a huge balcony with tiered cushioned seating, a relic from its former use, and lounges and rooms around every corner. The place could easily fit a few thousand people, and from the looks of things as we entered the club, it felt to me like Suzanne Bartsch had it packed to capacity.

I had been to many Halloween parties over the years, but never had I seen one where the attendees were so invested in doing their part to create a true spectacle. Everyone was in a costume, and none of them were phoned in. It felt as if each person had worked as intensely on their presentations as Fred did, and that was saying something. The energy in the room felt like a circus on acid with no demarcation between performers and guests. The beats blasted through the room and the bass shook the floor. Making our way through the crowd was an impossibly slow process. Normally I'd be frustrated moving at such a creeping pace. But everywhere I turned there was someone or some *thing* capturing my attention, and much like a museum, I was inspired to get lost in the wander.

We miraculously found our crew and dropped our pills together, then worked our way through the feathers and the glitter until we found a spot on the dancefloor. My teeth began to chatter as the ecstasy washed over me. Random creatures grabbed at my bare ass and I loved every second of it. I felt myself embodying my character, a sex demon risen from the alleyways of the underground, and there among all the glorious drag queens and tricked out club kids, Fred and I still managed to stand out. Tom sent around his vial, sending us over the edge. Time and space melted away. The Palladium became its own wild, kaleidoscopic universe. Fred and I flew though it like dark queer angels in our harnesses and horns until all that flying left us feeling parched. We temporarily parted ways with our crew and made our way to the bar.

"Look over there, David, behind that fluorescent scarecrow. It's Thierry Mugler."

He was even sexier than I had remembered from our darkened encounter at the bathhouse. I caught him staring back at me. "I want to go say hello, Daddy."

"Wait. How fucked up are you? I don't want you to embarrass yourself." Embarrassment was a feeling I had yet to experience, and I certainly wasn't going to start now.

We walked toward him, circling past The-Wizard-of-Oz-On-Mushrooms gang, until I stood right in front of him. It felt as if he towered over me. He was bigger than I remembered too, maybe because we were mostly horizontal when last we met.

He reached out with one hand to stroke my horns and placed the other against my naked ass. "Wow. You look so gentle, like a precious little lamb." His French accent melted me.

I quickly replied, "You weren't exactly gentle with me when you had your fingers up my hole at the Westside Club a few weeks back."

For a moment he froze, and I thought I had ruined my chance to get to know my idol less biblically. My blind confidence had left me, and I stood there in silence, terrified I had blown it, until he threw his head back and let out a deep, sexy howl of laughter.

"You're no precious lamb," he exclaimed. "You are a mighty nocturnal beast!" He smacked my ass hard and I knew it would leave a mark. I was thrilled to be branded by him.

I couldn't contain my excitement. "We're such big fans of yours, Mr. Mugler. You're basically my idol. Both of ours, actually. I'm David and this is my boyfriend, Fred."

"It is nice to meet you both again under these new, more colorful circumstances. But don't you think Mr. Mugler is a bit formal considering where my fingers have been. Please call me Manfred. My friends call me Manfred."

I let my index finger dangle from my mouth, dramatically mimicking a self-aware, teenage seductress. "Does this mean we're friends, Manfred?"

"Why not, nocturnal beast?" He continued to stroke my horns and my

ass with his square hands, his fingertips lighting up the skin on my backside where his handprint was slowly rising. "These headpieces are fantastic. Who designed them?'

"Fred made them for us. He's a great designer too!"

"David cut it out," Fred said to me.

"Cut what out? You are great, Daddy." I turned to Manfred and said "He made all of the pieces we're wearing. He's so talented."

Manfred looked us up and down and said to Fred, "I would have to agree with your wild beast. Everything is polished, more clothing than costume."

Fred chimed in. "Well, everything but David. I wouldn't exactly call him polished."

Manfred laughed and nodded in agreement. "I would imagine he's a handful of a beast." He smacked my ass again, only harder. I was getting harder, too. The head of my dick came poking out of my codpiece. "It looks like the beast is in heat tonight!"

"He's always in heat," Fred replied. I was so turned on, being objectified by my man and Manfred Mugler at the same time. They spoke as if I wasn't even there, and it was driving me crazy. It was a rare moment when I kept my mouth shut.

"Good! I love wild animals! Domesticated beasts belong in a zoo, and zoos are so boring. This horny beast needs to be uncaged and free to roam the night."

"I couldn't tame him if I tried. But I love him the way he is." I stood there silently, obediently, soaking up each moment as the skin on my ass grew hotter and hotter from Manfred's manhandling.

"So, Fred, you are a designer?"

"Well . . . "

I wasn't about to let Fred fall prey to his own insecurities so I broke my silence before he could utter a word of self-deprecation in front of the legend himself. "Yes, he's a great designer. I design too. I'm his apprentice. We've started a line. It's some really cool stuff."

"These headpieces are much better than 'really cool stuff,' mighty beast," he corrected me. He turned to Fred and added, "This is an original idea, Fred. That makes you more talented than many who proudly and falsely call themselves designers. You should embrace your talent."

I became overwhelmed by the enormity of the moment and found myself welling up. "See Daddy. I told you you're amazing."

"Aw, look at those tears. It seems he is a gentle beast after all!" Manfred smacked me a third time, harder than the previous two combined, and my tears of joy were replaced by tears of pain, courtesy of the stinging sensation that shot through my skin. I loved it, and Manfred knew it.

And then it was over. "I must go now, gentlemen, but I am pleased we had a second opportunity to meet, this time with actual conversation."

"Wait . . . please," I begged him. I pushed my way to the bar and asked the bartender for a piece of paper and a pen. I wrote down our names along with our phone number and the address of the little store that wasn't even ours yet. "I hope you'll give us a third opportunity one day." Overcome with gratitude and overwhelmed by the poetry of the universe, I threw myself upon Manfred and embraced him, knowing full well it would probably be for the last time. "Thank you for seeing my man the way I see him." I said as I handed him the paper. "Here's our number and the address of the store we're going to open soon."

Manfred gave Fred a hug and disappeared into the colorful masses, leaving me in a state of humble euphoria mixed with wild ambition. For the rest of the night my head didn't stop spinning and I barely spoke a word. I just moved to the beat in a hypnotic flow state. I felt myself being elevated by a lunar pull, filled with a growing sense of purpose that carried me past the moon on solar winds and blew me through an endless cosmos of possibilities, potential, and dreams. Fred and I bathed together in the pool of our powerful, magical union until we walked out of the Palladium and into the mid-morning sunlight.

In the days that followed, I was certain Manfred would take us under his wing. It was, after all, part of the Sodomy Gods' plan. We were destined to meet him — not once, but twice — and he was destined to call. But the phone never rang.

* * *

On the third of November, a box arrived at our apartment. Fred and I opened it together, with Piggy between us. Inside was a black binder, trimmed in gold, with the words CORPORATE RECORDS written in gold across the cover, and NASTY PIG, INC stamped in gold along the spine. Inside the binder were notices and filings, by-laws and stock certificates, all of which pertained to our newly formed business, and none of which I actually understood. But one document jumped out from the others. It was the Certificate of Incorporation

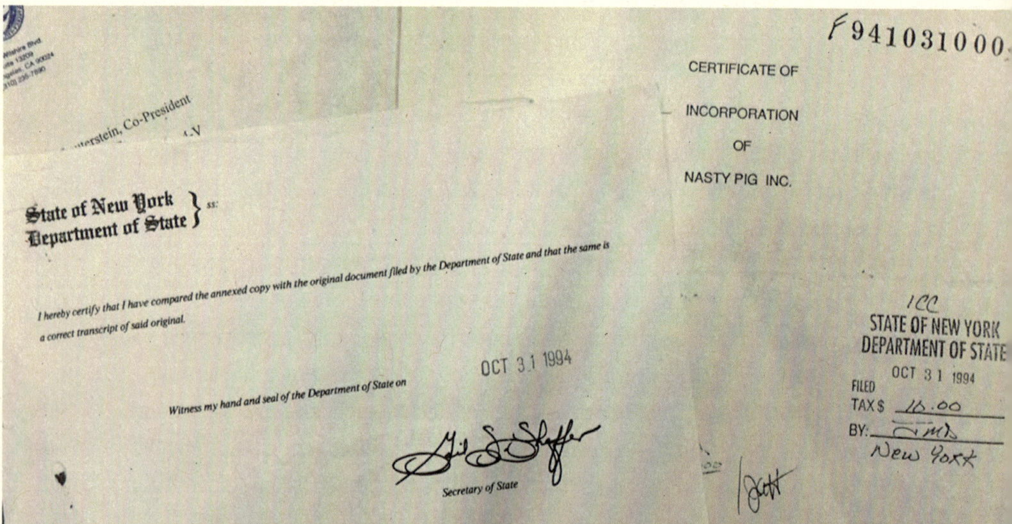
F941031000
CERTIFICATE OF
INCORPORATION
OF
NASTY PIG INC.
State of New York
Department of State
ss:
I hereby certify that I have compared the annexed copy with the original document filed by the Department of State and that the same is
a correct transcript of said original.
Witness my hand and seal of the Department of State on
OCT 31 1994
Secretary of State
STATE OF NEW YORK
DEPARTMENT OF STATE
FILED
OCT 31 1994
TAX $ 10.00
BY:
New York

of Nasty Pig Inc., by the government of the United States of America, indicating the exact date our corporation was officially formed: October 31, 1994.

Nasty Pig was born on Halloween. The poetry was writing itself before my very eyes. The Sodomy Gods were watching over me, confirming my faith in their glory through an undeniable series of symbols and signs. There was no turning back. We were officially in business.

The following morning, I took all our corporate documents to Chase Manhattan bank, along with the check I had gotten for my investment with Tommy D, and waited outside the Chelsea branch for 30 minutes until they opened at 9 a.m. I strutted over to the teller and deposited the check into my personal account, then I opened a business checking account for Nasty Pig, with the branch manager. "Nasty Pig . . . that's a wild name," she said. *Well, I am a wild beast,* I thought to myself. *Just ask Manfred.*

Once the check cleared, I returned to the bank, corporate records in hand, to transfer the money I had deposited in my personal account to Nasty Pig's account to act as seed money. The teller handed me back my deposit slip, my golden ticket, and I sashayed out of the bank feeling like a boss-ass bitch. I made a beeline to the nearest payphone, fed it a couple of quarters, and dialed his number by heart.

"Dunn Partners. This is Michael Dunn."

"Michael, it's David Lauterstein, your favorite pain in the ass. I've got some good news for you. We're ready to take that lease."

"That's not exactly good news for me, David," he replied, "because I'm gonna have to deal with you for the next two years." We both had a well-deserved laugh at my expense. "Congratulations. You have yourself a store. I'll get the lease all prepared with a start date of December 1 and have it sent over to you ASAP. How does that sound?"

"Literally like a dream come true, Michael."

"Perfect. Let's start with the name of your business."

"It's Nasty Pig, Inc."

There was silence for a moment. "Did you say . . . Nasty Pig?"

"I most certainly did."

"I gotta tell you David, I want to close this deal. But I can't have the words 'Nasty Pig' hanging on a sign outside my property. It's too obscene. What happened to that other name you gave me?"

re:visio

“Oh yes re:vision. Don’t worry, Mr. Dunn. ‘Nasty Pig’ is just the name of our corporation. Our store will be called re:vision,” I assured him.

“You promise, David?”

“If you don’t believe me, Mr. Dunn, you can put it in the lease. Let’s close this deal.”

“Okay David. But I gotta ask: If your brand is called ‘re:vision’, why did you name your company ‘Nasty Pig? It’s a pretty wild name.”

I looked down at our Corporate Records binder, our name stamped proudly in gold on the spine. “Well, Mr. Dunn. I'm a pretty wild beast.”

Thirty-Six

In the weeks that followed Daddy and I worked furiously. If we weren't at our day jobs or sleeping, we were buying fabric, making and correcting patterns, cutting out and sewing up samples. Once Fred felt we had each one right, he would grade our size medium pattern to a small and a large. That was just for tops. Grading pants took a lot more work and we didn't have very much time. I was determined to open before Christmas, so we sent our size 32 pant patterns to a professional grading service, and we got back a 30 and a 34. I knew making so few sizes wasn't ideal, but we didn't have much time *or* money left.

I had convinced Mr. Dunn to give us the keys to the store upon signing the lease. With only about two weeks left until the first of December, I figured there was no harm in asking. He knew from experience I wouldn't take no for an answer, so upon my third call to his office he said yes.

Building out the store was relatively easy, simply because there wasn't much we could do with 64 square feet. We had enough space for two four-and-a-half foot racks on either side, a curtain for a dressing room in the back right corner, and our small Singer sewing machine across from it. Fred thought the sewing machine was ugly there. I felt it would be cool that people could see us making things. Fred thought that was a stupid idea because there was nothing sexy about seeing a man sew. I thought Fred was clueless about where fashion was headed: toward real experiences with authentic brands. We had a few fights about it.

We began to fight more than ever. Turned out owning a business together added a whole new layer of shit for us to argue about. I was so headstrong in wanting to move quickly, and he was determined to make sure everything was as close to perfect as possible. "If you want me to be part of this you better learn that I'm not going to sign off on anything I don't believe in. It's got to be right to be ready. If you want it fast and janky, then find another business partner." Fights like that were early indicators of just how messy working with my boyfriend would turn out to be.

We found our groove, but all the teamwork in the world didn't seem sufficient to get the store open by December 1st. Fred thought my deadline was unrealistic. I thought his pessimism was counterproductive. But one night, in a rare bout of clear communication, he explained himself to me. "My dad and I used to do some contracting on the investment properties he bought when I was in high school. You learn fast that renovations and build outs take twice as long and cost twice as much as you think they will." Fred was right. It felt like there weren't enough hours in the day to get through what I had hoped for, and the number of days until December 1st were dwindling rapidly, along with the initial investment we'd made in Nasty Pig. It felt like time and money were in a race to the bottom, and no matter which resource won that race, I would end up as the loser.

I also had a stark realization that once we did open, sales were going to have to come in quickly or I'd be forced to shutter our dream. I pictured myself sitting in a store full of clothing, devoid of customers, as the city grew cold and dark with the onset of winter. The thought of having to move out, to take down the racks and the dressing rooms and put them in the trash, began to haunt me. In my gut was a combination of chronic unease, nausea, and fear. For the first of countless times to come, I was totally stressed out about money.

I was startled by a knock on the door, and I peeked out from behind the curtain to see Jeff standing there, sexy as ever in a motorcycle jacket and jeans tucked neatly into a pair of black leather lace up boots. I had no idea what the Sodomy Gods truly looked like, but the Christian kids I grew up with described their God as this old white guy with a long beard who lived in the clouds. I imagined the Gods I prayed to looked a lot like Jeff. I unlocked the door and immediately began fantasizing about what he might do to me in that two-foot-by-two-foot dressing room. My stress had magically disappeared. At least for me, even the thought of sex made everything feel better.

"Hi, honey," he said before entering. "If you're busy, I don't want to disturb you."

"You can disturb me anytime in any way you want, Jeff." We embraced each other and made out passionately. I was taking a risk. Fred could show up unexpectedly at any time. But the idea of getting caught turned me on as much as it terrified me. I loved the thrill of taking risks, a necessary quality for any entrepreneur. Risky sexual encounters thrilled me just as much. Eventually Jeff had to be the one to let go, and it was probably for the best. Neither of us wanted to, but neither of us wanted to disrespect Fred either. Both of us knew that doing so would put an end to our relationship, and neither of us wanted that.

"It looks like it's starting to come together in here." He reached for the pair of tiger stripe vinyl pants hanging next to me. It was the only garment in the store. We had used it to measure the height for the racks. "These are *amazing*. I love them. I'll be buying a pair of these once you open for business."

"Yeah, I love them too. And I'll definitely give you a family discount."

"A discount? Already?" He looked at the price tag. "$89?" he exclaimed, visibly taken aback.

"Do you think that's too much? I don't want to scare people away and make things too expensive. But we really need to make some money."

Jeff laughed. "No, honey. They are *not* too expensive." His answer should have comforted me in the way of his embrace, but my stress had already returned. I wanted to grab him. No, I wanted him to grab me and throw me against the wall, pull down my pants and turn me around and fuck that awful feeling out of me. I needed something to take its place. I had always been a fearless dreamer, but as my dreams turned into stark realities with all their associated costs, my blind confidence had been replaced with a looming sense of failure.

"You okay, honey?" Jeff asked me.

"Honestly Jeff, I'm not okay. I'm a mess. I could really use a little magic. I'm not sure if it's something I can ask for, but . . . "

He looked at me, then into me, probing behind my dampened eyes, searching for something intently. His face went through a series of expressions, reacting to whatever he was seeing or sensing, until finally his eyes changed. They became knowing. He had found what he was looking for, and his eyes connected with mine in a state of certainty. "Okay honey, I'm gonna make you a doll. Tell me what you need."

"Like a doll to play with?" I trusted Jeff implicitly, but I was also very confused.

"No honey. I'm not gonna make you a toy!" he laughed. "And if you accept what I'm offering, it's best that you don't play with it when it arrives." He nodded, back to being serious, as if he was agreeing with the gravity of his own words. "You're gonna want to pray to it."

That was sounding like the magic I was hoping for. "I understand Jeff, and yes I accept your offer. I'd love a doll from you."

"Then tell me what you need."

I knew exactly what I needed. I didn't know whether my answer would be okay with him and the Sodomy Gods and whatever other forces were listening behind the veil of my existence. But I knew what was happening behind the scenes at my young business: I was almost out of cash. "Jeff, I know I should ask for world peace or something noble like that, but what I really need right now is money. Is that okay?"

"Of course it's okay! There's nothing wrong with wanting money. Money isn't even real, honey. It's just an illusion. It's like this thing we all agree upon to represent the output of our energy. It keeps us from having to barter for everything. So if I make dolls and you make pants, and you need a doll but I need chicken breasts, without money, we're shit out of luck. But cash lubricates the transactions. I can trade you the doll for money, and with that money I can get my chicken breasts. You get your magic, and I get my dinner. Voila!"

"Wow. I never thought about it that way."

"When you tell me you want money, well you're just asking the universe for some energy to help you manifest your dreams of making people feel good. You're not just gonna hoard it. People who do that, greedy people, just suck that energy out of the universe and lock it up. They don't share it. They covet it. And all that energy goes bad, honey, It expires when it stagnates. It gets real ugly. But I know you. You're gonna trade it, move it around so that it can multiply, so you can give it back a thousand times bigger. So yes, you can ask for money, and lots of it."

"I don't need lots, just enough." I thought twice. "Well maybe a little more than just enough."

"How about we let the universe figure out the details."

"Totally. I'm great with that. Thank you, Jeff — for everything."

"Of course. It's my pleasure watching you show up and be present for yourself." He grabbed me and held me close. "You're gonna make all those dreams of yours come true. I can feel it."

"I can feel it too."

"Okay, then, my work here is done. I'm gonna head home and get stoned." He looked me up and down. "And you should too, honey. You look exhausted!"

"Honestly, I could really use a break."

"Well then meet us at The Lure tomorrow night. It's gonna be *amazing*."

"I tried The Lure a few weeks ago. They wouldn't let me in because I was wearing sneakers. It was lame."

"Tomorrow night is this new party called Pork. A few of our friends are throwing it. They want to bring a whole new energy to that scene and trust me, they won't care if you're wearing sneakers or not. You and Fred are *exactly* the crowd they're after."

"You sure Jeff? I'm not up for a second round of rejection there."

"I'm sure. You're going. I'll put you guys on the list." He kissed me goodbye, gently at first, almost platonically, but we couldn't help but give in to our shared desire for more and we mauled each other on the street in the glow of the light of Nasty Pig's little headquarters.

Thirty-Seven

Fred looked so fucking hot. He was wearing a tight black tee shirt, jeans with his matte rubber chaps over them, black leather boots, and a motorcycle jacket. Such a Daddy! I was wearing the exact same look that denied me entrance the last time I went to The Lure. It deserved to be seen, and Jeff assured me it wouldn't be a problem. As we approached the front door, I noticed the difference immediately. The doorman was wearing motocross pants, a vintage Crisco Disco tee shirt, and he looked about my age.

"Welcome to Pork, faggots. Ten dollars each," he said with a thick Italian accent.

"We're on the list." I replied.

"Of course you are. Who isn't. I don't know how the fuck we are going to make any money when every cunt in town thinks she's a V.I.C. What are your names?"

"David Lauterstein and Fred Kearney. Jeff Rose put us on."

"Oh. That queen. I love her. Javier is a pain in my asshole, but I love her too. Go in. Have fun. Try not to get AIDS."

"I didn't think that was funny," Fred said as we checked out coats. "There's nothing funny about AIDS." He was totally right. AIDS was terrifyingly serious. But "try not to get AIDS" was just about the funniest thing I had ever heard. For the very first time, I allowed myself to laugh in that fucking plague's face. It felt remarkably liberating.

The Lure was as dark and seedy as I had hoped. The few lights that were on were mostly red and blue, and the place smelled like an elixir of leather and sweat and sex. The DJ was playing a mix of grunge and punk and new wave. There was art on the walls, images of guys fucking in bunny suits and clown costumes. After going to countless gay bars, all of which bored me to no end with their sterilized straight-acting atmospheres, I had finally found a place that felt like me. And the guys there felt like me too. The place wasn't totally packed, but what Pork may have lacked in quantity was more than made up for with quality. The men were geared up for sure, but they put their own spin on things. Some of them wore leather and latex, but others wore vinyl and spandex singlets. A couple of guys wore Lucha Libre masks. And one guy other than me was wearing a pair of baggy jeans and a harness. We looked at each other, smiling, cruising.

"Is that Javier and Jeff?" Fred asked me. The two of them were in a giant crib between the bar and the DJ, wearing harnesses and diapers, throwing baby food at each other. I took Fred by the hand and walked him over to their play pen to say hello.

"You two are fucking crazy," I said to them.

They bawled at me in baby wails. Javier hit me in the head with a pacifier. It bounced off my helmet and landed between them. Javier grabbed it and stuck it in Jeff's asshole. It was incredible. I stood there for another moment, but when it became clear they weren't going to break character, Daddy and I walked to the bar to get a couple of beers.

The bartender was shockingly hot. He was Latin, with a ring in his nose that made him look like a bull. He wore nothing but a jockstrap, which made it obvious that his dick was pierced too. And his ass was so fucking big and hairy that it almost made me feel like a top. I turned to Fred, who was mesmerized by that ass, and said, "I love it here, Daddy." Judging by his hypnotized state I doubted that he heard me. Also judging by his hypnotized state I got the feeling he loved it there too.

"What can I get you hot fuckers?" the bartender asked.

"Two Coronas, please." I think I drooled as the words came out of my mouth.

He came back with our beers and a trio of tequila shots. "On the house for the two hottest fuckers in the place." All three of us downed them together.

"I bet you say that to all the boys," I told him.

"Just you, boy. And this man you're with. He's all Daddy. Oof. I'm Paul. Welcome to Pork."

"I'm David. This is my Daddy, Fred."

"David and Fred. I'll remember that. This is my Daddy, Phil." He called down to the end of the bar and gestured to Phil to join us.

Phil was British, jacked all the way up, and as sexy as his boy was. The three of us hung out near Paul, who continued feeding us shots as we got to know each other. As the night went on, Phil and Fred flanked me on either side and took turns putting their hands down my pants and fingering my hole. Our dicks came out. We stayed until the place closed and waited outside for Paul to get off. The four of us went back to Phil's place and shed any unnecessary garments. We fucked in our gear until the sun came up Thursday morning. That was Thanksgiving, and damn did I have a lot to be thankful for.

Thirty-Eight

The first of December came and went, and we were nowhere close to opening the store. Our little company bank account was bleeding out like a slaughtered pig being processed for its meat. It was all I could think about when I was alone. When I was with Daddy though, when we were creating, all that fell away. One night I asked him how he could remain so calm while I was forgetting what it felt like to sleep. "Life is going to push boulders in your path, Angel. You can either panic about how you're never going to be able to move past them, or you can grab a pick and start chopping away at them as they come, one by one, bit by bit." When we were creating together, it felt like we weren't just chopping away at those boulders. It felt like we were chiseling them into sculptures.

Slowly but surely, the little store really did begin to come together. The nine feet of rack space displayed our menswear line: vinyl tiger stripe pants, matte rubber chaps, vests made from rubber diamond plate flooring we found at Canal Rubber, black wet look shirts, a trio of "Hello Kitty" baby tees, and these incredible rubberized superhero tank tops that Fred spent hours constructing. Each was one of a kind, with a graphic star or a lightning bolt on the front chest. Both of us wore them to Factory the Saturday after he made a few, hoping to get noticed and generate some buzz for our store opening. The response was immediate, and I said to Fred, "We definitely need to get some business cards printed up." Screaming out our address to a bunch of people rolling their tits off to the massive sound system at Factory was just about the most challenging "word of mouth" advertising I could think of.

But people remembered. Along with our friends, who would pop by at night to say hi and see how things were coming along, strangers began to knock on our door to find out when we'd be open for business. "Soon" was the best answer I could come up with. They also asked for our phone number, an expense I couldn't yet cover, along with our store hours so they'd know when to return. One person asked a particularly poignant question: "What's the name of this place?"

"We need to get a sign for the door, David," Fred insisted. "I love that people are interested but we keep getting interrupted while we're trying to work and you love to talk while I'm waiting for you to finish cutting out fabric." He wasn't wrong. I loved talking to every single potential customer about what we were doing in the hope that they would return once we opened, but slowing Fred down was the opposite of achieving that goal.

Louis stopped by to bring us a store-warming gift and tell us he was finally moving out of Tom's apartment. "I just can't live there anymore. Tom's always circling the drain in a fucking K-hole. It's getting kinda dark." He looked at me and followed up with "like my unbleached asshole." I loved Louis's sense of humor and everything he said made me crack up, so I did my best to laugh like everything was normal.

But nothing was normal. Louis had changed so much. His strong cheekbones and angular features, physical traits of his Native American heritage that made him so gorgeous, had started to work against him. His face was sharpening as his skin retreated to his bone structure, a consequence of the weight he had lost elsewhere. I had noticed it happening to his body since the summer. At first, I complimented him on finally being a size two and we both howled as he did his best Naomi Campbell back and forth across the end of the Christopher Street Pier in early September. But when he took off his coat at Eddie's birthday brunch in October, I realized that none of it was his choice, and it wasn't something to joke about anymore. The fact that we couldn't laugh about it together just made things more uncomfortable for both of us. We never talked about it. We just stopped laughing.

"I better go home and walk Piggy before she craps on the floor. Talk about shit getting dark." I did my best to banter back with Louis and he smiled, but we both knew I was running away. I didn't hug him. I didn't kiss him goodbye. I couldn't bring myself to feel his absence beneath his winter jacket or touch my cheek to his. I was scared that his skin would be cold, or his cheek bones would dig into my healthy flesh, literally face-to-face with the reality of what was happening. Louis was there but he was evaporating. He was expiring like a quart of milk, left out on the counter and forgotten as it changed its consistency and soured. All of it was just too much for me. I briskly walked home and put a leash on Piggy and the two of us walked a couple of blocks. Once I felt safe from the possibility being seen by Louis or Fred, I found a stoop to sit on, picked Piggy up and cried into her fur until her scruff was saturated with my failure to be human to my friend who was dying right before my eyes.

Once I got that out of my system, I made my way home and found Fred in the bedroom, under the covers with the lights out. I put Piggy on the comforter next to him and he scooped her up and nuzzled her up to his face. I took off my clothes and got under the covers with him. We were quiet for so long it felt like the silence had fallen down upon us like a boulder during a landslide. I wanted to say something but this silence was so much bigger than me. I was pinned beneath it. I couldn't find any words to meet whatever horrifying moment we were facing together in the darkness. Finally, Fred spoke up. "Everything okay, Angel?"

"I'm fine, Daddy. You okay?

"I'm fine, too."

I'm not sure either of us slept much that night, but we woke up in the morning and I made us breakfast as we went to our day jobs like everything was normal. At least for us homosexuals in New York City, that *was* normal.

Thirty-Nine

We finally opened our little shop at 6 p.m. on December 23rd, with Jeff's magic voodoo doll mounted on the back wall. Though it was just two days before Christmas, Fred still took the time to decorate the store for the holidays. The lights and ornaments made the store feel polished. It glowed with promise. We stood inside together, taking up most of the room, and held each other as I played our song. *Do you believe in the wonder? Do you believe in the wonder? Do you believe in the wonder . . . the wonder of love?*

"Ok, Daddy, now get out. We need to make room for our first customer!" I said as a man peeked into our window, dressed in a manner best described as dapper. Fred left to go work on a couple more pieces that didn't quite get finished in time for our "grand opening" and I welcomed the dapper gentleman as he walked through our door. I kept myself busy fumbling at the sewing machine, pretending to change the needle so that he didn't feel like I was top of him, even though I was.

"I've passed you guys on my way home for the past few weeks and I have to tell you this has got to be the smallest clothing store I've ever been in," he said to me.

"Well, it's not how big it is, it's what you do with it," I replied in my typical David show schtick. "If you have any questions or you need a tour of floors two through 98 let me know!"

"Bless your heart," he said a bit smugly. "Is this your own line?"

"Yes. It's my and my boyfriend's line. He's the guy who just left. We make all these pieces ourselves." I wanted to read him badly for that "bless your heart" dig but I swallowed my pride in hopes of eating into his bank account.

He thumbed through our two racks, turning the garments inside out, looking at our construction. Fred had taught me that was a sign of someone being in the fashion business. I immediately went on guard, nervous that this man had come to knock off our designs before we even got started. But then he revealed himself. "You guys know how to make clothing, for sure. I'm a buyer for Nordstrom so I see a lot of designers. You know what you're doing."

"No way. Do you want to carry our line?" I said with all the naivete in the world.

His smug little smile gave way to laughter so condescending I could feel it crawl all over my dreams. "I don't think this is the type of line that the Nordstom customer would . . . appreciate." Now I hated him and his matching paisley tie and pocket square.

"No problem. My customers don't really shop department stores anyway," I fired back. Any joy he felt from his half-ass read wilted away beneath the darkness of my shade. The fact that I didn't have any customers yet didn't faze me one bit.

"Well best of luck to you,' he said as he put on his overcoat. "Before I go, let me give you some valuable advice," he said, not that I was requesting any. "When you're in the clothing business you make all your profit between Thanksgiving and Christmas. That's why the Friday after Thanksgiving is called Black Friday. It's the first day you'll turn a profit for the year. Your numbers go from red to black. Opening this late in the season isn't the soundest of business strategies."

He irked me. A lot. He also didn't know me. I was the king of longshots. I loved being the underdog. Back me into a corner, and I'd come out swinging.

"Thank you for the unsolicited advice," I quipped. "But I'm a bit confused so perhaps you could continue to educate me. How is running a business where you only have four weeks to turn a profit a sound business strategy?"

He thought for a moment, trying to find a crack in my logic. "Well, that's our business model. Perhaps you should have thought of that before you became part of it."

"No, honey. That's *your* business model. My business is going to make a profit *every single day.*" Truth be told, he did teach me something valuable about the industry, and from that moment onward I knew I had to treat each and every day as its own opportunity to win. Pinning your hopes on Santa to reward you come Christmas felt more like a myth than a business plan.

I noticed two guys outside our door looking in. "Speaking of, it looks like I've got some customers outside waiting for you to leave. Happy holidays!" I said as I opened the door to let him out. I welcomed in two cuties from the brisk winter evening and sat back down at the sewing machine. "Let me know if you guys have any questions."

"I actually saw you at Sound Factory wearing a sick rubber tank top like this one," he said, pulling a blue and white one with a lightning bolt on the chest from the rack. "Can I try it on?"

"Totally. Just step into our expansive changing room," I said as I swung open the curtain. "And if you need anything else just holler and one of our sales associates will be happy to help."

They both laughed, appreciative of my campy routine. We bantered back and forth as they tried on practically everything in the store. I was amazed at how well all the pieces fit. Fred was right to make sure everything was perfect before it ended up on our racks. It was one thing to sell clothing to friends, but here were two strangers whose measurements we never took, and still they looked amazing in every single piece they tried on.

"I love your line so much," the bigger one said to me as he admired himself in the mirror wearing a pair of black vinyl pants and a green and black rubber tank with a star on the chest. He turned to his friend and said, "I walked in a mere mortal and now I feel like a superhero!"

"More like a superhomo," his friend replied.

"Your jealousy is showing, girl." He closed the dressing room curtain, put his clothes back on, and handed me the pants and the tank. "I'll take both – and she's paying. Thank you for the Christmas gifts, girl. I *love* them." I did my best to fold his items on the sewing machine before carefully placing them in a black paper shopping bag. I took out a receipt book, then listed each item. The total came to $149. My hands were shaking as I tore off that slip and handed it to the friend, terrified he would see the total and call the whole thing off.

"$149 for handmade pieces? That's it?" My hands continued shaking, only now they vibrated with excitement.

"Why are you so shaky?" he asked as he handed me $150.

"I'm kinda gagging because you guys are literally our first customers." I dug into my pocket, pulled out a dollar bill, and went to hand him his change.

"Keep it. Tape it on your wall for good luck."

He may have been our first customer, but he sure wasn't the last of that night. We sold another rubber tank top to another Factory queen, a shirt to a kid who worked at the Big Cup, and a necklace to a girl who lived down the block. I closed up shop at 9 p.m. and basically ran home to my Daddy, busting into the door of our apartment. *"Holy shit, Daddy. We made $278!"*

"You're so cute, Angel. I love seeing you excited," he said as kissed and held me.

"I just can't believe it. Like random strangers bought our stuff and it was so cool to see them try things on and feel good about themselves. We made them so happy and it felt fucking incredible."

Making money paled in comparison to making people feel good. I vowed to myself that I would never, ever lose sight of that.

Forty

Over the coming months, re:vision became a thing. We'd have a couple of customers on weekday evenings and a few on Saturdays. Sundays were touch and go, so I chose to treat them as optional. Factory was a great place to spread the word, and since I had business cards made, I was able to actively point folks in the right direction. Sometimes I would just party with them until we left together and walked right to the store, our pupils larger than the square footage that housed our line. I'd put on house music and we'd just keep carrying as they tried on our gear and fell in love with it. There was something truly powerful about dressing these guys up in our unique blend of streetwear and fetish. Watching them try on chaps for the first time, looking in the mirror at themselves, amazed at what was staring back, was deeply gratifying. They'd ask me what I thought, and I'd always say, "Don't ask me. Look in the mirror and ask yourself. If you like what you see, if you smile and feel your dick getting hard, then it's a total fucking yes." Often, I saw plenty of smiles and plenty of hard dicks, and one by one, I began to build a little army of sexually empowered faggots right there in our tiny shop.

We also began attracting a following from the crowd at Pork. Young, kinky guys seemed to love what we were all about, and Pork gave them a space where they could wear our gear without fear of getting turned away by some old-school, gatekeeping doorman. We even made fans out of a few hardcore Leathermen we met there, including a smoking hot guy named Joe, his husband Joel, and their boy Doug, who looked about my age. I recognized the three of them from the neighborhood, and Doug and I ended up hitting it off thanks to our shared love of dark humor and dominant tops. The three of them would come by the store every couple of weeks to say hi, browse our racks and try things on, until one weekend each of them picked out something they liked and made an actual purchase.

"I gotta tell you, I'm so fucking psyched to have you as customers. I didn't think guys like you would be into our style. I actually kinda figured you'd hate it," I said to the three of them outside on the street, as the store wasn't big enough to host the four of us comfortably.

"Really? Why do you think we keep coming over here?" Joe asked.

"Because you wanna fuck me in the ass," I replied confidently.

"Well, that's definitely true," Joe said as he and Joel groped at my butt, "but we like the gear too. Especially Doug. He loves it." Each of them kissed me. They smelled good and tasted even better. "Will we see you at Pork, sexy boy?" Joe asked.

"Most definitely, guys." Fred and I had been going to Pork religiously since it opened. I loved the underground fetish scene there as much as I loved the underground club scene at Factory, and through our creations, we were pulling both of those influences together and refining a style that was uniquely our own.

I was also refining my style of being a businessman. What I lacked in experience, I made up for with an in-your-face attitude that was unabashedly gay as fuck. I took my sexuality and threw it in people's faces, not for shock value, but to get them comfortable with gay people on gay terms. We were fearlessly wearing our sex positivity on our sleeves, and I walked the Nasty Pig walk by literally talking the Nasty Pig talk. But I offset that militant take-no-prisoners attitude by humbly sharing what I had learned about queer history and gay sex magic. I packaged it all together as my unique philosophy and served it to the masses every opportunity I had. While I might not have had an MBA, I put my poetry degree to good use and told stories. I did my best to have our customers walk away with a tale they could share with their friends. I didn't just want them to look gorgeous, I wanted them to feel gorgeous, inside and out. I instinctively knew our path to success would be making sure our clothing was like a memento of the Nasty Pig energy we were putting out into the world through our 64 square feet of commercial real estate in Chelsea.

One Sunday afternoon, post-Factory, Kevin came by the store with a few other members of the House of Aviance to kiki on the street. I was overjoyed to see him.

"How's business, girl?" he asked me.

"Kinda slow today, but whatever. It's still earlyish."

"So what does one do to entertain oneself on a slow day at re:vision? Don't get me wrong, girl. She's real fierce. But you can only remerchandise her racks in so many ways before you run out of options." We all laughed. Kevin wasn't reading me. He was just being funny.

"Mostly I write poetry when I'm here alone. I actually finished one up before you all stopped by."

"Well let's have it Miss Thing! I'm all ears."

I probably would have said no to anyone but Kevin, as I kept my poetry mostly to myself and I *never* recited it. My trauma from elementary school had left some deep scars. But Kevin was Kevin, so I got up the nerve to recite 32 lines of rhyming queer philosophy from memory to him, the Aviances, and Fred. The words flowed from my soul, through my vocal cords and out my lips with the same rhythmic pace they held in my head.

dancing on the finest of lines
delicate with my rhymes
gentle and aggressive is my special delivery
progressive linguistic imagery
artfully intertwines
the cock and the ass
with the heart and the mind
seal it all together with a tender ballsy kiss
back up my philosophy with skilled impassioned fists
limp wrists suit this nasty pig just fine
erect a sect of worship in which
hard and soft combine
with brut affectionate force
both confrontational
and sublime
humble and cocky
graceful and stocky
hairy like a mythic Himalayan beast
smooth like times of peace
this flipping style
i lease from Gods
their mercy keeps my ass in line
blessing me with the wisdom
anal sex is just divine
took me from behind the scenes
laid in me the tools
with which to shine
both hard
and soft
im so much better off

a cock sucking
ass fucking
man of the cloth

"Wow, Miss Lauterstein," Kevin practically whispered, fluttering his dramatic, perfectly applied lashes and shaking his bald head. "The goggles. The garments. The poetry. You just keep coming for me, girl. And here I thought I was just coming over here to ask you queens to make me a dress."

The thought of Kevin, the ringmaster of Sound Factory, wearing a dress by us and telling everyone where he got it, lit up every single one of my entrepreneurial instincts. "Oh my God, Kevin, we'd be honored to make it!"

In typical Fred fashion he loudly and sternly interjected, "Oh we would, would we? Glad I'm included in this decision, being that I'm the one who's going to do most of the work." He wasn't wrong in his assessment of the situation, nor was he delicate in how he handled it. Kevin and I froze, unsure of what would happen next, each hoping the other would break the awkward silence, but fortunately Fred did it for us.

"I'm happy to make a dress for you, Kevin. It would just be nice if my boyfriend asked me before he said yes."

"I'm sorry, Daddy," I said quietly, hoping my cool, subservient vibe would bring the temperature down a bit.

Sensing an opportunity to shift our communal gears, Kevin interjected, "So about this dress, what are y'all thinking?"

I looked at Fred, allowing him the opportunity to express any ideas he might have, but after an ample amount of silence I spoke up, "What are *we* thinking? You just told us you wanted one a second ago, queen. So what are *you* thinking?"

"Well it's gotta be something I can move in. And I definitely want it to be pink. But it's gotta be something major if it's coming from you queens. I wanna wear it and make the girls gag like *oh no she didn't!*"

I had no idea what it was going to look like, but I knew exactly what it needed to be. "Okay, queen, I get it. We're gonna make you an *oh no she didn't* dress."

Kevin put on his oversized green bomber jacket, thanked us, and kissed us both goodbye as he began to head down 22nd St. But before he got too far, he turned to us and said, "If I'm really feeling it, girls, I'll wear it when I debut my new track *'CUN-TY'* at Factory in a few weeks."

"Cunty! Are you kidding me?" I gleefully cheered.

"No, Miss Thing. CUN-TY. Period." With Kevin's help, the Factory children were about to get the Nasty Pig message at a whole new level.

But some of the gay adults living in Chelsea weren't particularly happy about what we had to say.

Forty-One

An envelope was taped to the front door of our little shop. Inside was a handwritten note that read:

> YOU'RE FUCKING GROSS.
> THIS IS NOT WHAT OUR COMMUNITY NEEDS.
> STOP MAKING US LOOK BAD
> AND STOP SPREADING AIDS!!!

I must have read those words a hundred times. Fred read them too, over and over again. We had very different reactions to our first piece of hate mail.

Fred didn't want to be hated at all, especially by people within our own community. I think he had felt enough hate for a lifetime after living through the most vitriolic years of the AIDS crisis. He wanted everything we did to be seen as universally positive. Sometimes I wondered if he'd prefer we fly under the radar and not be seen at all. His fear of negative attention was what led to the "demise" of the M.F.A. in the first place. The very idea of us self-identifying as faggots triggered way too many ugly memories for him, all the way from his formative years right through adulthood. Holding the note in his hands, tears filling his eyes, his lower lip pouting forward, I could see all that trauma and pain coil up inside of him, constricting his heart.

I was enraged. We were two gay men, totally in love, starting our own business, using our creativity to inspire queer people to reconnect with the joy of their authentic sexual selves, after a decade and a half being unfairly shamed for our desires. And yet, someone within our own ranks took it upon themselves to accuse *us* of making *our* community look bad, accusing us of adding to the very plague we were fighting against with sex positivity. It wasn't like I hadn't felt that type of judgment before as I interacted with strangers who walked into our store. For every person who came in to shop and show us love, there were a dozen who showed up just to snicker with their friends and make bitchy comments about our designs. That buyer from Nordstrom might have been the first, but he certainly wasn't the last. I constantly fielded questions like, "does anyone actually wear this stuff?" and "is this a Halloween store?" But things got really pointed when we put out a couple of tee shirts that boldly said "NASTY PIG" across the chest.

That seemed to really touch a nerve. The offhanded comments got more confrontational: "Why would you encourage anyone to identify themselves in such a derogatory way?" . . . "Do you really think we deserve to be treated like a bunch of animals?" I found myself going from defending our designs to defending our way of thinking and living. It seemed like there were plenty of queer people, from our community leaders to the masses following them, who wanted our sexuality to be erased from our identity so the world could forget about what we did in the bedroom. Heteronormativity was considered the goal and our shared ability to blend in was the benchmark by which to judge its progress. But I had seen my fair share of heteronormativity, from its hypocrisy to its misogyny, and those were qualities that felt far from aspirational. No, we would not be hypocrites. We would be honest about our natural desires for intense sexual connection, about our craving for cock and ass. At Nasty Pig, we proudly and literally wore that truth on our sleeves. But those handwritten words that had been left on our front door made it abundantly clear just how strong of a sentiment there was for us to deny our nature as blessed faggots.

Head down, his eyes unable to look into mine, in a broken, wounded tone, Fred expressed himself to me with uncharacteristically simple clarity. "I don't like this, David." He caught me completely off guard. The rage that was ripping through me dissipated. I could see and feel that he had no fight left within him. He was too crushed by that note to do battle. So instead of grinding him further into the ground, something inside me softened. I realized, maybe for the first time, that I didn't need to fight for what I wanted. I needed to fight for my man and help pull him back together. I sat down on the stoop in front of the store, took his hand as he sat down next to me, and put my arm around his shoulder.

"I can see how much this is hurting you, Daddy. I feel it."

"I just don't understand why you want to be so confrontational, David. I hear you in the store and it's like 'ass fucking' this and 'sodomy' that and it's a lot for people. It's a lot for me. I want to be supportive because I know your heart is in the right place, but you're so different from everyone else." Finally, he looked up from the street and stared into my eyes. "You don't see it, Angel, but I do. A lot of people don't get you, and it's like you're oblivious." He wasn't wrong. I was oblivious to other people's opinions of me, but that was because I truly didn't care. Why live my life in service of other people's approval when I wanted to spend whatever time I had on this planet living authentically, fearlessly in pursuit of my dream to make my queer community feel sexy and empowered again?

"Daddy, I want to explain something to you, okay? I know I'm a lot, and I know that I'm different. I've known I was different since I was a kid."

Fred interrupted, "It's not that, David. I knew I was gay when I was a kid too. This is about *you*."

"Daddy, can I finish, please?" I gently asked. He nodded, so I continued. "When I was like 11 or 12 years old, my grandma sat me down in our living room one afternoon and told me we needed to talk about something that was very important. She told me there was a reason my parents pushed me to study a lot and get good grades and be the smartest. That I'd have to work extra hard my entire life and go out into the world being the kindest person possible — and it was all because I was Jewish. She let me know that while our family had a very good life in New York City where we could feel safe, most people in the world hated us just for being who we are, and the reason we were both sitting there together on that couch was because some of my ancestors had settled in The States after fleeing the pogroms in Russia and Austria. Pogroms were like precursors to The Holocaust, Daddy. But not all of them left. Some of them stayed behind, because they thought if they blended in and just acted like everyone else that no one would care. They ended up being killed anyway. She told me I can never, ever hide being Jewish because if people liked me for who I pretended to be then one day they would end up hating me for who I truly am."

"I'm sorry, Angel. I didn't know that about your past. I had no idea."

"It's okay, Daddy. It didn't scar me for life or anything like that. But it stuck with me — that I was always gonna be different and hated just for being me. And in case you haven't noticed, I'm not just Jewish, I'm also like really, really, really gay."

"Oh, I've *really* noticed, David," he said with a smile.

"I guess what I'm trying to explain is that I'm not going around saying things for shock value. I'm being brutally honest about who I am. Who we are. This is our truth, and within the truth of our existence lies its beauty. That's what I want Nasty Pig to be all about. This mixture of art and activism and truth. And it's all in service of making queer people feel amazing about who we are and getting straight people comfortable with what we do when we're naked. It's not always gonna be pretty, but it's always gonna be honest."

I took a deep breath and laid my cards on the table. "I don't want to do this without you, Daddy. But if you can't be brutally honest like me, then you have to be comfortable with my brutal honesty about myself. I'm done hiding."

Fred laced his fingers in mine and nodded. I wondered if that meant he was done hiding too.

Forty-Two

Keeping up with our little line became more and more challenging as word about us began to really spread around the city. *HX* magazine ran a feature on the store and traffic surged overnight. Our racks were getting depleted quicker than we could replenish them, so Fred reached out to a seamstress named Mary who he knew through his day job, and we began feeding her piece work to keep up with the demand. But even with the extra help, Daddy and I were getting stretched thin.

Things were a bit easier for me as my workload at Sonic Assembly had slowed down tremendously and there wasn't much for me to do. When there was nothing on my plate Paul told me I could use my Mac to work on designs, and I began pumping out graphics that I'd print out onto transfer paper and iron onto baby ringer tees to hang from our racks. I was heavily influenced by the guys from GFS and the entire streetwear scene, and I loved the way the medium allowed me to visually comment on queer culture in ways only we could understand.

But while I was having fun with my work, Fred was miserable with his. He hated his boss, he hated his coworkers, and after being moved into the quality control department at his company, he hated his job as well. He went from doing something he enjoyed, quietly making patterns by himself, to spending eight hours a day in various factories in Chinatown measuring garments and arguing with the sewers when they made things incorrectly.

One Wednesday night, after a particularly strong evening of sales at the store, I closed up shop at 9 p.m. and walked home. Fifteen minutes later, Fred came through the door, dropped onto the couch next to me, and sobbed into my shoulder.

"Baby, what's going on?" I had to ask him a few times before he could pull himself together to get a few words out.

"I can't do this anymore, David. I can't keep working at this fucking job for this miserable bitch then come home and be creative or even sew anything. I look at the store and the racks look sad and I don't even have the time to feed enough work to Mary. And I feel like I'm letting you down, Angel. That's the worst." He put his head in my lap as if to block out the world and returned to his tears. I hated seeing Fred so distraught. I knew the work he was doing was crushing both his creativity and his soul, and I needed both those things intact for our relationship, let alone our business, to thrive.

Before I could think twice, I gave sound to the first idea that came into my head. "Just quit, Daddy. Make Nasty Pig your full-time job."

His crying stopped and he picked his head up to look at me and gauge my seriousness. "I can't quit my job, Angel. I love you for saying that, but I can't do that to us."

"Yeah, you actually can. You're not doing anything to us. You'd be doing it for us. Business has picked up and we keep missing sales because of all the sizes we *don't* have. It's like we're losing our opportunity to grow almost every day."

"But can we actually afford it?" He asked, posing a very valid question, one for which my brain didn't have answer. I led with love and let my heart do the talking. "I dunno, Daddy, but we'll make it work somehow." I reached over to the coffee table and picked up the phone and handed it to him. "Just do it right now, before I change my mind!" So he did it. He called his boss and left a message on her machine informing her that he couldn't come in the following day or any day thereafter. The entire time he looked at me with his gorgeous eyes. They appeared to be filled with happiness, but his smile didn't match. It never matched. It felt genuine and dishonest at the same time. I knew it was hiding something, and since I had just agreed to support him as our business continued to find its footing, I felt like I could finally just ask him: "Daddy, why don't you ever really smile at me. Are you just never all that happy? I don't get it."

He took a deep breath. Then he took another. And another. I did my best to prepare myself for some god-awful story from his childhood that scarred him so badly he could never fully smile again. Maybe he was beaten when he showed too much happiness, or his drug-addicted dad just sucked a lifetime's worth of joy out of his system. But after a few more deep breaths, he took hold of his thick upper lip and pulled it upwards. "My teeth are disgusting. I'm so embarrassed, Angel. I don't let anyone see them, ever. I hate my smile so much."

He then went on to explain to me that after breaking up with one of his ex-boyfriends, he packed his stuff and got in his car and drove away. There was a snowstorm that night, and he lost control of his car. He hit the guardrail and went right through the windshield, knocking out all of his front teeth and a few of the back ones. His dentist at the time did the best he could with what little was left, using a combination of bridges and crowns and poorly made implants. But the work was coming undone. The enamel was wearing away, revealing the hodgepodge of materials and techniques that were used to put Fred's mouth back together again, and I understood why he had trained his facial muscles to never let it all be seen with a fully formed, unbridled smile. I kissed him until he kissed me back. "You're the most handsome man in the world to me, Daddy." I took the phone from his lap, called the answering machine at Sonic Assembly, and left a message for Paul that I needed to take the following day off. "Let's go out and celebrate, Daddy. You're free! I'm gonna go douche and get ready. You're a full-time Nasty Pig employee now!"

He smiled at me, still without showing any teeth, but more genuinely nonetheless. "So how exactly does celebrating my freedom end up being about you getting fucked in the ass?"

I smiled back at him, ear to ear, and replied, "Shouldn't everything end up about me being fucked in the ass?"

* * *

Pork had gotten steadily more crowded over the months since it started. Its rise in popularity coincided perfectly with ours, and more and more people would show up wearing our re:vision gear and Nasty Pig graphic tees. It was incredible to see, and it never got old. I'd go up to every single guy wearing our stuff and thank them. They all remembered me from the shop, and I did my best to do the same, but between my horrible case of face-blindness and our growing fan base, it became more and more difficult to keep up. But I spotted Joel and Joe and Doug from across the bar, as they were impossible to forget. I grabbed Fred by the hand and led him over to the three of them so I could flaunt our matte rubber chaps and shake my furry bare ass in their faces. After some very passionate kissing, groping, and fingering, Joe finally took notice of what I was wearing from the waist down. He asked me about them, and once I explained that they were off the rack, machine washable, and cost $125 dollars, he said to me, "You know what? You guys should get a booth at IML."

"What's IML?" I asked.

Joe went on to explain to me that IML stood for International Mr. Leather. It was some sort of contest for Leathermen, where they would dress up and show off their gear, talk about the community, and get judged to determine the winner. “It sounds like a beauty pageant to me,” I said half-jokingly.

He laughed and replied, “Oh, it’s definitely a beauty pageant.” He then went on to explain its origins and history, and how it held together the community during the darkest years of the AIDS crisis. I was very intrigued, but I still didn’t understand how our little brand fit into any of it until he talked about what went on at the hotel where IML was hosted. People from all over the world showed up for the event and booked rooms at a place called The Congress Hotel, which Joe described as “haunted.” While the contest itself took place on the Sunday night, the entire weekend became this massive gathering for kinky guys looking to socialize, party, fuck, and shop the vendor market set up in the hotel ballroom. The market was a place for businesses that catered to the kink community to sell directly to customers. Now that *really* intrigued me.

“You think they’d like what we do? Stuff like this?’ I asked Joe as I moved his hand to the back of my leg.

He took a moment to reply. “Honestly, David, a lot of them won’t. A lot of rule breakers don’t like it when their rules are broken. But you’ve definitely tapped into something new, and we could use some new blood in the scene after so much of our blood has been spilled.” He looked around pensively. “That’s why I love coming here. You kids are doing something new.” He moved his hand from my leg to my ass and said, “And even if they hate what you sell, they will definitely love this.”

I was sold. I relayed all this information to Fred and told him we were going. He went through his usual process of pointing out all the unknowns, including what it would cost, how we would make the inventory, and whether or not the event would even want us there. I went through my usual process of apologizing and backpedaling as he took down my excitement with the pesky details of reality. I pivoted. “How bout I get us a couple of beers, Daddy.”

Paul was working, and he gave us the beers on the house. I left the $10 bill I was going to pay him with on the bar as a tip, but he slid it back to me. “Just let me take that big Daddy dick attached to your man again.”

I slid the money back to him. “How about you take both?” *Keep the energy circulating,* I thought to myself.

“Deal, you hot fucker.” He stuffed the ten into his jock and asked me, “So what have you been up to, you sexy talented boy?”

“You know, conquering the world, making my dreams come true. Oh, and Daddy quit his job tonight to go full time with Nasty Pig. And I wanna go to this thing called IML that Joe just told me about. And I need to find a dentist and a big pile of money, too."

Paul served up three shots of tequila, each with a lime wedge, and said "Here's to the full-time Nasty Pig Daddy!"

"Don't we get any salt with that?" Fred asked.

"Yeah, just lick my sweaty butt cheek." Paul hoisted his big meaty ass onto the bar and me and Daddy did just that. The three of us downed our shots and Paul continued, "You guys should definitely have a booth at IML. Me and Phil are going again so we can show you the ropes. The four of us fuckers would have so much fun." Paul was such a troublemaker. We got along famously, and it didn't bother me one bit that Fred had a big ol' crush on him.

"I'm thinking maybe IML might not be such a bad idea after all," Fred said to me, staring hungrily at Paul's massive, hairy ass as he went to help another customer. I snapped my fingers in front of Fred's face to get his attention and we both had a good laugh. He picked up his beer and said, "I'm going to take a piss. Try to be here when I get back, please."

"Yes, Daddy." Paul returned and poured us a second round of shots. "When I first told Daddy about IML he wasn't into it, but your ass *literally* changed his mind," I said to Paul. "Now, if you can find me a dentist and a pile of money you'll be three for three tonight."

"I can't help you with the money, but me and Daddy Phil go to this sexy little fucker down in the West Village, Dr. Montrose." Paul reached over the bar and grabbed me by the back of my head, pulling my ear close to his lips to whisper, "Don't say anything, but he's a secret fisting bottom pig boy. He doesn't tell anyone because he's afraid of how it would look to his patients if they found out." He switched his accent to an absurdly incorrect attempt at sounding British. "She fancies 'erself a respectable lady."

"Well then how do you know? Does he come in here?"

Sticking with the British accent he replied, "Oh 'eavens no! She's much too respectable to go out to the pubs and the clubs."

"Well then how?" I pressed him.

Switching back to his deep, sexy voice he replied, "Well, she may be too respectable for The Lure but every couple of months Daddy has him over and he disrespects that pig boy dentist ass all night long. But don't tell anyone, you little fucker, or Daddy will kill me, okay? You promise?"

"Oh, I promise," I replied, grinning from cheek to cheek.

"Ok, fucker. Ugh, I can't believe I just opened my big fucking mouth.

Oh well, *c'est la vie,*" he said as he innocently shrugged it off with his broad shoulders. He opened a Corona and put it down in front of me. "Now about that pile of money you need . . . "

I cut him off. "Gracias, guapo, but I don't think I'm gonna need it anymore."

* * *

I sat in the busy waiting room reading a copy of *Time*, wearing my black leather motorcycle jacket over a simple white tank top, matching black leather motorcycle boots, and a thick metal cock ring beneath a skintight pair of 501s with a red hanky placed conspicuously in the back left pocket. It was a good 30 minutes before my name was called. "Mr. Lauterstein?" A woman in a light blue set of scrubs announced. I stood up and she noticeably did a double take. I didn't blend in with the elderly ladies and preppy professional types that surrounded me, just as I had hoped for. "The doctor will see you now. Please follow me." She walked me back and led me to a room at the end of the hall. "Have a seat and the doctor will be in shortly." But I didn't have a seat. I walked to the far end of the room, past the dental chair to the window, and gazed out onto the street. I didn't give a fuck about the scenery. I just wanted to make sure Dr. Montrose saw me from behind when he walked in. About a minute later I heard the door open. I didn't turn around though. I gave the good doctor a minute to take it all in. I could feel his eyes all over me.

"Hello Mr. Lauterstein, I'm Doctor Montrose."

I turned around slowly, aiming my pretty green eyes directly into his brown ones, and said "Nice to meet you, doctor. Thank you for seeing me." He was a hot fucker, just like Paul said, and I served him up my very best devilish grin. I loved watching as he struggled not to cruise me right back. He was so tightly wound, working overtime to keep his composure. He fumbled with my chart, looking downward as he flipped through the pages, all in an attempt to check out my dick unnoticed. It was adorable watching him fail. He was too flustered to remember to ask me to be seated, so I took it upon myself to come up next to his chair. I felt myself taking control from him. I knew he wanted to submit, but everything within his environment was designed for him to be in charge. We were on his turf and that made everything even hotter. Sensing an opening to further exert my dominance, I took off my jacket and handed it to him. "Would you mind hanging that up for me, doctor?" I asked.

"Um, no, not at all. Why don't you have a seat, Mr. Lauterstein." He dropped my jacket the first time he went to hang it, then he bent over to pick it back up off the floor. It definitely wasn't intentional, but he ended up bent over in front of me nonetheless. He got it right the second time and apologized for his clumsiness.

"Don't worry about it, doctor. I enjoyed the view. And please call me David." I sat down in his chair and he sat down right next to me.

"Okay, David. Looks like you're a new patient."

"That's correct." I was so turned on by the tension and the need for formality. I soaked up all the power I was owning, and it rushed right to my dick, which had gotten visibly erect in my jeans. He tried so hard not to stare at it. He was squirming in his seat. I couldn't believe it, but I loved being a dominant top.

He cleared his throat. "So, what brings you in here, David. Are you having any issues I should know about?"

"Nope. Just wanted to come see you, doctor."

"Okay, well according to your chart you just had a cleaning last month so you're not due for another until the fall. I'm happy to examine you and give you a cleaning, but I don't want to take advantage of you David. Do you want to rebook this appointment with my receptionist?"

"It's okay to look at my cock, doctor," I said with all the confidence in the world.

He didn't say anything back. He froze. Then slowly, very slowly, he peered up from my chart and gave in to his desire to just fucking stare at it. I began to massage it through my jeans, squeezing it and stroking it for him. His lips parted, barely, and I knew I was in his head. I was also in his pants. His dick was as hard as mine.

"Dr. Montrose, may I call you Anthony?"

"Okay."

"I've got a problem, Anthony, and I'm hoping you can help me out. I've got a boyfriend and I love him very much. But he never smiles, and that makes me so sad." I kept stroking away at my cock, working up my precum. The denim by the slit of my dick started to turn a darker shade of blue. "Turns out he was in a pretty bad car accident a few years back, and his dentist at the time did his best to fix things up, but he didn't do such a great job, so now my man is embarrassed to smile. I want to see him smile again, Anthony. Don't you think that's fucking sweet?"

He was sweating, nervous, and leaking precum just like me. He didn't take his eyes off my cock. "Very fucking sweet," he said under his breath.

"Here's my problem, Anthony. My man and I just started our own business and money's really tight. I would imagine you can relate, Anthony. I'm sure things were tight when you first opened your practice."

"Yeah, I get it. I can relate."

"Good," I nodded. "I guess we have more than one thing in common then."

"We do?" he asked as drool literally fell from his lips and hit the floor before he had the chance to suck it back in.

"Yes, Anthony, we most certainly do. Both of us are business owners, and both of us want me to fist your ass for hours and hours and hours." I put my finger beneath his chin and lifted his gaze to meet mine. "I'll be on call for you, Anthony. You just tell me when you want it, where you want it, and I'll be there with fucking bells on. It'll be our little secret. No one's gonna know, I promise. All I ask in return is that you give my man his smile back."

I booked Fred an appointment with the receptionist at the front desk then walked straight to Jeff and Javier's place. Fortunately, they were home. "I need you to teach me how to be a fisting top, Javier." I explained what I had done, much to their delight, and Javier gave me a crash course in how to fist along with a softcover copy of *Trust: The Handbook: A Guide to the Sensual and Spiritual Art of Handballing*. As I put on my jacket to head back to our apartment, Javier took me by the shoulders authoritatively and said, "David, you must tell Fred everything, darling, everything. As soon as you see him. Do not keep any of this from him or your secrets will rot in his mouth." His words made perfect sense to me.

When I got home, I sat Fred down next to me on the bed and told him he was getting a brand new set of teeth from a dentist named Dr. Montrose, and then I told him honestly how I was going to make that happen. He objected repeatedly, but each of his objections were met by my insistence. There was simply no world in which my Daddy wasn't going to smile. No way. Not on my watch. I handed him the appointment card, got up, and went into the kitchen to make him some dinner.

Over the next few months Dr. Montrose drilled away at Daddy's mouth until he got his smile back. I became a fisting top, drilling away at the good dentist's cavity until he, not I, determined my debt had been settled.

Forty-Three

"Oh my God, you're Frankie Knuckles, right?" I didn't have to ask. I knew it was him, and he was standing right there in front of me in our store. Me and the Godfather of House face to face. It felt unreal. Like most New Yorkers, I was unbothered by celebrities. I had passed plenty of them on the streets of Manhattan and didn't look twice. But Frankie Knuckles wasn't a celebrity. He was royalty.

"Yes, that's me" he replied with a beautiful, gentle smile that lit up his face and then mine. He radiated warmth and humility and I felt myself lifted by his very presence. "I'm your neighbor."

"Wow. You're my neighbor, and you're here in my store? Holy fuck . . . Frankie Knuckles!" I was dumbfounded by the moment. I didn't know what else to say. Thankfully, Frankie did.

"And you are?"

"Oh, I'm a designer, along with my boyfriend. This is our line."

"I was hoping to get your name," he said in the most gentle, disarming manner. Like most New Yorkers I was used to defining myself by what I did. Leave it to Frankie Knuckles to humanize me in person, just as he had done with his music for so many years.

"Oh, I'm sorry. I'm David. David Lauterstein. And I'm like a *huge* fan. *Huge*. "'Tears' is one of my all-time favorite songs!"

"Okay, David," he said as he nodded his head at me. "I'm impressed. Most people around here know me for 'The Whistle Song,' but it sounds like you know your records."

"I love that song, too! Don't get me wrong. I love everything you do. I mean you're Frankie Knuckles! You invented house music."

"People like to say that, but I had a lot of help from all the artists who came before me. All those great records, there'd be no house without them."

"Yeah, I love when I'm dancing to one of your sets at and I hear samples of the old disco and funk records my Dad used to play. Brings me back to dancing with my sister in the living room. I still can't believe you're here."

"In the flesh." He was so soft, so human.

"Welcome to my little store. Here . . . please take this." I took one of the necklaces Fred had made off the wall and handed it to him. "It's a gift. You've moved me on so many occasions. So this is our energy, in return."

"Thank you, David. That's very kind of you. What's re:vision all about?" I told him about Fred and our dreams and our vision for queer culture. I asked him about his experiences, hungry to learn anything I could about our history from one of my elders. There were so few around, and there was only one Frankie Knuckles. We talked for almost an hour. It was surreal and yet so real at the same time. The Godfather, wearing our work, talking to me about house music. I felt like the most blessed queen in the world.

"Well, David, I have to go, but it's been a pleasure to meet you, neighbor."

"Oh my God Frankie, the pleasure was all mine. For real. Can I give you a hug."

"You sure can." I hugged that man so hard and for so long. "Listen, I'm throwing a party on the fourteenth at my apartment. I'd love for you to stop by if you're interested."

"That all depends on who's DJ'ing," I said, throwing out a little bit of the David sass. He had a good laugh over that. I handed him a business card and a pen, and he wrote out his address along with the date and the time of the gathering. Then he left, and for the rest of the day, after having met the Godfather of House himself, I could barely function. I almost couldn't fall asleep that night. My alarm clock went off at five the next morning. I practically climbed on top of Fred. "Wake up, Daddy. It's time to go to Factory. Today's the day!"

* * *

Factory was still packed when we got there at 6:45 a.m. It was one of those mornings when Junior was so on fire that no one was leaving. The scene on the floor was pure, chaotic, and gorgeous. People were throwing down and hollering in the best possible way. Fred and I dropped a pill and dove right into the madness. Junior was delivering one banger after another, sometimes two at a time, sometimes three. The loops and the layers got stacked and called back to each other in a synthesized symphony of breakbeats and samples. The speaker stacks shook the room. It was furious. Mind bending. Junior had us under his spell — all of us — united in rhythm under one roof. He built up the energy, higher and higher, and we on the floor just went up and up with him. With my pill washing over my brainwaves, I felt like I was being sonically edged. The floor was on the verge of Junior's tribalistic orgasm, and just as he was ready to make us all cum together in one massive release of orgiastic energy, he fully cut the music and the lights, leaving us in a darkened void of silence. We *screamed* like an unruly mob with Saturn-sized blue balls and no beat in which to unload our surging endorphins. In a combination of agony, ecstasy, and protest, we stomped our feet together in a four on the floor revolt. We could see his silhouette in the DJ booth, faintly backlit by the only light left on in the whole fucking club. Faced with our raucousness, he remained still and unmoved. He wasn't budging and neither were we. With each passing minute it seemed as if he was content to be locked in a brutal standoff with his devout cult of followers for the rest of the day. But then the light behind him turned red and we erupted in wild anticipation as we watched him pull a record from his massive collection and place it on one of the three turntables he used to make us insane. The needle hit the vinyl and every speaker in the house boomed with Kevin's voice: "*CUN-TY. CUN-TY. CUN-TY.*"

Kevin materialized on the elevated runway wearing his bubblegum pink, one-of-a-kind, custom *Oh No She Didn't* dress. It was skintight, showing off all his gorgeous muscles, and the open back was laced like a corset but scooped out so low it revealed the top half of his ass. Every single human being packed into Factory went wild, and Fred and I stood together in the center of it all, hand in hand, our lives united, and drowned ourselves in their overflowing excitement at what we had created.

About an hour after his performance, we found Kevin in the lounge hanging out with Cesar and Howie and the rest of his crew. "This dress gave me mother fucking *life* tonight!" he shouted at us as we approached. "You girls turned me out. Talk about feeling CUN-TY." Kevin took Fred's hands into his own and said to him, "The children are *gagging* on the gown, Miss Fred. Thank you, queen." He then turned to me and said, "And yes, Miss Lauterstein, I tell them it's from your shop on 22nd Street."

"I'm just happy you like it, Kevin," I said.

He turned back to Fred and said, "Who does she think she's fooling, little miss businessman over there lookin' at me like a billboard. Girl, you have a money manifesting voodoo doll hanging over your head at the store," he said to me. "So don't even try it with that happy queen bullshit."

He wasn't wrong, and so I replied, "What can I say, girl? I don't have an advertising budget, so you it!" I spotted Javier and Jeff and waved them over to hang with us while Fred passed our bumper around the group and

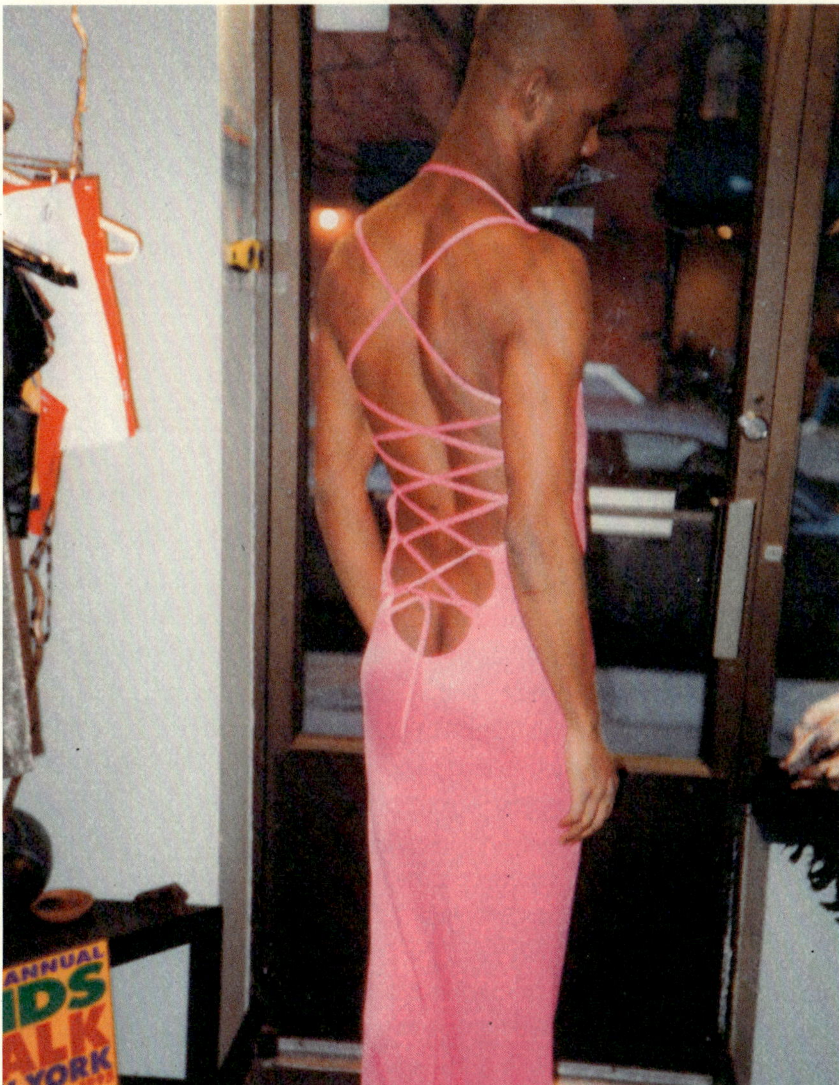
ANNUAL
YORK

powdered everyone's noses. I looked around at the crew of friends I had made on my own, independently of Fred, and realized they were kind of like my chosen nightlife family of freaky queer artists and hookers. I quietly, joyously said to myself, "The House of Nasty Pig."

Junior must have cued up a song for Kevin's follow up performance, so he grabbed Cesar and said, "C'mon queen, we gotta get to the stage like now. Thank you again for the dress, girls. Let's continue the carry after Miss Vasquez is done with me."

Cesar interjected, "And let's kiki up in the loft after this place closes. Y'all wanna come over?"

I was about to say yes for both because I wasn't about to miss the chance to hang with the artist collective that made Sound Factory happen, but I looked at Fred and said, "I'm so into it, Daddy, if you are."

"I am too."

"Okay, it's a total yes for me and Fred."

"Jeff and I shall join as well," Javier added.

* * *

Junior played his last record at 2:45 p.m., and we all met up outside Factory, sunglasses on to shield our dilated pupils from the afternoon brightness. Cesar brought us to a manual freight elevator right next door to the club and we piled in. He closed the gate, pulled a large industrial lever, and I watched the bricks and the windows of the shaft pass by as we ascended to the sixth floor of the building. It all felt so gritty and distinctively New York. "Sixth floor. Ladies' lingerie, cosmetics, faggotry, and favors. Everybody off," Cesar said as he pulled back the gate and unloaded us all.

The loft was massive, taking up the entire floor above Factory, and I immediately knew it was originally built for commercial purposes. Large windows flanked both the north and the south sides of the space, a necessary feature for workers to get as much natural light as possible while keeping electric costs down. The wood floors were well worn by decades of industrial use which only added character to the space. The floor vibrated to a pulsating bassline. "Sounds like Miss Junior is giving the stragglers one more track," Cesar told us.

"Wait, you can feel the Factory all the way up here," I asked him.

"Girl, we feel the Factory everywhere in this place."

I had only been there a minute and already I did too. Turned out Sound Factory, shaking our energies from six stories beneath our bodies, had plans for us that afternoon. She didn't gather us up for a kiki. Something else happened. Something important and genuinely major. She had us come together to realize we were all creatively united in our passion to reclaim our existence from the omnipresent horror of the human immunodeficiency virus, relentless in its quest to define every square inch of our identities with its incessant darkness. It wanted to take all our spaces, public and private. It wanted us in totality, infecting our dreams and fantasies with its very real nightmarish vengeance. It wanted to murder us, decimating our glory for its pathological success. It had broken our connection to our queer ancestors. It had broken the freedom of our sexual revolution. It had broken our collective heart into countless bloody pieces then it built up psychic walls in our individual minds to ensure those pieces remained separated and alone, unable to ever truly heal. It wanted to make us subservient and secretive and shameful and sick.

And we were so fucking over it. We wanted to slap the dying shit out of AIDS, tell it to fuck all the way off, and take back what was rightfully ours: our unique, glorious, shining queer identity. We didn't want to blend in and fade away. We weren't interested in being tolerated or accepted. We wanted to be respected and celebrated as a necessary part of the fabric of humanity. We wanted to be exalted for our differences and claim our rightful place in society. And most of all, we wanted to harness all the energy being channeled through that building — from the top floor loft down to the basement that housed the legendary Sound Factory — through our shared creativity and spark a cultural queer revolution. We knew we were early to the fight, and we knew it would be measured in decades, not years. We accepted we wouldn't be the true beneficiaries of our efforts. We weren't in it for ourselves. We were showing up to battle for our future queer descendants. "Doing the Lord's work," is what Jeff and I called it. The lords that governed my soul were the Sodomy Gods, and I was dancing, creating, working, fucking, and living in their name.

Forty-Four

Our application to show our line at IML was approved, barely. I had spoken with a gentleman by the name of RJ, the coordinator for the vendor market, and he said all the booth spaces were booked up. He took my number and told me he would contact me for the following year. I didn't want to wait, so I turned on the charm and did some begging. "C'mon RJ. Can't you do anything for me this year? I don't need much room. Just one tiny, little booth somewhere. *Please?!* I promise everyone there will love us! And if they don't, I'll give away blow jobs instead." He was amused by the David show. The following day he called to get my credit card number and the address where he could send the paperwork for our 8'x10' space, 16 square feet more than I had in the city.

"I have to be honest with you, David. Your booth is gonna be in an offshoot room on a separate floor from the main vendor area. It's not a great location, but it's the best I can do," he told me.

"You're best is better than anything I hoped for. Thank you *so* much for making this happen for us. I'm super excited for my first IML!"

"I'm excited for you to attend. Honestly, we need some new vendors to shake things up, but don't tell anyone I said that. You ready with a credit card for me to reserve the space?"

"I sure am."

"Okay, what's the name on the card."

"David Lauterstein. And the company name is Nasty Pig."

"That's such a great name for a company. I think the attendees will love it."

* * *

We had no idea what to expect from IML, but with our limited manufacturing capabilities we decided to focus on a tight collection of five styles and bring a few dozen of each. Four of the styles would come in our machine washable matte rubber. The fifth style would be a graphic tee featuring four humping pigs on the front left chest and a mock can of Nasty Pig ham on the back. Even though we had been selling our line under the name re:vision in New York City, I decided our corporate name would be better suited for the customer base at IML. I printed custom labels and hang tags with our new

Nasty Pig branding made especially for this run of products.

We contracted Mary to do all the sewing and Fred and I painstakingly applied all the hardware ourselves. My decision to bring us to IML was great in theory, but in practice it meant a shit ton of work that mostly fell upon Fred's shoulders. It also meant that our energies were being pulled away from the store and the racks were visibly suffering. On a regular basis Fred would say, "This better be worth it, David." Things escalated from there, and in the ceaseless tension of it all, Eddie packed his things and moved out. With him gone, I had the bright idea of pushing the couches together in the living room and laying a 4'x8' sheet of plywood across them to serve as a makeshift cutting table for fabric. I thought it would help speed things up with production, but it just made our apartment a mess. One night I came home from the store to find Fred holding his head, slumped over the plywood in a pile of pattern paper and fabric scraps. "I can't do it anymore, David. It's too much for me."

"The table isn't working?" I asked.

He looked up at me. "I know you're trying, David, but I don't need a cut table. I need your help." Between my nine-to-five with Sonic Assembly and running the store on nights and weekends, help was something I couldn't give him. There weren't enough hours in the day. I had no time left. So I did what any sensible person with mounting expenses and a precarious household income would do. I called Sonic Assembly, left a message for Paul that I was quitting my job, and doubled down on what mattered the most: making Fred and my dreams come true. After I hung up the phone, I fully expected Fred to freak out and insist I call back so we'd have at least one steady source of income. But Fred just put his arms around me and quietly thanked me. "I love you so much, Angel. We're going to make this work."

"Daddy, I need to go to Pork and get us some drinks before I realize what I just did and change my mind."

"You're not going to change your mind, Angel. This is what you always do. You go for what you want and you just figure it out when you get there. It's one of the things I admire so much about you." Fred wasn't generous with compliments, so when he gave one to me it really counted.

"That means a lot to me, Daddy." We kissed each other, two artists versus the world. "Let's go out and celebrate being full time Nasty Pigs. I know exactly what I wanna wear." I pulled out my big rubber chemical clean-up boots. "Time to break these bad boys in!"

* * *

After showering and cleaning out, I began the process of building out a look around the boots. My instinct was to wear them with nothing but one of my jocks, so I tried each of them on in front of the mirror. Something wasn't quite perfect, though. I was very particular about my proportions. So I tried on a matte rubber codpiece Fred had designed that made my ass look so round. I added a leather harness and an armband and topped it off with a GFS cap. Queer superhero meets streetwear had become my signature style, and my look was delivering big time. My outfit wasn't exactly street legal, though, so I grabbed a pair of baggy jeans to wear for the walk downtown. I took off my boots, put the jeans on over the codpiece, then put the boots back on. But just as I went to button up my fly, I noticed something interesting. My jeans were standing up on their own, slumped down against the tops of my boots. My ass was almost fully exposed from the back, as was the codpiece from the front. I went to the mirror to get a look at what was happening — and *goddamn* did I look sexy as all hell. It appeared as if my jeans were about to fall off, and mixed with my leather and my baseball cap, I had found the perfect balance of b-boy swag meets power bottom presenting for the world. There was something fantastically disheveled and equally put together about what I was serving. Best of all, I had never seen anyone wearing anything remotely like it. Fred sized me up and down and said, "That looks really interesting." Interesting was a good thing for Fred, and I earned my *second* compliment that night. Being full time Nasty Pig employees seemed to be making things between us better already.

As soon as we walked into Pork, I took my shirt off, tucked it into my belt loop, unbuttoned my pants, and let them drop. With my jeans hovering around my thighs and my fuzzy butt on full display, I couldn't help but put a little runway in my walk. Paul saw me coming and couldn't help but clock me for it. "Category is: Supermodel with back hair. Show 'em how it's done, hermanita!" But once I got up close to him he switched gears. "Wait a minute. What are you wearing, fucker?"

"You know . . . this," I casually replied.

He nodded in approval. "You win for best dressed tonight, you hot little fucker." I looked around the bar and he wasn't wrong. I told him the good news about me quitting my job, and he poured us a round of tequila shots, complete with his signature salt lick, and we raised our glasses in a toast to Nasty Pig.

I made my way through the crowd slowly, feeling other bodies pressed against my own, covered in sweat, smelling like leather and armpits. Strangers groped at me. Sometimes I stopped to grope them back. Sometimes we kissed, then moved on with our lusts. It was intoxicating for me. So simple. So natural. So intrinsic to my being. I felt genuinely high on the speedball of endorphins, testosterone, and pheromones. Suddenly I was jolted from my glorious delirium by the stinging smack of a hand making contact with one of my ass cheeks. "What the fuck?!" I exclaimed as I twisted my body around.

"Did I hurt you, wild beast?" It was Manfred again, and instantly the skin on my ass stopped stinging in pain. The sensation shifted to a combination of heat and intensity, my nerve endings firing, alive and ready for more. I felt myself blushing, my face reddening to match the handprint he had certainly left on my ass.

"I'm sorry. Do I know you, sir?" I asked nonchalantly, doing my best to contain my excitement, knowing full well he could see it all over my face anyway.

"Let me remind you again. Turn around." I did, and he reminded me so fucking hard on my other ass cheek. I then heard him ask me, "What is this you are wearing, beast? Turn for me. Let me see you." I did as he said, again, and his eyes moved over my body with careful focus. He grabbed at the waist of my jeans and picked them up. He let them drop. He ran his hand over the fold I had placed near the top of each of my boots, exposing its neutrally colored underside, contrasting the dark industrial shade of green of the rubber. "Beast! *This* is style, an original look. *Fantastique!* Is this from your collection?"

"Well, not the boots . . . or the jeans . . . or the hat. But the rest is ours."

"Are you here with that Daddy of yours?"

"Yes, of course. He's over by the bar. Can I go get him and bring him over?"

He looked me up and down once again. *He was admiring me.* "Nah, beast. Best if I follow you so I can enjoy you from behind." I led Manfred through the crowd, looking behind me way more than necessary to ensure he hadn't disappeared. It was all so insane, an audience with my idol. I would have asked him to pinch me had it not been for the throbbing sensation his thick, French hand had inflicted on my ass, already letting me know I definitely wasn't dreaming. I saw Fred waiting for me by the bar, looking a bit pinched due to the length of my absence. But once he saw me with Manfred, the anger lifted from his face.

We spent the night together, the three of us at the bar, and casually talked as if everything was normal. We just *hung out* until about 3 a.m., when he had to leave. *He* thanked *us* for our company. *He* thanked *us* I thought to myself. I grabbed my wallet from my jeans and pulled out a business card. "I know you must be so busy all the time, but if you're ever in Chelsea, I'd love it if you'd stop by our store and let me show you our line."

He took the card from my hand, held it up to his face, then tucked it into my codpiece. "Keep it, wild beast. I still have the napkin you gave me last time."

The Sodomy Gods had sent me yet another sign and I thanked them for continuing to show me I had their approval. Fred and I finished our beers, said goodbye to Paul, and made our way north towards Chelsea. It didn't matter that neither of us would be getting a regular paycheck anymore or that our bank accounts were practically empty. We were flying without a safety net, but at least we were flying. I took his hand in mine, wings intertwined, and we soared home together.

We were two full-time Nasty Pigs — with nothing left to hold us up and nothing left to hold us down.

* * *

It was one of those hot and humid New York City afternoons with so much moisture in the air you kind of had to swim through it. We couldn't afford an air conditioner for the store, so on days like that I would sit on the sidewalk next to the front door swigging a two-liter bottle of Diet Coke. We couldn't afford a mannequin either, so I served as one with my carefully curated looks. I had become a bit of a fixture on 22nd Street, and I did my best to put on a good show for the public. On that particular afternoon, I was wearing a highlighter-yellow rubber tank top with electric green insets, and a pair of matching booty shorts with a reverse applique NASTYPIG sewn straight across the ass.

With my soda bottle empty and my bladder full, I stood up, locked the door, and walked around the corner to the Big Cup to take a leak. The kids that worked there had all become fans, and I gave them hefty discounts for letting me use their bathroom and for rocking our gear while working at the queer social hub of the city. On my way back to the store, I reupped on my Diet Coke at the deli, and as I unlocked the front door, I heard someone call

out at me: "Nasty Pig! There you are my wild beast."

It was Manfred. With a smile on his face and my napkin in his hand, he crossed the street, walking toward me, and my heart thumped in my chest like a booming kick drum layered with a sub-bass beneath it. I was stunned, exhilarated, terrified. The master himself had arrived and he caught me completely off guard. I had dreamed of him stopping by the store, but I never took the time to think about what that might be like. "I can't believe you're here," I said.

"I needed something new to wear and Barneys has gotten a bit blasé." He glanced over my shoulder and into the store. "Aren't you going to invite me into your *atelier?*"

"Of course! Welcome," I said as I opened the door for him. "It's not Barneys, but it's ours."

He stepped inside and I followed, trembling as he meticulously fingered through every single garment on our well-stocked racks. I was extra grateful that I had quit Sonic Assembly and devoted all my time to our line. "You don't want to be Barneys, beast. Trust me." He went back in for a second pass, pulling out a pair of rubber racing pants, a matching racing vest, and a sleeveless white supplex shirt, turning each piece inside out to examine our finishing skills. "I will try these." He handed them to me, and I hung his choices in the tiny dressing room. He went inside, closed the curtain behind him, and I stopped breathing as the greatest designer alive took off his own clothing and stepped into ours.

"Yeah, I like these." He pulled open the curtain and took a couple steps back to get a better view of himself in the mirror. "This is Fred's design?"

"They're all Fred's designs, except the graphic tees. Those are mine. But Fred's the talented one. He makes all the patterns too."

Manfred ran his hands over the seams as his gaze switched back and forth between the mirror and his legs. "The construction is fantastic. Very complex. Please tell Fred I'm impressed with his work." I was doing my best to keep it together. He tried on the other pants and the shirt quietly, giving each garment the same level of scrutiny. "I will take all three, wild beast. You'll need to do the following for me." He began rattling off the adjustments he required: a half-inch off the sweep of the shirt, a quarter-inch off the back of the knee of the racing pants, and so on. I scrambled to write down every one of his requirements. Fred and I had a house rule that we didn't customize our clothing for customers, but Manfred wasn't a customer. He was Mugler.

He changed back into the clothes he'd arrived in, and I carefully bagged up his purchases and inserted the instructions into the bag before stapling it shut. I told him that he didn't have to pay for anything, but he insisted and paid me anyway. As we stepped outside the store to say our goodbyes, I said to him, "Can I ask you a question? Why did you tell me that I didn't want to be Barneys? You mean like carrying a bunch of other people's lines?"

"No, wild beast. I meant don't get so big, so corporate. It's not what you want."

"Easy for you to say, Manfred. Your house is gigantic. It's incredible. You get to do everything. Why wouldn't I want that too?"

He put his hand on my shoulder and for the first time called me David. It was like a parent addressing a kid, a sign of caring formality to ensure attention was being paid. "David, this world of fashion . . . it's nothing but smoke and mirrors. It all looks so fantastic and aspirational, but behind the scenes, there's an industry that feeds on people and eats them alive. What you have here is what fashion should be about. The designer in connection with the customer. Everything in between — the department stores and the magazines and the shows — it's garbage. It's brutal. My advice is to keep things small. Keep designing for the people who love you and don't waste your energy convincing the rest of the world to do the same. They will find you when they are ready. And you will be ready when they find you." I soaked up every drop of wisdom from the man I had idolized for so many years. "Speaking of ready, I will need these before the holiday you Americans celebrate at the end of the month."

"You mean Memorial Day right? That's no problem. We're gonna be closed that weekend anyway so I'll make sure you have everything before then. We're going to this thing in Chicago to show our line to a bunch of new customers, so I really appreciate hearing your advice. It kinda confirms my decision to drag us out there without knowing what the hell I'm getting into."

"Are you going to be at IML?" he asked.

I was shocked by his question. How the hell did Manfred Mugler know about IML? "Yeah, we're going. Hopefully it will be good for us."

He gave me a wicked smile. "I think it will be very good for you, beast," he said as he put on his sunglasses and kissed me on both cheeks. "I have a final request. Once you've tailored my pieces, bring them with you to Chicago and I'll pick them up from you at your booth."

Forty-Five

I didn't think Amanda was serious about using us for a shoot. She lived a couple doors down from the store and had come in a few times to talk to me about some photography exhibition she was working on. "I just want it to be like *so* New York City," is how she described it. I chalked Amanda up as someone who was big on ideas but light with specifics, a talker. New York City was filled with talkers, and generally speaking, they were high on my scale of annoyances. So I was shocked when she came in to give me some actual details. She wanted to shoot pieces from our line, but she wanted *us* to be the models wearing them. "You know, you and your boyfriend, and a couple of people you guys hang out with. You're all so rad," she told me. "Don't take it the wrong way, the clothing is great, but you guys have to be the subjects. You bring the style to life. You're what New York City is all about." She wasn't wrong, so I complimented her intuitiveness and asked for more details

"The shoot would have to be this Sunday, the fourteenth. I know it's only a few days away, but I snagged the studio as soon as they had an opening. I've got a backup plan in case you say no. But don't say no. It's going to be amazing, I promise." I asked her the time and the location of the studio. "I'd need you guys to be there from 10 to 4. The studio is close by on 12th and Washington." We had Frankie's party on the fourteenth, but it wouldn't start till late, and the studio was right around the corner from Jeff and Javier's place. "It's called Industria." And with that I had heard enough. Industria was just about the coolest studio in the city, and I wasn't going to pass up the opportunity to have our first photo shoot at such a legendary location.

"We're in. We'll be there. See you on Sunday."

* * *

Convincing people to skip Sound Factory for a Sunday morning photo shoot would be a challenge. Convincing people to skip Sound Factory for a Sunday morning photo shoot at Industria would be effortless. I figured I'd get a little pushback from Kevin though. "Industria? Girl, are you serious?" he said to me. "I can give Miss Factory a day off for that level of cunt."

The night before the shoot I packed up a suitcase with nearly every garment we had on our racks, and at 10 a.m. sharp the following morning,

Kevin, Jeff, Fred, and I met outside of Industria. "Okay, kids," I told them, "I want us to get in there and serve up some iconic queer superhero realness. Think Triple X-Men. Fantastic Fourway. We're saving the children of Gotham and we're doing it *fiercely*, you got it?" I didn't have to ask though. I knew they fucking got it.

We buzzed the front door, Amanda welcomed us in, and my jaw hit the floor. All of us turned to each other, equally gagged. The set up was official, high fashion. The room was huge with a sweeping white background, not a scuff or a footprint in sight. Judging by the smell in the air, I knew it had been freshly painted just for us. She had about half a dozen lights set up at multiple heights, and she introduced us to both of her lighting assistants for the day. There were four make-up tables off to the side, one for each of us, and a couple of rolling racks, and a steamer for our garments. She got us settled in and I began to unpack the looks until she introduced me to *our* assistant who would take care of all the prep work and get us anything else we needed. "Just ask," she said to us. "The only thing I want you guys to focus on is being yourselves and delivering."

From 11 a.m. until about four in the afternoon, in one set of sick looks after another, we came through like the true New Yorkers she desired to document. We gave her everything she could have wanted and more. Geared up in the fast-forward, high-octane aesthetic that Fred and I had cultivated together, the four of us transformed into the New Mutant Assfucking Avengers. We delivered sex demons and *Charlie's Angels* all at the same time. I felt unstoppable, indestructible, a man of steel practically chosen by the Sodomy Gods to conquer the world with my queer superpowers. Our show got so severe, she had to send out one of her assistants to grab a few more rolls of film. Her shutter kept on clicking until the manager of Industria had to throw us out. Before we left, she thanked us repeatedly for what she said was the best shoot she had ever experienced. "That was something special," she said. "Beyond my expectations."

Kevin chimed in, "You told us to be ourselves and deliver, girl. What else did you think was gonna happen? These girls bring it to the runway every mother fucking time." Every mother fucking time was right. We came. We saw. We slayed the house down.

* * *

We dropped the suitcase of clothing off at the store, and Fred and I walked home to eat a little dinner and get ready for Frankie's party. Fred cooked up some chicken and vegetables, put our plates out on the cut table, and turned on *Female Trouble* for about the 10th time. Unable to afford cable any longer, we disconnected our service and got into the habit of cycling through the movies we had on VHS tapes. I took a few bites of my meal, mostly just pushing the food around on my plate, and Fred said to me, "You're not hungry?"

I was hungry, but so was my hole. "I ate a big breakfast and had a slice of pizza at the shoot. And I kinda wanna douche before we go out."

"Of course you do," he said. Sometimes I felt like Fred kind of shamed me for my sex drive, but I believed that if he felt like it was too much to handle, he was welcome to let all the other hotties in New York help relieve him of its burden.

"Is that a problem for you, Daddy?"

"No," he said, "I just didn't realize it was going to be that kind of night. Today was a lot for me and I figured we'd go to the party for a couple of hours and call it a night." Fred was an introvert, and the photo shoot was probably a big drain on his energy. But I was an extrovert, and after the exhilarating day we had at Industria, I was totally charged up and ready to celebrate. An early night was never in the cards for me.

We walked to Frankie's loft on 19th Street, gave his doorman our names, and just as if we'd been going to an actual club, he pulled out a clipboard with a guest list and checked us off. We got on the elevator with a couple of other people who were clearly headed to the party too, and we all got off on the top floor and followed the beats to his apartment. His place was huge, with a wall of windows that offered up a stunning view of the city. The ceilings were high and the lights were dimmed low. The room was bumping, filled with a mixed crowd of New Yorkers who had been blessed enough to know our legendary host, dancing to a deep house groove that was pumping through the speakers. I saw Frankie through the crowd and took Fred over to introduce them to each other. I noticed he was wearing the necklace that I had given him and the poetry of the universe overwhelmed me. My life was just so beautiful, almost too beautiful to be real. I had been given a calling, shown my true purpose, and a series of exquisite symbols and signs manifested themselves to encourage me to follow my path fearlessly. The magic had me spellbound. It was the only thing that felt truly real. The more I gave it my faith, the more it showed its faith in me in return. Fred and I danced together to the lushness of Frankie's vinyl collection, and there within the cinematic skyline of my city, I truly believed in the wonder of love. "Take me home Daddy. I need to feel you inside me."

We burst through the door to our apartment and barely let go of each other as we stripped ourselves naked. Fred backed me into the bedroom, turned me around aggressively, and folded me onto the bed with my head down on the sheets and my ass spread wide in the air. He put his lips on my hole, kissing it gently, teasing it, and once he had me thoroughly worked up and gyrating hungrily, he used his tongue and his mouth to eat it and devour me. He slapped my hole with his monstrous dick. "Beg for it, boy." I begged and I begged, lost in my ravenous desperation for his cock to feed my pulsating hunger. He began to move his body away from mine to retrieve a rubber from the nightstand, when unconsciously, uncontrollably, my mouth gave voice to the careless, prohibited desires that I had kept locked away. "Put it in me raw, Daddy," I said. With those six words out in the open, hanging in the room like an executed felon, the intertwined, fully heated filaments that connected us together were exposed to the air and extinguished.

Fred sat down on the edge of the bed, facing away from me, shoulders slumped, his head to the ground. He was silent. I flipped myself over and sat beside him, placing my hand upon his thigh next to his understandably flaccid penis. We were right next to each other, two sweaty, naked full-time Nasty Pigs in a dysfunctional three-way relationship with a microscopic virus whose constant mindfuckerry kept us permanently wedged apart.

"I'm sorry I said that, Daddy. I know it's wrong," I offered him quietly.

He took a couple of deep, labored breaths, doing his best not to shatter. "You don't understand, Angel. If anything ever happened to you I . . . I wouldn't be able to . . . I don't know what I'd do without you. I love you so much." I stayed quiet, allowing him the space to express anything else he needed to. But he just kept breathing, eyes down.

"I know that, Daddy. I guess what I don't understand is why we just can't go get tested. I mean I know you explained it to me before, but if you don't think you have it then let's just find out and get it over with." I paused for a moment and gave his thigh a squeeze so he'd lift his gaze and look me straight in the eyes. "Daddy, if there's something that happened in the past or if you haven't been totally honest with me, then just tell me." But just as the words left my mouth, I knew how unnecessary they were. Fred may have had all sorts of baggage, but dishonesty was not in his character. He never lied to me or anyone. It was one of the reasons I loved and respected him so much.

"I would have told you, Angel. You know all about my past, my exes. I kind of just drifted from one monogamous relationship to another. I've barely been single since 1980, and even then, I wasn't really fucking or getting fucked. Most guys got a look at my dick and just wanted to suck me off." He didn't spend the 80s pushing his luck in sex clubs and bathhouses in Manhattan. He hid from the plague in New Jersey with the Hudson River between him and his deathbed in a string of long-term relationships that kept him safe from the carnage.

"I'm sorry I even asked, Daddy. I know you always tell me the truth and I know how much you hate doctors. But we're both negative, Daddy and . . . "

"How do you know you're negative? You've never been tested, either." I knew I was negative. There was no way I could have seroconverted. I only had a few hook-ups before Fred and none of them involved any fucking. Fred and I were always safe. Always. Safe sex worked. Fred and I were living proof.

"You're right, Daddy. So let's just both get tested. I'm good with it. I wanna know for sure. And I'm so fucking ready to stop using rubbers with you. I wanna feel that big raw Daddy dick inside me so bad." I understood the importance of safe sex, but much like in every other area of our new life together, I was done playing things safe.

He smiled at me, fully, openly, and it lit up his face. His new teeth were beautiful, and he had gotten rid of all his shame. "I want that too, Angel. I want to give it to you and make you happy."

The next day we walked down 6th Avenue to St. Vincent's Hospital where we met with an HIV specialist named Dr. Johnson. She was awesome. She asked about our sexual histories:

- How many partners have you had?
- How many partners have you had that were HIV-positive?
- How many times did you give oral sex?
- How many times did your partner ejaculate in your mouth during oral sex?
- How many times do you receive oral sex?
- How many times did you ejaculate in your partner's mouth during oral sex?
- How many times did you have anal sex?
- How many times . . .

- How many times . . .
- How many times . . .

The list went on and on and on. I asked her what she thought upon reviewing our answers, hoping to get some indication as to our risk. “I can’t tell you whether or not you have HIV. The only way to know for sure is with a test, and if you take one today, we’ll have the results in about two weeks.” *Right after we get back from IML* I thought to myself. She looked up from my chart and continued, “That being said, based upon your health and sexual history, I think you’ll be okay. HIV is easy to transmit, but condoms are almost 100% effective at preventing that, and transmission through oral sex is very rare, especially if your partners don’t ejaculate in your mouth.”

“What about, Fred?” I asked with all smiles. Despite his gorgeous new teeth, Fred wasn’t smiling with me.

“To be honest, we don’t see many people anymore in your age group, Fred, at least not who were sexually active as far back as 1980. But if everything you told me about your health and sexual history is true, I’d say you made a lot of good decisions and dodged a bullet.”

“It’s all true Dr. Johnson. My man doesn’t lie.”

With that, we rolled up our sleeves and she drew our blood to be sent off to a lab. Despite everything I knew about my past, my absolute certainty that I was negative, I left the hospital terrified. That I had been so safe didn’t make a lick of difference when faced with the realization that I had just submitted myself to a life-or-death blood test. My mind went racing backwards to all the guys I had hooked up with before Fred, those terrifying moments when we kissed and maybe I had brushed my teeth a bit too hard. Maybe my gums were still bleeding on a microscopic level. There was that one guy who made my mouth all salty and I realized after he left that it was his precum. Or that guy who had me face down and he was fingering my ass and at one point I thought maybe he put the head of his dick in me? I had a panic attack on 7th Avenue and 18th Street, and Fred had to sit me down on a stoop with my head between my legs to keep me from hyperventilating. After about 10 minutes my breathing returned to a steady rhythm. “How are you so calm, Daddy?” I asked him.

“One of us needs to keep it together and it doesn’t look like it’s going to be you.” We shared a good laugh together and Fred gently kissed me. “I’m actually glad we did this, Angel. I need to take better care of myself now that I have you.”

Forty-Six

It was a mad dash to the finish line getting ready for IML. We were sewing and applying grommets and snaps right up to the Monday before the event, the same day my Humping Pigs tee shirts arrived from the screen printer. Fred and I packed up our inventory — along with a pair of collapsible rolling racks, two boxes of plastic hangers, a little boom box for music, and a half a dozen receipt books and pens — and we lugged it all to the UPS store using a hand truck we borrowed from our super. I had underestimated the number of boxes it would take to ship out our setup, and when the UPS clerk tried to run my Nasty Pig Amex to pay for the shipment, it came back with a decline. I used cash from the store instead. Crisis averted. I tracked the packages, and everything arrived without incident two days later. The only thing left to do was get us to the event. We were taking a big risk, sinking so much money into inventory for just a few styles and closing the store for six days. It felt like the price tag for IML just kept going up.

We landed in Chicago and took a cab to the Congress Plaza Hotel and Convention Center. "You're right by The Magnificent Mile," our driver told us. "It's gorgeous over there." But as we pulled up to Congress, the first thing I noticed was that it wasn't particularly magnificent. The building itself felt stately and historic from the outside, but once we made it through the lobby, I quickly understood why Paul told me the place was haunted. It felt from another era, and while probably quite grand in its heyday, the years of wear and tear had taken its toll and left it a shadowy ghost of its former glory.

We found our room tucked behind a row of vending machines and next to a pair of doors held together by a locked chain. The word *NO* was spray-painted across them. Fred and I looked at each other, and he said to me "And here you thought getting an HIV test was scary." We unpacked our bags and I hooked up my hose to the showerhead. We grabbed our sewing machine and the Nasty Pig banner Howie had made just for us, and we headed downstairs to find the Vendor Market.

Up an escalator, down a hallway, and through several sets of doors, we got to our off-shoot room nowhere near the main market. Unfazed by our remote location, we got right to work, assembling our racks and hanging our inventory. Everything was black, so it all merchandised nicely together. Fred

NAST

PIG

set up his sewing machine, and I unrolled our Nasty Pig banner, hanging it from the pole and drape behind us. It looked sick, an X-rated take on that underground, New York City Sound Factory vibe. I stood back a few feet, admiring what we'd accomplished, and I said to Daddy, "We're about to put our stamp on this mother fucking function."

A heavy-set gentleman with an incredibly kind face and a leather vest covered in enamel pins entered the room. He walked up next to me as he checked out our banner and said, "So this is Nasty Pig. Is one of you David?"

"That would be me!" I said gleefully.

"Pleasure to meet you, David. I'm RJ. We spoke on the phone about getting you this booth."

"It's great to meet you RJ. Thank *you* so much for doing this for us. I'm so excited to be here. That's my Daddy, Fred, over there." Fred approached us to shake RJ's hand. "So, what do you think, RJ? Are you ready for Nasty Pig?"

He walked through our booth and checked out our gear. He pulled out a pair of our chaps. "Are these really $139?"

I panicked. "Do you think that's too expensive? They're totally machine washable, and we can hem them on the spot."

He put the chaps back onto our rack. "Honestly, David, I think you could get a little more for them. But it's your first year, so just see how things go."

"I just want us to do well here. I want people to like our Nasty Pig vibe."

RJ paused as his eyes wandered over our booth, a smile on his face the entire time. Nodding his head he said to me, "David, I think *a lot* of people are going to love Nasty Pig, but a lot of people aren't going to be too thrilled. That's just what we need around here, so welcome to IML."

* * *

At noon on Friday, a loudspeaker boomed: *The IML Vendor Market is now officially open.* All the other vendors in the room applauded, and then it got very quiet. No one was playing any music. *WTF?!* I popped a cassette of a bootleg Junior Factory set into our boombox and cranked up the volume as Armand Van Helden's Cardiac Arrest mix of "Heartbeat" broke through the unnecessary silence. I turned to Fred and announced, "Straight from the streets of New York City . . . Nasty Pig is in the house and we about to get *busy!*"

That turned out to be rather prophetic because within the hour our booth was crowded. Customers had never seen anything like our matte laminated rubber. It landed somewhere between leather and latex, while also being different from both. I pitched that it was machine washable, and that landed as a huge selling point. I quickly figured out that these guys were used to having pieces of gear that made them feel sexy but weren't exactly ideal for the rigorous sex they were actually having. Fred's unparalleled construction skills meant our garments fit almost everyone right off the rack, and my Humping Pigs tee delivered that streetwear edge — the flavor of the Nasty Pig brand. Once people looked at our prices though, it became the shot heard 'round the world of IML. Customers purchased two and three garments at a time, sometimes one of everything, then an hour or two later they'd return with their friends who wanted to get a piece of the Nasty Pig action. Fred went back to the room twice to get more inventory. By the end of day one, Daddy and I were totally wiped out from hustling nonstop. We were drenched in sweat and dehydrated from the retail marathon we had just run. But none of that mattered: we were a *fucking hit!*

With the market opening at 11 a.m. the next day I knew I couldn't have a long night, but there was no way I was turning out the lights and going to bed. I wanted to check out the madness, and I wanted to do so wearing Nasty Pig. With both of us wearing tri-color matte rubber motocross pants, we exited our room and went downstairs to the lobby.

The scene down there was nothing short of surreal. The dated, *grand dame* aesthetic of the lobby had been turned on its ass by the juxtaposition of hundreds of old-guard Leathermen in their fetish finest. Their oversized cigars, ill-fitting chaps, and macho-man personas stood in humorous contrast to the giant chandeliers above their heads and the Louis XIV replica chairs upon which they sat. Much like the Congress itself, most of the men looked as if they once shined but had since lost their glory as their own community moved on and marched past them. These were the real men associated with this scene, not the romanticized version I had fictionalized while jerking off to classic Falcon Studio porn and old copies of *Honcho*.

We got a couple of beers, toasted our successful debut, and started pointing out to each other the guys who were wearing Nasty Pig. After only a minute or two, we realized there were quite a few of them. More than quite a few. I was overcome by the moment, flooded with thoughts of gratitude for our customers and their newfound belief in what we were doing. But then the voice of my soul, the voice I was learning to trust, spoke to me from a place deeper and more evolved. *If you really wanna honor the poetry of the universe, get out there and give thanks to the people themselves. They're the ones who truly deserve to hear it.* I put my beer down on the bar, walked over to the first guy I saw wearing our gear, introduced myself to him and said, "Forgive the interruption but my name is David, and this is my boyfriend Fred. We own Nasty Pig, where you got your pants. I just want to thank you for choosing to spend your hard-earned money with us."

I spent that night thanking as many of our new customers as possible, but more importantly I had the opportunity to listen to them, to learn about their experiences. What I discovered was fascinating. These kinky gay men, the pariahs of my plagued community, were very down to earth. They came from all over the country, traveling many walks of life. While on their journeys they had to overcome a tremendous amount of shame to arrive at a place of comfort and pure fucking joy — at this place — surrounded by their own kind in the lobby of the Congress Hotel. The battle to come out of the closet was an almost universal experience for practically every queer person who even dared to fight it, but these guys had to do it twice. The acceptance that many of them found by their fellow, liberated homosexuals was revoked when they opened up about their true sexual desires. *They* were the people who made *us* look bad. But *they* were just being themselves, and that was supposed to be what we were all about. We championed tolerance and acceptance in general, but down toward the bottom of that social contract, AIDS had inserted some fine print: *unless you champion the ass-fucking part out loud and proud.*

I learned that their innate curiosity about what they could experience through their bodies meant they were genuinely curious people in general. They were free thinkers, business owners, artists. Many of them were carving their own way in the world outside of their bedrooms or their dungeons or whatever set up they created in their basements and their garages to explore their desires. They loved the transformative nature of the clothing they wore. They were using fashion to feel sexy and empowered. It turned out they were a lot like me, right down to the hairy ones who didn't shave their bodies. It was refreshing to see all the relatable hairy men who stood in sharp juxtaposition to the shaved and chiseled sculptures that dominated New York City.

I mentioned my observation to one of our new Nasty Pig customers and his knowledge of its root cause left me stunned. Like just about every other aspect of our identities, AIDS had its fingerprints all over our metamorphosis from the natural hairy aesthetic of the 70s to the statuesque and perfectly smooth ideal of the 90s. I found out that we flocked to the gym to prevent ourselves from wasting away, and we shaved off all our body hair to prove we weren't hiding any lesions. The men I met that night, fearless in their identity and inspiring in their integrity, had nothing to prove and nothing to hide.

Fred and I headed back to our room to rest up for day two of the Vendor Market. I thanked the Sodomy Gods for allowing me to serve the ranks of the kinky and condemned who made the pilgrimage to Chicago on the last weekend in May every year. Maybe it was business suicide, but I decided I was going to use our brand to champion these people as well. We would be messiahs for the pariahs. My community may have relegated them to be our sacrificial lambs, but I was going to celebrate them as our fearless Nasty Pigs.

* * *

Our second day in the vendor market made day one look serene. From the moment we opened, we were slammed with customers. The word on Nasty Pig had spread Friday night, reaching all the attendees who had landed in Chicago after the market had closed at seven p.m.. It felt like they all showed up at once on Saturday, and we had to ask people to form a line that wrapped around our booth. I thanked them for their patience as we served as many people at a time as we could. Fred gave up on hemming pants and chaps for our customers as they waited. We chalked the correct lengths, put them into shopping bags, stapled their receipts to the outside, and told them they needed to return the following day to pick them up. Some people grumbled about having to wait, but not a single customer walked away from the opportunity to snag the hottest new products at IML.

That didn't mean others didn't walk away grumbling about what we were offering. Many of them grumbled right to our faces. "This isn't real leather" was a common judgment. "There's no way this stuff is going to fit right" was another. We were told that our line wasn't fetish, that we were a flash in the pan, and that our quality wasn't up to par with the traditional vendors who had been coming for years. Of all the negative comments, "This is a bunch of disco clothes" was my absolute favorite. "Bless your heart," I responded, an expression I had picked up from Jeff that fit the moment perfectly. It seemed that for every person who loved what we were all about, there were another five who balanced it out with some real vitriol for our brand.

Nasty Pig became a big topic of conversation, and everyone had an opinion. It seemed that our divisiveness had followed us west. In New York City, it was based upon our fearless sex positivity. In Chicago, it was rooted in a question of our authenticity. Not that I was mad about it. I loved the combination of positive and negative attention. We had people taking sides and that meant they were invested, whether they liked us or not. Hating on Nasty Pig seemed baked into our brand DNA, and our detractors unwittingly spread the buzz about our little company on our behalf, free of charge.

"You were right," I said to Joe, the Leatherman who had convinced me to come to IML in the first place, when he stopped by our booth during the last 10 minutes before we closed. "There are plenty of people here who *really* aren't liking what we're doing."

"Yeah, I figured," Joe replied. "But how are sales? We tried to stop by three times today, but we couldn't even get in. You guys were packed."

I just smiled and flashed them a wad of cash, happy as a Nasty Pig in shitloads of new customers. "I guess we're doing ok."

* * *

Down in the lobby, we ran into Paul, our favorite bartender from The Lure. "Well, well, well! If it isn't the Nasty Pigs," Paul announced. "Where have you two fuckers been hiding?"

"Behind a wall of customers in our booth," I replied.

"Tell me about it. We tried to get in there yesterday, but the line was too long and we weren't on the list," he laughed. "You guys are killing it. Everyone's talking about you and I'm spotting so many sexy men wearing your gear."

"It's been fucking amazing. We sold out of so much product. I'm so glad we came. But let me tell you, *mija*, it's been grueling. We've been working our tits off. And you know what they say: All work and no play makes David a hungry boy."

"I can help with that, fucker." Paul walked away and returned with a hairy muscled-up Daddy who I remembered from the booth. He had a thick Long Island accent and an equally thick, uncut dick I had discovered while fitting him for the Nasty Pig chaps he was now wearing before me. "David and Fred, this is my new friend Anthony."

Inserting himself between me and Fred he said, "Nice to meet you studs. You're the Nasty Pig boys right?" He grabbed my bare ass and said, "You helped me with my new chaps."

He put his other arm around Fred, and they started making out. He turned to me, and I looked up at all six-foot-three of him, struck by the level of sexy that he was effortlessly oozing. I felt up and down his leg, my hand running over his purchase, and I said to him, "Thanks for buying these. You look amazing in them."

He took his hand off my butt, lubricated a finger with his spit, and slid it up my hole. "I'm gonna look amazing in you too, boy." We lasted about five minutes, the three of us mauling each other, before we said our goodbyes to Paul and Phil to head to our room. As we walked away and headed to the elevator I heard Paul shout at me, "You're welcome, you little ungrateful fucker."

I turned around and shouted back at him, "Buenas noches, *mija*. Muchas muchas gracias!"

* * *

We barely had anything left by the time we opened on the final day of the market. We had completely sold out of most things, and the little we had left barely filled a single rack. Most of those pieces went to returning customers, many of whom showed up wearing their previous purchases. The overwhelming consensus was that our product withstood any abuse inflicted upon it. I wished I could say the same for my asshole, which felt a bit sore after hours of pulverizing courtesy of Fred and Anthony. *Worth it,* I thought to myself.

One guy came through the booth and asked us what was on sale. "Nothing," I told him. I thought his question was odd, but then another guy came through and asked the same question. Then another. "Why isn't anything on sale? *Everyone* marks down the stuff they have left on the last day so they don't have to bring it back with them," he said.

Flanked by a few returning customers, I explained, "Why would we do that? It's like you're punishing the customers who appreciate you the most for getting their gear early. Why would I give you a discount when these guys showed up first and paid full price and keep coming back for more?"

He looked at me dismissively and said, "Well that's just how it is. All the other vendors do it."

I tilted my head, wagged my finger back and forth and replied, "We're not the other vendors, honey. We're Nasty Pig." My three returning customers howled at my sass and applauded my stance. When the announcement came over the loudspeaker that the Vendor Market was closed, I stepped outside the booth to admire the four lonely garments we had left to send back to Manhattan.

"Where is all your merchandise, wild beast?" I turned around and there was Manfred, finally, looking as gorgeous as ever. "I hope you didn't sell my Nasty Pig couture!"

I grabbed his shopping bag from underneath the table and presented it to him. "Of course not! I would never do that to you." He came into the booth and embraced each of us. "I'm so happy to see you," I told him. "I figured you didn't come."

"Nah, beast, I've just been busy." I knew exactly what he meant. "And it looks like you've been busy too. All the boys are talking about Nasty Pig. You and Fred are the stars of the show." Manfred took off his clothes to try on his customized gear, staring intently at each piece in the mirror to make certain of the fit. "Perfect tailoring, Fred. I am a very satisfied customer." Fred lit up with his approval, his perfect smile on full display.

"We aim to please," I replied.

"Thank you for the special treatment, my Nasty Pigs. Are you going out tonight to celebrate your success?" Manfred asked.

"Fuck yes! We're going to the closing party at the Eagle. How about you?'

"Of course! Let's all go together, yes?"

"That would be amazing." I was gagging so hard I could barely speak.

"It's a date. Meet me in the lobby at 12:30, gentlemen. I will leave you to finish up here." He left our booth, holding his Nasty Pig shopping bag for all the world to see. Even Fred couldn't help but practically jump up and down in excitement. We threw the four pieces of stock we had left into a shopping bag, broke down our booth, and boxed it up to ship back to New York City.

"Thank you for your blessings, oh mighty Sodomy Gods." We gathered up our stuff and as we exited, I looked to Fred and proclaimed, "We will *definitely* be back here next year"

"Well, not exactly," I heard RJ say from behind us. "I'll be moving Nasty Pig to the main floor. It's where you belong."

We got back to our room and ordered some dinner. Fred took a nap, and I took it upon myself to count all the money we had made at IML. I was astonished. In four days we did about three months' worth of sales at the

shop. Manfred was right: forget about the industry standards and bring Nasty Pig right to the customer. That's exactly what we had done with IML. Black Friday came six months early for Nasty Pig, smack dab in the middle of May.

I had to call Rich and tell him about what we had just pulled off. "Dude, you don't even understand. These guys ate us up! We made so much money! All the clothing here is so fucking expensive, and it's hard to take off and its all gotta be customized. Our stuff was fitting everyone perfectly the moment they tried it on. And they can throw it in the wash. We are like a third of the price. We sold out of everything. I'm fucking shocked!"

Rich schooled me. "Don't be so shocked, D. It sounds like you pulled off the best business strategy of all. Nasty Pig is what's known as a disruptor. You built a better mousetrap with your product. It's what companies dream of doing. Congrats, you little faggot."

* * *

We met Manfred in the lobby as planned and the three of us stepped out of the Congress into the cool Chicago wind. The air felt uniquely gorgeous as it swept across my face, a quality I attributed to being directly across from Lake Michigan. But I soon realized it wasn't the breeze that held a special character. It was that I hadn't left the hotel once since we arrived four days ago. The air wasn't uniquely gorgeous. It was just fresh.

Feeling like a big shot with a pocket stuffed with cash, I insisted on paying for our car ride over to the Eagle. Manfred thanked me for my generosity, informed me that he had already taken care of our transportation, and led us to his stretch limousine parked in front of the hotel. We pulled away from The Congress and Manfred rolled down the windows. "Chicago holds the promise of what an American City can be," he told us. "The architecture is magnificent." Manfred and Daddy struck up a conversation about patterns and construction. They spoke in a language I had just started to learn. It felt truly unbelievable, *my* man and *the* man speaking casually about the mechanics of fashion together. I didn't contribute much as we drove toward our destination. "You're terribly quiet tonight, beast!" But I had no words for the moment I was experiencing. It was poetry so transcendental it bordered on the divine.

I was snapped out of my heavenly state when we entered the Eagle, glowing red and packed to the rafters with sweaty devilish men determined to make the most of their last night at IML. The dancefloor was wall-to-wall bodies, sliding and grinding up against each other. The place was so heated, condensation was dripping down the walls. And there were so many guys all decked out in Nasty Pig.

I bought a round of drinks for the three of us and we raised our bottles. Manfred made the toast "To Nasty Pig!" and I poured a little beer out for my queer ancestors who had passed, then I guzzled the rest down. We headed to the dancefloor, but somewhere along the way we lost Manfred. "Should we go find him?" Fred asked me. "I don't think so, Daddy. He has a way of finding us when he wants to. Besides, I'm ready to drop a pill and do a big ol' bump!"

The substances washed through me. It seemed like the club got darker and darker. The music got heavier. The energy in the room thudded hypnotically. The guys around me began groping each other, pulling their cocks out, playing with each other's butts. Some of them began blowing each other. And then I saw something I had never seen before, something that consumed my fantasies when I jacked off alone. The men around me, swept away in the sex-charged atmosphere, started fucking each other, pants around their knees, simple, fast and easy. Paul had told me I would see this happen. He explained to me that there were a lot of positive guys who went to IML to find each other so they could experience the pleasure of what was prohibited by our health experts and our community leaders and our fear of a lethal virus. They went there to let loose and fuck each other raw — what I wanted to do so badly — give in to the heat of the moment and just let go. But when faced with my deepest fantasies, instead I froze. It was the only thing I could think about. It was the only thing I wanted to see. If it right in front of me, I went looking for it everywhere. Like an accident on the road, dark and horrifying and captivating, I couldn't take my eyes off the carnage. It felt like it was happening to everyone — and no one seemed to care except for me. Despite its deadly nature, I couldn't help but long to be swept away right along with them.

Not that I would ever cross the event horizon and fall into the black hole of the thing I most wanted. Its monumental gravity, no matter how incomprehensibly strong the pull, wasn't enough to overtake my fundamental desire not to get AIDS and die. Still, I spent the night in a purgatory of conflict that overshadowed all our accomplishments of the weekend. The Sodomy Gods had blessed me everything I wanted going into IML, then cruelly flaunted for me the one thing I knew I dared not have.

"This isn't fun for me," Fred said. "I'm ready to leave."

"Why, Daddy? There's still another hour to go."

"Because I might as well be here by myself. You're lost in your own little world, and I know what's going on and I'm over it. I don't want to be around this anymore. It's too much."

He was right. I hadn't said a word to him since we separated from Manfred. I was spinning out so hard due to what I was seeing that I lost sight of why we were at IML in the first place. I had lost sight of rejoicing in our tremendous success with my Daddy. I had even lost sight of myself. If I really was a champion of sex positivity, then I needed to recognize that these guys were just championing a sex positivity of their own. It felt forbidden to me because it was. But it wasn't forbidden to them. They were connecting with each other while they still had time to do so. They were just having fun. I might not be able to participate in that kind of fun with them, but I had to figure out how to let go in a different way and celebrate it for them. And if I was some sort of sexual superhero, then I needed to stand up and be a hero for these guys too. They were our customers, our new fans, and over the course of the past four days they put enough in our pockets to last for months. I had no right to be jealous or afraid of them. I had to stand up for them too, learn from them, and serve them up our Nasty Pig magic while they were still here and alive.

"I'm sorry I checked out, Daddy." I kissed him cautiously until I felt him kiss me back. We made out on that dancefloor for the rest of the night. We danced together and we celebrated. We thanked our new customers. We partied until they closed the place down.

* * *

Safely back home in New York, my mind raced with ideas about where to go next with Nasty Pig. I couldn't shut my brain off. I felt like we were going to conquer the world. I had no idea what that would look like. I just knew we were destined to be a success. It might take ten or twenty or even thirty years for the world to catch up to us, but I was okay with being that far ahead of our time. One day all our work would pay off. We would lead a queer army of sex-positive lovers and we would build it ourselves, one Nasty Pig at a time. And with the results of our HIV tests coming soon, the final barrier between me and my Daddy was about to give way.

Forty-Seven

I woke up the next day, back in my own bed, to the sound of the apartment door closing. The clock said 1:46, and it took me a minute to put two and two together. That it was sunny in the bedroom meant it was the middle of the day, not the middle of the night. I never slept that late. I also never woke up without Fred by my side because I always got up before him. IML had taken as much out of me as it had given. I laid there in the rays of sunshine that came beaming through the plants, dappling my face in the warmth and the light of springtime in New York.

Until I heard Fred crying, sobbing, and suddenly everything went cold. Dr. Johnson had told us she would call when our results came in, and I vaguely remembered hearing the phone ring at some point earlier in the day. I didn't think he would go to the hospital without me, but over the past two weeks, I had wondered just how scared he was of getting his results. He seemed so calm, but under the surface, somewhere in his mind, I knew he was getting ready to face his greatest fear. He would no longer be blissfully ignorant as to whether or not he was destined to waste away and die. He had to be preparing to face his other greatest fear: losing the man he loved. He must have been terrified that his Angel would fly away. Even though I was sure we were both going to be fine, somewhere in my mind I was getting ready to face whether I would lose him too. I buried my face in the pillow and cried as quietly as I could before I got it out of my system. I wiped my eyes dry with the comforter, prepared myself for the news, got up out of our bed, and opened the door to the living room. Fred looked at me with swollen, bloodshot eyes. His breathing was labored by the weight of the tragic ending to our love story.

I couldn't bring myself to sit next to him. I couldn't move. "Daddy, just tell me what the doctor said. It's gonna be alright, I promise." I was lying through my teeth. It wasn't going to be one bit of alright. I wanted to run away from that moment as fast as I could, but I was trapped there in time. My mind ran round in circles trying to outpace the overwhelming panic and fear that had washed over every synapse in my brain.

He managed to interrupt his uncontrollable sobbing just long enough to get out the mortifying news. "Louis is dead," he told me. The ringing I barely remembered hearing had come from the morgue. They called to ask Fred to identify the body.

* * *

I did my best to support my man, but we were almost equals in the heartbreak. Fred had lost his best friend, and I had lost his best friend, too. I was so caught up in my reality that I lost sight of Louis's finality, despite knowing it was on its way for months. Now that it was finally here, neither Fred nor I knew how to navigate Louis's passing. We were together, yet completely alone in our devastation.

We got dressed and walked over to Louis's tiny studio apartment that he had rented on Ninth Avenue. It now all made sense why he walked away from living with Tom in his amazing two-bedroom apartment in the West Village. Louis needed to get away from the decadence. He needed to get away from Tom. He needed his own peaceful space in which to quietly die.

Fred and I went through what few things Louis had taken with him. We did so sometimes silently. Sometimes Fred would break down and I would console him. Other times it was me. The bouts of unrelenting sadness kept us in his place for a while though. I was shocked to open one cabinet in the kitchen and see dozens of bottles of painkillers and homeopathic remedies. There were hypodermic needles, both unopened and used, strewn messily about together in a dresser drawer beneath a small stack of perfectly folded sweaters. It contrasted the organized simplicity of everything else around me, a reminder of the dark chaos he must have been experiencing beneath his composed surface. There were no rules for our existence as gay men. There was only chaos.

Fred gathered up the porn magazines he found in the nightstand along with a couple of dildos and some lube and threw them into a trash bag. He emptied the fridge of its contents. Louis had asked Fred to get his apartment ready for his parents before they arrived, a ritual that I realized was commonplace within our ranks. Upon learning of his passing, they would come to the city, retrieve his things along with his body, and do with them as they saw fit. Perhaps they would pick and choose the things they wished to remember him for and throw the rest of his identity into the trash. Fred knew he wouldn't be invited to the funeral. He wouldn't be made aware of the location of Louis's grave. Fred was tasked with honoring the man he truly was — a beautiful queen with a dark, angled face and a dark, wickedly pointed sense of humor — right there in his apartment before the real Louis disappeared.

In a small box, Fred packed up a set of red Depression-era glass dishes they had purchased together at a flea market and a picture of the two of them dressed in white, taken hours before Louis told Fred he had HIV on the dancefloor of the Roxy.

"Are you sure that's all you want, Daddy?" I asked Fred.

"I'm sure." And with that we closed the door on the physical life that Louis had led and walked out into a world without him. We got back to our place and laid down in our bed together. I held my special man in my arms until he fell deeply asleep. Eventually, I left as I couldn't contain my tears any longer. I managed to make it out our front door where I collapsed to the floor of the hallway and burst apart. I had always considered Louis my guardian angel, sent to me from heaven to personally shake some sense into my gay ass and tell me never to let go of Fred. I would never forget the look in his eyes when he told me I had landed a lifer. All along I thought he was trying to protect me from making a rookie gay mistake — walking away from the best man I would ever find. But I realized he was also trying to protect his best friend from the life he knew Fred would have to lead once he had died. Both things were true at once, beautifully, tragically tangled together. It all made sense, not that it made anything better. Society had ignored us for so many years. We were left to figure out this horrid plague on our own, fighting for our lives as we buried our dead *en masse.* The burials may have slowed in recent years, but they hadn't stopped. In my short time as an openly gay man, I had lost my share of friends, but none as close as Louis. My sadness mixed with anger that turned into a raging fury. I ground my knuckles into the marbled gray carpet beneath me. It felt as if the acid in my stomach had gone rogue, burning right through its lining, and eating away at my insides. I didn't know where to channel it. I didn't know how it would ever be contained. But after a couple of days of it ripping apart my heart and my brain, I turned my poet's soul to process and make sense of my pain.

we are left

dedicated to louis ybarra

this tree falls with so much sound
he quietly comes crashing down
we are left with less to breathe
we are left to grieve
this sadness does not leave but grows in its stubbornness
the tears still come every few days
the pain stays and haunts us when the stars fall
when the images on the wall are covered
when hypodermic needles are discovered hiding in the cupboard
we cannot help but cry
we are left to wonder why the compassion has been lost
why our pain is tossed away and given no weight
why the dead are victims of hate more so than disease
we are left to wheeze and pray for breath

these trees come quietly crashing down
they fall with so much sound on a nation of deaf ears
the death of queers is common and accepted
sustain your justifications and turn your back
you lack humanity
you lack god
you mock the death of my boy king
i will honor him and hold fast to his presence
never will i forget his life meant more than a ribbon
more than a quilt
i will not let anger stain his beauty
i will let his spirit intoxicate me!

In Louis's honor, I would stay on my path and follow the universe's poetry as it led me forward. I would keep on fighting. I would never give up. I was done with a society that viewed me as second class for taking it up the ass. I was done with those in my own community who wanted to erase our queer sexual identities in the hope of being accepted into that very same society, the one that was happy to let us die in the streets. I was done with everything that looked to hold us back and I was done with living beneath the terror of AIDS.

But AIDS was just getting started with terrifying me.

Thursday

The next day, we found out Fred had HIV.

Everything we knew cracked apart like thin ice, and we plunged into the freezing waters below. We wanted to hold onto each other, but we were so numb that we couldn't help but sink together, next to each other yet so far apart.

I was negative, not that it mattered much. Everything I wanted for myself hinged upon a life lived with Fred. I had put all my hopes and my dreams into us. They felt so unbound, so expansive. But *us* now meant me, Fred, and AIDS, and when filtered through the prism of our damned reality, our limitless possibilities evaporated. Our dreams became delusions. *Us* became finite. Sooner or later, Fred was going to die. We were now keeping time with a doomsday clock as it methodically ticked its way down to the inevitable. I imagined its face to be the circle I had drawn on that stained and crumpled piece of paper, the circle that contained the only three things that mattered to me.

At first, those things represented what I needed to leave behind so I could move to Philadelphia and get on with my life. Then they felt like the only things in the world that mattered, that truly *gave* me life. Now they were just a stark reminder of everything I was condemned to lose.

But there was one more thing I could lose as well: my own life. If I chose to stay with Fred, it meant every single sweat-drenched intimate encounter between us could be the first of my last. All it would take would be one flaw within the manufacturing of a condom. One drop of precum. If one microscopic virus jumped from his body into mine, I would suffer the same fate as Fred. The same fate as Louis. The same fate as countless numbers of my gaunt, lesion-covered queer ancestors.

My Jewish ancestors ran. They knew what was coming and they ran to The States. They ran for their lives. How could I dishonor them and knowingly put myself in the crosshairs of harm's way? How could I do that to my Grandma? How could I do that to her daughter, my mother, and to my father, and to my sister? I had introduced them all to Fred. I told them he was my friend. But I suspected they knew. I wasn't yet out to them, but I felt sure they knew who I really was and who Fred really was. And I bet they were quietly terrified, too. I bet that terror was so quiet they didn't dare speak about it to one another. It just loomed in the backs of their minds like a dormant demon that no exorcism could possibly vanquish. One flaw would be all it took to stoke that demon out of its slumber and make it monstrously real for everyone in my family. They didn't deserve that cankerous fate any more than I did, or than Fred did.

Or than Louis did. Louis prophesied all of this. I know he was telling me to stay with Fred, but maybe I read the poetry wrong. Maybe when he told me I landed a lifer, the universe was testing my ability to divine a different truth. Maybe I was supposed to interpret it as a play on words. A lifer, after all, is a person who'd be imprisoned until the day of their death. Fred had been sentenced to the unappealable incarceration of AIDS. Even if I was crazy enough to stay with him, even if he didn't take me down with him, for as long as he stayed alive, I would be his prison wife, incarcerated and chained to his inescapable fate as well.

We barely spoke that day. From the moment Dr. Johnson convicted him until the time we got into bed with each other, AIDS right there between us, alive and dead at the same time, as is the nature of a virus. All I had to do was move an inch or two closer to him in the full-size bed he had originally gotten just for himself and I would be able to touch it. I couldn't *not* touch it. The bed was so small. He didn't buy that bed for the two of us. We barely fit in it. And that was before we became opposites, incompatible, pushed apart, serodiscordant. That was what felt like a lifetime ago, the time before we became death's bedfellows.

Both Fred and I clung to our sides of the bed that night, each afraid of falling asleep. Falling asleep would lead to waking up, and waking up meant the day we had experienced wasn't just a wretched nightmare. Waking up would mean the beginning of the end of our dreams, so still as corpses, next to each other, we laid. Above our heads, Fred's black velvet canopy became the inside lid of our casket, destined to close upon us one way or another.

Friday

We rose like the dead and ate breakfast. I left to go open the store, business as usual, and Fred stayed behind to finish up some sewing. I had a few customers and robotically put on The David Show for them. It didn't take much anymore. I could do it in my sleep if I had to, if I ever slept again. Everything had changed yet it hideously stayed the same. The world turned like nothing even happened. The hours passed, the daylight stopped, the night began. I closed up shop, locked the door behind me, pulled the gate down, and wandered my way back to what no longer felt like home.

Fred was making dinner. It smelled good. I took my shoes off and put on *Dangerous Living.* We ate our food next to each other as we stared past the screen. None of the funny parts of the movie made us laugh. We forced ourselves to laugh, though. We had to. But it was uncomfortable and totally dishonest and both of us knew it. It was as necessary as it was unbearable.

After dinner, Fred told me he wanted to go to Sound Factory Bar. I agreed to that. How could I not? How could I deny him anything ever again? How could I talk about my long-term plans for the business, or saving money for an apartment, or our future? How was I supposed to talk at all? Or act? Or be real? Both of us showered. Neither of us douched. We didn't wear anything from Nasty Pig. Not on purpose. It just happened. I noticed. I wondered if Fred noticed too.

We walked into Sound Factory Bar. I didn't want to wave hello to Frankie. I didn't even want to dance. I didn't know what we were doing there. "I want to get high," Fred told me. Of course he did. He always wanted to get high when we went out. I guess so did I, so I agreed to that as well. If I stayed with Fred, I would be saying yes to everything he wanted, for better or for worse, in sickness and in health, until his death do us part. We dropped a pill, and he asked me to dance and I didn't want to at all. I still said yes.

I tried to take my problems to the dancefloor. I hoped the music would lift me up or at least drown the world out, but it wasn't working. I felt the shudder of my pill and I tried to let go but I couldn't. I couldn't let go of the truth. I wasn't a superhero or a champion. I wasn't even a man. I was just a delusional kid who had done way too many drugs and along the way convinced himself to believe in magic and worship the made-up Sodomy Gods. What was I thinking? Like anything could protect me from my stupid choices, let alone from fucking AIDS. I had managed to romanticize everything that was happening in my life as some sort of cosmic poem. That was until the tragedy of my reality showed up, indelible writing on the wall. It was scrawled out before me in cold, succinct prose. I had done a terrible job of reading the signs, but they were doing a spectacular job of reading me.

And then something happened. Something managed to cut through the bitter, incessant dialogue I was hearing. Something began to shake me up and alter the arrhythmic noise that was rattling through my brain. My mind began to get quiet. It was reorganizing itself around a booming external sound that took me over with its vibrations. It was a resonant bassline that leveled everything around me and inside me before it pulled me back together and grounded me in its thunderous groove.

A woman's voice came through the speakers and she sang to me:

Keep pushing on.
Things are gonna get better.
It won't take long.
Keep on moving to the top.
You gotta keep on moving.
You gotta keep on moving to the top.

She sang it to me again and again, hypnotically, until she had me under her spell. She made me sing it with her. "Keep pushing on. Things are gonna get better. It won't take long. Keep on moving to the top."

Then she sang:

Don't give up.
Don't give in.
Keep on pushing and you'll win.
Don't give up.

Don't give in.
Keep on pushing and you'll win.

I sang it with her again and again and again. I looked to the DJ booth and I could swear Frankie was looking right at me. Maybe he wasn't. Maybe I was just as high as the sky, but I couldn't deny the authenticity of the moment I was living through. I couldn't deny the poetry, even if I tried. Even if I wanted to. But I didn't want to try. I wanted to believe in it. I wanted to have faith. I wanted it to be real. Frankie kept that song on loop for twice as long as any other that night, and I firmly believed that he kept it on just for me to listen to it, just for me to hear. The universe wanted me to keep pushing on even though I didn't know where on earth I was headed. So, when Fred told me he was ready to head home I said yes. We walked up 6th Avenue, and for the first time since Thursday morning, I reached out my hand and grabbed hold of my man's. We headed home together, touching each other again.

Saturday

We rose from our bed like two men and ate breakfast together. We talked a little. We even laughed once or twice. It almost felt warm, like we had managed to swim to the surface and claw our way back up onto the ice. But our ice was still so thin, though, thinner than Louis on his deathbed. Thinner than my skin. AIDS was still there with us. AIDS was still going to win.

We resumed business as usual. We put on the show.

That evening, after a day at the shop, I put on *Dangerous Living* again. Then I reached for *Female Trouble* and then for *Pink Flamingos*. We had seen them all so many times, so I went with season two of Absolutely Fabulous instead. The funny parts made us laugh, even though we had seen them all before. "We should really make a list of movies like *Thelma & Louise* that neither of us have seen and I'll bring it with me next time I go to Blockbuster." Those words came out of my mouth. They weren't about long-term plans for the business, or saving money for an apartment, but they were about the future. Whatever it held, our future was heading straight for us.

Fred told me he wanted to go to Sound Factory. Both of us showered. Both of us douched. Fred slipped into the living room and returned to our bedroom with a gift, perfectly wrapped in silver and black. No card. We weren't there yet. Neither of us knew if the next card would be a birthday card or an anniversary card. Maybe it would be a get-well card. Maybe it would be blank, leaving space for lengthy explanations and mournful apologies. Maybe it would have just enough room to say goodbye. A gift wasn't required to say anything at all. It just had to be opened, so I opened it. Inside, folded behind delicate grey tissue paper and sealed by a sticker that said Nasty Pig, was a one-of-a-kind, blue, red, and yellow rubber superhero tank with an S on the chest, the symbol of the Superman. I lifted it from the box and held it out in front of me. My hands were trembling. My heart was trembling too. It was remarkable, out of this world.

"Do you like it An . . . ?" He was going to say Angel, but he didn't. He just left it alone to linger as he awaited my reply.

"It's amazing." I slowly shook my head back and forth. "I love it. I love it so much." I just didn't know if I deserved to wear that S on my chest.

We walked into Sound Factory. I said hello to everyone because it felt like everyone was there that morning. Javier and Jeff, Paul and Phil, Kevin and Cesar and Howie and Serenity, Axel and William and Leslie and Lucy and Tom. Even Carl and Paul were out. Everyone but Louis. Louis wasn't there and we all knew it. We saw it in each other's watery eyes. We felt it when we held each other three times as long. We shared an unspoken wish, that he would fall from the stars, straight into our arms, but we knew it could never be granted. We came out to dance with his spirit instead, just as he had requested. "I won't be able to come down to you bitches so you better haul your pussies to Factory and get so fucking high you make it all the way up there to turn it the fuck out with me fiercely." A question entered my head. I asked myself what Fred would want us to do for him when his time was getting close. I told the crew I needed to take a piss and I ran as fast as I could to the bathroom where I locked myself in a stall and cried out all my hearbreak to the poetry of my favorite Frankie Knuckles track.

so many . . .
so many tears . . .
they're drippin and droppin and droppin and drippin
and drippin and droppin and droppin and drippin
and drippin and droppin and droppin and drippin
and drippin and droppin and droppin and drippin . . .

I pulled myself together and joined back up with the crew. I wanted to dance. I knew exactly what we were doing there. "I want to get high," I told Fred. Of course I did. I would one day have to let my beloved man go rest in his peace, leaving me behind to futilely try to reassemble my life with only half the pieces left. He might leave me behind, infected with his death sentence. I wondered if he would let me stay with him now, even if I wanted to, knowing what that would mean for me. I wondered if he could live with that. We all dropped the same pills together and I asked Fred to dance. He said yes, so along with our chosen queer family, we took our pussies and all of our problems, and we brought them to the dancefloor to honor our fallen angel Louis.

We found a spot by the stage and one by one we let go in submission to the patterns of the drums and the undulating bass. The pills were clean, glorious, so fucking strong. We all started rolling together, one family under one roof, united by the grooves in the vinyl that ignited in sound as the needle tore across them like a matchstick. Tom took out his magic vial, inhaled a bump of ketamine and sent it round our circle. When it returned to him, he did another bump and went to send it round again. "We gotta make it up there," he said as he pointed to the heavens. "She's waiting and you know how pissy she can get." We all had seconds, and just as Louis had requested, we got so fucking high and we danced our pussies off like there was no chance for tomorrow.

Fred was dancing harder than all of us. I had never seen him move before with such power. He was *going the fuck off* and I wasn't the only one who noticed. All of our friends began to call it out. "Let 'em have it, Fred!" "Work it out, bitch!" "You better fucking do it!" All of us except Javier who just stood there in mystical, wide-eyed amazement and observed his transcendence, his transformation.

Javier took Fred firmly by the hand and said, "Come with me." They disappeared into the crowd. I figured Javier had something necessary to say to Fred, some powerful insight or piece of wisdom too important to impart surrounded by thundering speaker stacks where some words might get lost to the music. Maybe it was about Louis. Maybe he picked up on the thing in Fred that had changed. But then Paul tapped me on the shoulder and pointed to the stage. "Look at that fucker go!" he said. Javier was up there spinning his lights, putting on a show for the Gods and the Goddesses, adding to the spectacle that was Sunday morning at Sound Factory.

I shouted over the music, "I know, Javier is major."

"Not Javier, you dumb little fucker. I'm talking about your Daddy."

There on the stage elevated above the crowd, out of his comfort zone and in the center of attention, turning it the fuck out *fiercely*, was the man that I loved, one level higher than the rest of us and that much closer to his breathless best friend. His eyes were closed, his energy bursting open as he danced in what could only be described as a state of determination. He was determined to honor Louis in the way his family wouldn't. He was paying tribute to the true human being we had lost. There was more going on though. I just knew it in my soul. A giant boulder had rolled onto his path. It towered above him, practically blocking out the light of the sun. Fred was up there, bravely grabbing hold of the best tool for the job in his arsenal. It was a tool he had never used before, but that wasn't going to stop him from doing exactly what he needed to do, the same thing he had done his entire life when faced with the shadow of adversity. Fred was up there chipping away at the boulder of his terminal prognosis, and he was doing so by finally being fearless. He was gorgeous, so sexy and empowered. He was radiating light. He was shining.

Isn't that the only thing you ever wanted for him, David?

Everything around me just ceased. The lights stopped their flashing. The speakers froze in silence. The throngs of revelers around me vanished. There was nothing left in the club, or the city, or the whole planet. There was only me, my Daddy, and the voice of the Sodomy Gods coming at me. They were coming through me. They were coming *for* me.

Don't you want him to shine?

Fred was up there staring down his greatest fear, face first, head on. The boulder he was up against, an extinction-sized meteor that had burned through the atmosphere and landed before him, had landed before me, too. It existed for both of us, no matter what. It was our cold, hard, lethal fact. I could turn around and run away in fear, but that boulder would just roll and follow me wherever I went for the rest of my life. It would no longer be able to crush me, to kill me, and I would move on. That boulder would appear to get smaller and smaller in my rearview mirror. It wouldn't be shrinking, though. It would just be further away, but never would it be gone. It would always remain our cold, hard, lethal fact. And Fred would always be there with it, alone, every single time I looked back.

Or, I could get up on that stage with Fred and dance. We could chip away at that earth-shattering agent of destruction together. It would be a courageous, valiant display of love. HIV-negative men didn't date HIV-positive men. We certainly didn't let them fuck us. We stayed as far away as we could. But an HIV-negative man in his early 20s, in his very first relationship, giving up on his future, all for a man destined to get horribly sick and transform from boyfriend to burden to buried — that was unheard of. It wouldn't be courageous or valiant. It would be reckless at best, and deadly at worst.

What's it going to be, David? Love or fear?

I knew I had to make the most consequential decision of my life. There was no point in postponing it another minute. Nothing was going to change. Whether I was stone cold sober or high as a fucking kite, our cold, hard fact was our cold, hard fact. I took my eyes off Fred to hang my head and look down.

There upon my chest was that S, reverse-appliquéd to a rubberized tank, custom-made for me by the man I'd grown to love.

What's it going to be, David? Push has come to shove.

I spent the past couple of years finding my purpose. I swore that I'd spend my life serving my community. I branded myself a champion of sexual positivity. I made promises to my queer ancestors, to the queer kids yet to be born. I promised I'd fight for them to live in a world where they could celebrate their identities without stigma, without shame, and I would do so fearlessly. If I was unwilling to do that for Fred, for my Daddy, then everything I claimed myself to be was false. It was lip service. It was talk.

What's it going to be, David? Will you just talk the talk, or will you walk the walk?

I looked up at Fred, shining away, and I knew I had no choice. I said to the Sodomy Gods, "I'm not just gonna talk. And I'm not gonna walk. I'm gonna *stay.*"

I watched Fred dance to a couple more songs. I couldn't take my eyes off him. He was the most beautiful man in the world. Javier finished his light show, he motioned to Fred, and together they left the stage, descending to the floor, and returning to our circle. Fred and I locked eyes, and he froze.

I stepped to him, face-to-face with my future, staring into its murky green eyes. I threw my arms around it, around Fred, around love. "You're amazing, Daddy. I love you so much." His body pressed against mine. I wasn't letting go. I made sure that he felt it. He began to cry upon my neck. He wept into my ear, "I'm sorry, Angel. I'm so, so sorry."

I held his face in my hands, wiped his tears, and said, "Save your apologies for someone who needs them. All I need is your love." Then I kissed him and he kissed me back. He smiled brightly as he pulled at my rubber S, then he let go and it snapped back onto my chest, right where it belonged. "My Superman," he said to me. I shook my head back and forth in disagreement. "No Daddy, the S is for Sodomy Gods."

We danced until I couldn't take it anymore. I wanted to get my man home. I was hungry and I wanted to be under him so badly. We said our goodbyes to our family, hailed a cab, and headed back to our apartment as quickly as we could. Behind closed doors, safe together in our home, we did what defined us as gay in the first place. Fred got on top of me, and before he slid his cock into my ass he asked, "Are you sure, Angel?"

I felt the tip of his dick touching my body. "I'm so fucking sure, Daddy." He entered me, stretching me open. He started out slow, letting my body know I could take it. He took me over and pounded away at my hairy, greedy ass for a couple of hours. I couldn't get enough. Neither could he.

"I'm gonna cum, boy!"

"Me too, Daddy!" He pulled out and shot his load into the rubber and I shot mine onto the bed.

There in our magic jungle, beneath our velvet canopy with Piggy at our feet, we collapsed next to each other, breathing heavily, then steadily, then gently, our fingers intertwined the entire time.

The condom didn't break, and neither did we.

POWERHOUSE

Epilogue | *Letter from the CEO*

Had you asked the ballsy kid who started Nasty Pig if he thought one day he'd be honored at the White House, I know he would have had the blind confidence to unequivocally say, *"Yes!"* Had you asked him if Fred would be there by his side to share in that honor, whatever optimistic spin he would have placed on his reply would have been a facade. People like Fred got AIDS and died, full stop. Upon learning of his HIV-positive status, I began to think of his future in terms of years, not decades, until I learned not to think about his future — our future — at all. I chose to live all our moments in blissful ignorance on whatever borrowed time the Sodomy Gods had granted us.

Miraculously, Fred didn't die. He turned out to be a long-term non-progressor, one of the *very* lucky few whose bodies mysteriously had the power to keep the virus in check. So, day by day, year by year, decade by decade, as he survived, we survived. We even learned to thrive until 30 years later, when we received that honor at the White House together — hand in hand, side by side, as intended. I don't know if I would have made it to that moment without Fred, but I thank the Sodomy Gods that I never had to experience that alternate reality. That timeline is taking place in another of their infinite parallel universes, unfathomably far away.

Our $50 investment in Nasty Pig and our three decades of very hard work have paid off. After struggling for so many years to keep our small business afloat, we've recently gathered ourselves a comfortable nest egg, and I'm in the early stages of accepting that it's not all going to disappear. But the dividends Fred and I relentlessly pursued were never financial ones. All we wanted was to live in a world where queer identities were honored, and sexual positivity could be openly expressed. We have come closer to that reality than either of us could have hoped for when we started in 1994. Here we are today, a legally married gay couple living our authentic queer truth. I am, against the odds, a poet-CEO-author, writing a love story that includes plenty of good old-fashioned, divinely inspired sodomy.

Together, we championed queer sexual positivity long before it became part of the mainstream conversation. But all our advocacy would have come without victories had it not been for the hundreds of thousands of customers who saw us for who we truly are and believed in what we have stood for since day one. Wearing our brand took a lot of guts for many different reasons. Fred and I got many things right with our business, but we were terrible at public relations. We let the story about Nasty Pig be fictionalized by the uninformed opinions of strangers, and what they had to say about us was overwhelmingly unflattering. So, to those of you who chose to identify with our authentically messy dream, we are incredibly grateful for your belief in what we do, and we say *thank you, Thank You, THANK YOU.*

The kid who started Nasty Pig made a promise to his deceased queer ancestors that if he survived, he would pass down whatever knowledge and wisdom he acquired to younger generations of queer people to come. This book is part of that promise. Many men of my age bemoan the fact that younger queer people today don't have to face the struggles we did as portrayed in this memoir. I think that's fucking crazy. I wouldn't wish our identities of terrified isolation inextricably mangled by AIDS upon anyone. I will say this, however — countless brave humans sacrificed their lives in the fight for the freedoms and the rights about which some of you need not think twice. Your queer ancestors proudly marched and loudly died in the gleeful gaze of a murderous public eye so that you could brightly shine. Please do not forget their sacrifice. The uncloseted space we currently occupy within society's house is both fledgling and fragile, and it's being dismantled as we speak. Our queer identity is not a guarantee. It is a precious gift and a privilege. I urge you to treat it as such.

Let's seize this historic moment when we have access to queer generational knowledge to listen to and learn from one another. We are incredibly powerful. I truly believe that we are magic. Thank you for giving me the opportunity to share part of my magical journey with you.

Yours in Sodomy,

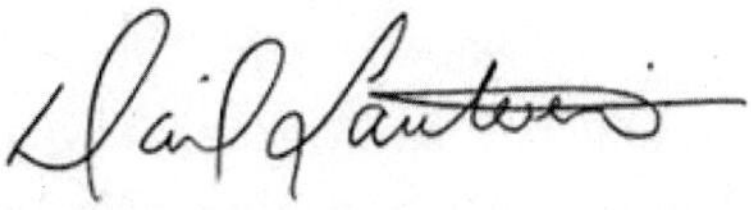

David Lauterstein
Founder and CEO
Nasty Pig

Acknowledgements

Thank you to my everything, Frederick Kearney. You have the strongest moral compass of any man I have ever met, and you took a chance on me anyway. You saw me for the human being I truly am, and I have spent a lifetime shedding my ego as I aspire to be as amazing as you. I love you *so so so so so so* much.

Thank you, Scott Wise, for being the impetus for this book, along with a whole bunch of other pretty amazing things that I've accomplished since you came into my life. I wouldn't have written *Sodomy Gods* if not for your tireless belief in me and your relentless desire to whore me out.

To Manfred: You are the master world-builder. I cannot thank you enough for encouraging me to build mine. I might not have understood your advice when you offered it but that didn't deter me from unquestioningly heeding it. I understand it now. The size of the world you build is irrelevant. The autonomy is the gift and the treasured customers who choose to populate your created world are the only people worth serving.

To Frankie: You are the Godfather of House. All of humanity has been blessed with your genius. Logically, I know you didn't spin "Keep Pushing On" that Friday night just for me, but magically I know you did. I took my problem to the dancefloor, and you let the music make my spirit soar. I'm still pushing on. Additionally, thank you Boris Dlugosch and Inaya Day for bringing that track into existence.

To Louis: Thank you for gifting me those four words — "you landed a lifer." I made Frederick my life and I'm still here with him. We both miss you but I'm sure you know that. You are unforgettable.

To my Witch Doctor, Jeff Rose: Honey, I wouldn't be me if you weren't you. Your philosophy courses through me, as does your magic. I will never be able to thank you enough. (P.S. . . . Obi is doing her job exceptionally well these days.)

To Javier: I don't know what dimensions you are traveling but clearly we are all 20 years behind you. Thank you for showing me the way, darling.

To Lee: Thank you for being my brother. You never let me down. You always build me up. I am so grateful for our friendship. I may be a self-centered dick, but I know I'm the one dick you really love, and I never forget it. I will have your back forever.

To my Old School Crew: Dwayne, William, Stephan, Nathan, Leslie, Franna, Eddie — you supported me from the get-go. You know where this journey started, cuz you were right there with me and Frederick. Thank you for those legendary times.

To Peter, Ken and Joe: Each of you had a hand to play in my journey from unemployed college grad to budding entrepreneur. Thank you so much for starting me on this journey of a lifetime.

To Kevin: When many of the children had forgotten you, you chose to remember yourself. When the children woke up from their amnesia, they did so with the whole world present. They *all* came together for the legendary recollecting. Who's feeling like an orchid now, girl?!

To Chad: When I was dreaming up Nasty Pig on the floor of the Factory, I knew it was going to be about fashion and music. It had to be. You made the music part possible. You listen to my crazy ideas and my shitty voice memos and somehow manage to make them WERQ. Thank you for making my sonic dreams come true.

Thank you KRS One and Chuck D. To KRS One: You instilled in me a desire to learn and educate. To Chuck D: You instilled in me the booming militance with which to own my truth. You are the truest poets, the realest MCs. I don't know who I would be had you not filled me with your power.

To my Black Duck Hoes: You know hoe you are. You are my amazing chosen family, and you are all truly batshit crazy. I wouldn't have you any other way obvi. The ridiculous, loving bond we share is unlike anything I've ever experienced. I hope that we spend every summer together until we all die. Hopefully, Jay will die first, and soon, and painfully, so that Dom and Fred and I can live happily ever after among your madness.

Thank you, Stephen Urice, my guiding light. You put two roofs over my head, one under which I learned to grow up and one under which I wrote about my journey. I am so fortunate to have you as a mentor. I hope that I always make you and Mark proud. And Rocqua, too.

To Dax: From CEO tips to spiritual partnerships to Roseland hair flips, our friendship is nothing short of cosmic. Thank the Gods I have my DHS to travel with during this lifetime. You inspire me so much.

To Dr. Karen Oates: Thank you for your counsel, your wisdom, and the outsized contribution you have made to my life. I may not have wanted to be a fine bottle of wine when you first brought it up, but I'm here now. My delicate sophistication is intoxicating. As usual you were right.

To Don Hershman: When I didn't have two nickels to rub together you put me on your dime every time you stayed on West 22nd Street. You told me that one day I'd have a dime of my own, a hundred thousand dimes a day, to be exact. I laughed at the absurdity of your words but in hindsight the absurdity was all mine. Thank you for never giving up on me, even when I once deserved it.

To Dennis: At a time when I had convinced myself that hating all the people who I assumed would hate me back would keep me safe from harm, you showed up and treated me with kindness. You taught me that I didn't need to pretend to be scary when I was so damn good at being sweet. Thank you for being my first ride or die.

To my Nasty Pig team: You don't show up to work. You show up to win. I am so fortunate that you choose to work with Frederick and me. Thank you for your dedication, your talent, and your drive.

To my Dad and my Mom and my Sister: You learned a whole lot about me from this book, but probably nothing that you found particularly surprising. Well maybe the part about me prostituting myself for Frederick's teeth. What can I say? You raised a real hustler.

To Patrick Davis: Thank you for giving sound to queer voices, including mine. You certainly don't have to do this — yet you do — and our community is better for it.

Notes & Credits

This work contains excerpts and references to specific works by other artists and such uses are made and intended as Fair Use of each such work under the United States copyright laws. The author and publisher provide the applicable attribution to these works based on readily available public information.

Chapter Six contains lines from R E O Speedwagon's song "Keep On Loving You." Lyrics copyright © 1980 by Kevin Cronin. Published by Fate Music, Inc.

Chapter Eight contains lines from Bill Wither's song "Lovely Day." Lyrics copyright © 1977 by Skip Scarborough and William H. Withers. Published by Golden Withers Music & Chappel Music.

Chapter Twenty-Three contains lines from Pink Floyd's song "Another Brick in the Wall, Part 2." Lyrics copyright © 1979 by Roger Waters. Published by Pink Floyd Music Publisher, Ltd.

Chapter Forty-Seven contains lines from Boris Blugosch's song "Keep Pushin'," featuring Inaya Day. Lyrics copyright © 1996 by Boris Dlugosch, Errol Rennalls, Jafan-Mousse T., and Inaya Yafan. Published by Plutone, Edition, and Peppermint Park.

Chapter Forty-Seven contains lines from Nu Colours's song "Tears." Lyrics copyright © 1993 by Frankie Knuckles, Robert Owens, and Satoshi Tomiie. Published by London Music, Ltd.

The author and publisher make no claim of any rights whatsoever to the works cited and excerpted for artistic and critical purposes in this book.

Image Credits

Page(s)	Image courtesy of:
30 - 31	Author, photographer unknown
45	Author
52	Author
53	Author
56	Author
66	Author
76	Author
81	Howie Keck
90	Author
119	Author
137	Author
139	*Paper Magazine*, courtesy of the author
157	Author
160	Author
169	Author
207	Author
210	Author
212	Author
226	Author
230	Author
252	Author
253	Author
262	Author
269	Author
276 - 277	Author
285	Author
303	Author

About the Author

David Lauterstein is among the most influential forces in queer culture, celebrated as an unapologetic champion for sex-positivity since co-founding the iconic Nasty Pig fashion brand in 1994. As its CEO, he has been honored for his trailblazing entrepreneurship, his philanthropic efforts supporting homeless queer youth, and by the White House for his decades of public health advocacy. A formally trained poet and house music producer, Lauterstein resides in New York City with his husband and Nasty Pig co-founder, Frederick Kearney. *Sodomy Gods* is his first book.

About the Type and Paper

Designed by Malou Verlomme of the Monotype Studio, Macklin is an elegant, high-contrast typeface. It has been designed purposely for more emotional appeal.

The concept for Macklin began with research on historical material from Britain and Europe dating to the beginning of the 19th century, specifically the work of Vincent Figgins. Verlomme pays respect to Figgins's work with Macklin, but pushes the family to a more contemporary place.

This book is printed on natural Rolland Enviro Book stock. The paper is 100 percent post-consumer sustainable fiber content and is FSC-certified.

Sodomy Gods was designed by Eleanor Safe and Joseph Floresca.

Unbound Edition Press champions honest, original voices. Committed to the power of writers who explore and illuminate the contemporary human condition, we publish collections of poetry, short fiction, and essays. Our publisher and editorial team aim to identify, develop, and defend authors who create thoughtfully challenging work which may not find a home with mainstream publishers. We are guided by a mission to respect and elevate emerging, under-appreciated, and marginalized authors, with a strong commitment to advancing LGBTQ+ and BIPOC voices. We are honored to make meaningful contributions to the literary arts by publishing their work.

unboundedition.com